Trevor Shannon

UNDERSTANDING THE PSALMS

A SPIRITUALITY FOR TODAY

Limited Special Edition. No. 12 of 25 Paperbacks

Trevor Shannon was a parish priest in Lancashire for seven years before becoming a school chaplain for twenty-two years. His last years as a parish priest were in East London. He still exercises his priesthood in North Norfolk, where he currently lives. Recently widowed, he has four children and a large number of grand and great-grandchildren. He received degrees in Theology from Cambridge University and London University, and has used the Psalms daily for almost sixty years. He retains many friendships from the years spent playing amateur football and league cricket, as well as from the parishes and school that he served. His great desire is to make the Christian faith accessible and attractive to all people.

In memory of Maureen, the light of my life, and dedicated to all church-goers who have been baffled or simply put off by the assumptions and insensitivity of some of us clergy.

Trevor Shannon

UNDERSTANDING THE PSALMS

A SPIRITUALITY FOR TODAY

With all good wishes and blessings.

Love, Trevor

AUSTIN MACAULEY PUBLISHERS™

LONDON • CAMBRIDGE • NEW YORK • SHARJAH

A CIP catalogue record for this title is available from the British Library.

ISBN 9781788488211 (Paperback)
ISBN 9781788488228 (Hardback)
ISBN 9781788488235 (Kindle e-book)
ISBN 9781528951319 (ePub e-book)

www.austinmacauley.com

First Published (2019)
Austin Macauley Publishers Ltd
25 Canada Square
Canary Wharf
London
E14 5LQ

I should like to record my thanks to those whose words I have quoted in the text of my book and to the many others whose words I have read but not quoted. Special thanks are due to Bishop Graham James of Norwich and to John Waine, one-time Bishop of Chelmsford, for reading my manuscript and encouraging me to publish.

Understanding the Psalms
A Practical Spirituality for
Christians Today

A Personal Introduction

I have read the psalms daily for many years and have experienced
uplift and wonder. I have also been distressed, amused, puzzled and
appalled. I am aware that many of my fellow Christians share those
varied reactions, and what follows is an attempt to address them.
After the introduction are my own reflections on the psalms, set
down, I hope, in a non-technical way. They are the sort of facts and
ideas I would take along with me to a parish study group, hoping to
interest and instruct, and expecting people to respond with their own
thoughts and questions so that we might all grow in faith and
understanding.

I was introduced to the psalms early. When I was four, my
eight-year-old sister used to take me to Sunday School. Morning
Sunday School was a mixture of hymns, psalms, Bible readings,
prayers and a talk. When the superintendent said, "On the red
cards..." we obediently, in unison, read Psalm 19; and we did it
every week. I knew that psalm by heart long before I could read it.
I realise now that its closing verses fitted very well with the stress
which was laid on being good and avoiding sin – aims which
permeated the whole service. Almost every week we would sing the
hymn, "Do no sinful action, speak no angry word..." The hymn
moved on to warn us, "There's a wicked spirit watching round you
still..." and then, "Ye must learn to fight with the bad within you,
and to do the right." So, conditioned by that hymn, I knew there was
bad within me, and it came as no surprise to be saying in Psalm 19,
*Who can tell how oft he offendeth? O cleanse thou me from my
secret faults. Keep thy servant also from presumptuous sins, lest
they get the dominion over me: so shall I be undefiled and innocent
from the great offence.* All that at four years old! The language of

the Book of Common Prayer and the Authorised Version of the Bible was no barrier. That is how it was in church and Sunday School, and we just accepted it, and by accident received some valuable education.

At four, and even at ten, I don't think I had much idea what the presumptuous sins of Psalm 19 might be. I certainly wasn't sure what the great offence was. But I had been naughty often enough and tried to cover things up, usually by saying that my sister had done it, so I knew what secret faults were, even if they weren't quite what the psalmist had in mind.

This was in the late 1930s and early 1940s, long before the Parish Communion had become the main service of the week in most Anglican parishes. We were a Morning and Evening Prayer parish, with an 8.00 a.m. Communion Service for those who were serious enough about their religion to get up fairly early after a much earlier start in the cotton mill on the previous six days – yes, six.

When morning Sunday School was over we paraded up to church to join our parents and we shared in what was left of Morning Prayer – probably more psalms and certainly hymns and a sermon. In the evening we went as a family to Evening Prayer with more psalms, hymns and readings from both Old and New Testaments as well as prayers and another sermon.

I am not sure what influence familiarity with the psalms had on me and my friends' spiritual development, apart from them being used to make us feel guilty so that we would be 'better children'. But alongside that, memory certainly stored up some wonderful words and phrases: *Keep me as the apple of an eye: hide me under the shadow of thy wings. (Ps. 17, 8); Mercy and truth are met together: righteousness and peace have kissed each other. (Ps. 85. 10); I will lift up mine eyes unto the hills: from whence cometh my help. (Ps. 121. 1).* And from an early age I was amused by *They go to and fro in the evening: they grin like a dog and run about through the city. (Ps. 59. 6)* I used to look for grinning dogs but never saw any. Those remembered words and phrases were a small but valuable legacy.

(*In this Introduction I have quoted so far from the Prayer Book version of the psalms – Miles Coverdale's wonderful words – because that was the version we used. From now on I shall generally use the words of the Revised Standard Version of the Bible.)

The Psalms in Worship Today

Times have changed. I think it is true to say that today the Old Testament is under-used, under-valued and not really understood by many Christians. It is also true that of all the books of the Old Testament the one quoted most often in the New Testament is the Book of Psalms. Jesus was clearly very familiar with the psalms, and as all Christians know, he used the opening verse, or more likely the whole of Psalm 22 as he was dying on the cross. Because of this, from the earliest days until now, the Church has used psalms extensively in its worship, both private and communal. In most Anglican parishes today the Eucharist or Holy Communion is the main service of the week and the one which most worshippers attend. In the modern Communion service a psalm or canticle is provided to be said or sung between the Old Testament and New Testament readings. Many other psalms stealthily find a place in the service as they are the basis of well-known hymns. The best known is probably "The Lord's my Shepherd, I'll not want…" (Psalm 23). In this case the hymn is a rewriting of the whole psalm in a metre suitable for a hymn. Other hymns use phrases, words or ideas from psalms, building on them a complete hymn. Examples are "Lord enthroned in heavenly splendour…" (Psalm 3.3); "O worship the Lord in the beauty of holiness…" (Psalm 29.2); "Glorious things of thee are spoken…" (Psalm 87.2-3); "Praise, my soul, the king of heaven…" (Psalm 103); "All my hope on God is founded…" (Psalm 127); "Let us, with a gladsome mind praise the Lord for he is kind…" (Psalm 136); "All people that on earth do dwell…" (Psalms 148 and 150). There are many, many others.

Psalms are also set to be said or sung at the Daily Offices of Morning and Evening Prayer. The revised prayer books of recent years have reduced the number of psalms that were set for each service in the Book of Common Prayer. There the pattern was that the whole Psalter should be said or sung each month. Thus on the first day of each month, at Morning Prayer, Psalms 1, 2, 3, 4 and 5 were said. The Prayer Book Lectionary also intended that, roughly speaking, the whole of the Old Testament should be read once a year and the whole New Testament twice a year.

The Book of Common Prayer of 1662 was based largely on the work of Archbishop Thomas Cranmer. He was a devout reformer, trying to bring all people (and virtually all people in England at that time were at least nominally Christian) into a closer relationship with God through a deeper knowledge of Scripture. It was a vitally important part of the reforming movement that the Scriptures were translated into English (as well as other languages in other countries) out of the Latin of the Vulgate Version. It thus became possible for people to read the Scriptures or to hear them in their own language.

The accessibility of the Scriptures was an important feature of the Reformation, and two of the great European Reformers wrote powerfully of the Psalms. Martin Luther said, "Where does one find finer words of joy than in the psalms of praise and thanksgiving... On the other hand, where do you find deeper, more sorrowful, more pitiful words of sadness than in the psalms of lamentation?" John Calvin wrote, "The Holy Spirit has here drawn to the life all the griefs, sorrows, fears, doubts, hopes, cares, perplexities, in short, all the distracting emotions with which the minds of men are wont to be agitated." This continental Reformation ardour for the psalms was reflected in the various revisions of the Prayer Book in England.

In pre-Reformation times there had been monks and nuns praying regularly, seven times a day (as it says in Psalm 119. verse 164), praising God and praying for all people. The core of monastic worship was (as it still is) the singing of the psalms. But the monasteries and nunneries had been dissolved, and in some cases destroyed, by order of King Henry VIII and Thomas Cromwell in the process of the separation of the English Church from the oversight of Rome. So Cranmer merged the various 'hours' of monastic prayer into the two longer services, *Morning Prayer* and *Evening Prayer.* In the Book of Common Prayer the rubric (or instruction) introducing the services requires all clergy to say Morning and Evening Prayer daily: "And all priests and deacons are to say daily the Morning and Evening Prayer either privately or openly, not being let *(that is, prevented)* by sickness, or some other urgent cause." That rule still stands for all Anglican clergy.

It was intended that Morning and Evening Prayer should be for everyone; public, not private worship. Again the rubric is very clear. "And the Curate *(that is, the incumbent)* that ministereth in every parish-church or chapel, being at home, and not being otherwise reasonably hindered, shall say the same in the parish-church or chapel where he ministereth, and shall cause a bell to be tolled thereunto a convenient time that the people may come to hear God's Word, and to pray with him."

The intention, clearly, was that the Scriptures, especially the Psalms, should be a part of the daily prayer of every Christian.

What a wonderful witness it is today to the people of a parish (even if most of them would not count themselves as Christians) when each day they hear the church bell tolling in the morning and evening reminding them that their parish priest is praying for them. It might also remind them that they in turn might pray for their priest.

A Worry about the Psalms

There are verses in some of the psalms which seem downright un-Christian. I said them at Sunday School and sang them in church without a thought, without a qualm. To give just two examples: the closing verse of Psalm 137 says, "*Happy shall he be who takes your little ones and dashes them against the rocks.*" It sounds like raw and cruel vengeance. Or Psalm 58, verse 10: "*The righteous will rejoice when he sees the vengeance: he will bathe his feet in the blood of the wicked.*" There is a great deal of this sort of thing in the psalms. What can we make of it?

Context matters a lot. When I was a child I accepted what I was taught and recited the verses from the book in my hand however bloodthirsty they were. Perhaps I wasn't just insensitive. There was a war on. The air-raid sirens sounded most nights, and we would try to sleep on a mattress under the dining table, or go to the local air-raid shelter. In the morning, on the way to school, we delighted to pick up pieces of shrapnel in the road. To a child it was exciting rather than frightening. We were used to violence and hatred and death; at least we were always hearing about them. It came as no surprise to us that the psalmist had 'enemies.'

But as time passed and I got older, and wars were either cold or fought at a distance from home, some verses in the psalms began to worry me. As thinking adult Christians we have to ask ourselves if or how we can use such words prayerfully and Christianly.

Philip Toynbee, writing in his published journal *Part of a Journey,* records a visit to an Anglican convent near where he lived in Wales. He knew the convent well. He liked to attend the services. He made many friends there and valued the help they gave him. In one of his diary entries, he puts the question about the uncomfortable verses in the Psalms very powerfully: "Evensong at Tymawr. Holy and loving sisters singing the psalms. Because St Benedict started the practice 1400 years ago. And this antiquity of the tradition is impressive. But what contortions of mind and heart must be needed to convert so much brazen self-righteousness, so much whining self-pity, so much bloodthirsty vindictiveness into a 'type' of Christ's passion or whatever meaning they give it?"

Toynbee poses the question for all who feel uncomfortable with the vengeful verses in the Psalms. And we can understand the omission of such verses by the compilers of recent lectionaries. But we must also ask ourselves whether we have the right to pick and choose in this way? If we do, are we not placing ourselves and our own judgement above Scripture? And may we not also be missing some important part of the teaching of the Scriptures?

Who Are the Enemies?

The vengeful verses are directed against the psalmist's enemies. Sometimes, they are called *the wicked* or *the ungodly*. Who are they, and how can anyone have so many enemies? First we have to remember that the psalms were composed over a very long period. Traditionally they have been called 'The Psalms of David'. In I Samuel (16.14-23), David was brought into the court of King Saul to soothe the king by playing the lyre – "Whenever the evil spirit from God was upon Saul, David took the lyre and played it with his hand; so Saul was refreshed, and was well, and the evil spirit departed from him." So David had a reputation as a musician and has been called 'the sweet psalmist of Israel'. (II Sam. 23.1). If he did write one or more of the psalms it would be dated before 1000 B.C. The content of other psalms places them many years later. For example, Psalm 137, *By the rivers of Babylon we sat down and wept,* places itself during or after the Babylonian exile, some 500 years later. Other psalms, by mentioning for example, the rebuilding of the temple after the return from exile, must be dated at a similar time. This means that the composition of the Psalter as a whole covered several hundred years.

Enemies of the Nation. In the long period of time during which the psalms were written, Israel and Judah, the two nations into which the twelve tribes of Israel formed themselves, were involved in many conflicts against surrounding nations, some of them small, some of them great powers. At different times, they were at war with Philistia, Moab, Midian, Syria, Egypt, Assyria, Babylon. There were many others. So there were plenty of national enemies to worry about. In the psalms the enemies are usually unnamed. This might be because the psalm was written as a prayer for use in public worship and could be used as different enemies threatened the life and faith of the nation.

Enemies of the Faith. The dangers posed by other nations were not just military, political or economic. It was the religious threat, the temptation to apostasy, that was considered the greatest peril. We should be aware too that it was not just the psalmists who felt deeply about the influences of foreign nations. The prophets did too. We need only read Amos's oracles against Damascus (Syria), Gaza (the Philistines), Tyre, Edom, Ammon, Moab to understand how perilously attractive some of the people of Israel found the religions of other nations.

Nor were the enemies posing only military and political threats. The cults of foreign gods had been brought into Israel partly by travellers moving between the different nations, but more significantly by royal marriages, bringing into the country a foreign princess and her religion, protected perhaps by treaty arrangements.

We should remember too that the Promised Land was not empty when Israel took possession of it. The people of Canaan had to be driven from their ancestral lands or compromises had to be made for the invaders and the people of the land to co-exist. In Zephaniah 1.4-6 we find a clear indication of how prevalent the worship of gods other than Yahweh was in the Judah of his day, which was at the time of Josiah's reform in about 620 B.C. He wrote what he believed were God's words, "I will stretch out my hand against Judah, and against all the inhabitants of Jerusalem; and I will cut off from this place the remnant of Baal and the name of the idolatrous priests; those who bow down on the roofs to the host of the heavens; those who bow down and swear to the Lord and yet swear by Milcom; those who have turned back from following the Lord, who do not seek the Lord or inquire of him." Or we can read in II Kings 24. 4-20 of the abuses which King Josiah had to deal with when he began his reforms under the influence of 'the book of the law' which had been discovered during the renovation of the temple. Ezekiel too, in chapter 8, gives a graphic picture of the foreign cults which had invaded even the temple in Jerusalem.

So, over many years, there was no shortage of national and institutional 'enemies' for the psalmists to worry about, and we should not imagine that the number of times they are mentioned, crowded together in the psalter, is an indication of paranoia in the poets. Perhaps, we might also reflect that politics today, and not only in the Middle East, continues to show signs of being faction-ridden, violent and corrupt.

Personal Enemies. The psalmists often speak of personal enemies. Before we start to try to understand or explain away these seemingly exaggerated concerns, we should consider the experience of Jeremiah. A prophet born into a priestly family, he seems to have supported the reforms of Josiah until he realised that keeping the Law could become a mere mechanical exercise without the spiritual and moral change that the Law expected. He spoke out, (for example Jeremiah 5. 1-5), and for his trouble was beaten and put in the stocks by Pashhur the priest (20.1-2). He was the target of an assassination attempt (11.18-19). Some time later he was charged with treason and put into a mud-bottomed pit and left to die (38.6). He was saved only by the compassion of a foreign court attendant who persuaded the king to let him save Jeremiah (38.7-13). So we know that personal enmities and attacks were not unusual in ancient Israel.

The psalmists' enemies seem to be people rather like those who persecuted Jeremiah. They slander, slight or even physically attack them. Time doesn't seem to change things very much. When John Henry (later Cardinal) Newman left the Anglican Church to become a Roman Catholic, he felt he was unjustly attacked and accused of dishonesty and disloyalty. He wrote, "I had for days a literal ache all about my heart; and from time to time all the complaints of the Psalmist seemed to belong to me." It still goes on. We might ponder how many people in public life today have been subjected to mud-slinging attacks, which might or might not be true.

We should also remember that in a psalm the poet may feel he is speaking only to God in private prayer, and he opens his heart, mentioning matters of which he probably did not speak openly. We might ask ourselves if we ever talk to God about problems or people who we feel are opposed to us or hurting us in some way. Do we mention them to God or even complain to God about them, possibly using terms or thinking thoughts we should hesitate to utter publicly?

And what about the many complaints of physical suffering? If we think that sometimes the psalmists exaggerate or are hypochondriacs, it is worth remembering that in their day, there were no anaesthetics or antibiotics, though no doubt there were many efficacious natural remedies.

The Psalms as Poetry. The songs of praise, the thanksgivings for victory, the pilgrim songs, harvest thanksgivings and the psalms of lament form a very mixed collection. As we read the psalms, we might feel as William Wordsworth felt as he listened to The Solitary Reaper singing songs, the meanings of which he could not be certain:

> "Will no one tell me what she sings?
> Perhaps the plaintive numbers flow
> For old, unhappy, far-off things,
> And battles long ago:
> Or is it some more humble lay,
> Familiar matter of today?
> Some natural sorrow, loss, or pain,
> That has been, and may be again?"

That is not an altogether inaccurate description of the Psalter, and as the psalms were central to the worship in the Scottish Kirk, the poet's 'solitary highland lass' may well have been singing psalms. Anyway, Wordsworth leads us conveniently into thinking about the poetry of the psalms.

Before we glance at some of the technicalities of Hebrew poetry, it will be helpful to remind ourselves of just how beautiful is the poetry of some of the psalms.

Psalm 19.1-6 celebrates the glory of creation:

The heavens are telling the glory of God: and the firmament proclaims his handiwork.
Day to day pours forth speech, and night to night declares knowledge.
There is no speech nor are there words; their voice is not heard;
Yet their voice goes out through all the earth, and their words to the end of the world.
In them has he set a tabernacle for the sun, which comes forth like a bridegroom leaving his chamber, and like a strong man runs its course with joy.
Its rising is from the end of the heavens, and its circuit to the end of them; and there is nothing hid from its heat.

Psalm 84 verses 1-3 meditates on the temple in Jerusalem:

How lovely is thy dwelling place, O Lord of Hosts!
My soul longs, yea, faints for the courts of the Lord;
My heart and flesh sing for joy to the living God.
Even the sparrow finds a home, and the swallow a nest for herself,
Where she may lay her young, at thy altars O Lord of hosts, my King and my God.
Blessed are those who dwell in thy house, ever singing thy praise!

Psalm 137 verses1-6 is the lament of Jewish exiles in Babylon:

By the waters of Babylon, there we sat down and wept, when we remembered Zion.
On the willows there we hung up our lyres.
For there our captors required of us songs, and our tormentors, mirth, saying "sing us one of the songs of Zion!"
How shall we sing the Lord's song in a foreign land?

If I forget you, O Jerusalem, let my right hand wither!
Let my tongue cleave to the roof of my mouth,
If I do not set Jerusalem above my highest joy.

There are many more equally beautiful passages.

We might say that what distinguishes English poetry from prose is metre and rhythm and often rhyme. In Hebrew poetry, the most distinguishing feature is *parallelism.* This means that commonly one half of a verse echoes the other half. To find an example, I simply opened my psalter at random and happened on the first verse of psalm 89 which says, *My song shall be always of the loving-kindness of the Lord: with my mouth will I ever be shewing thy truth from one generation to another.* The same thought is in both halves of the verse, *my song* balanced by *with my mouth,* God's *loving-kindness* balanced by *thy truth,* and *always* balanced by *from one generation to another.*

Such parallelism suggests that many psalms were designed to be said or sung antiphonally. For example the beginning of psalm 135 verses 1-4, might well be the priests' invitation to the worshippers to join in the praise of God. Then in verse 5 a worshipper begins his response. The whole of Psalm 136 lends itself to antiphonal singing.

When we read and pray the psalms it is always important to remember that they are poems, and they do not try or intend to convey their message in a prosaic, factual manner. They use similes and metaphors, and sometimes there is exaggeration and bias.

The psalms are not, of course, the only poetry in the Old Testament. Many of the oracles of the prophets are in the form of poetry, as can be seen simply by looking at the way the text is set out. The Song of Songs, most of the Book of Job, the Proverbs and Ecclesiastes are also in poetic form. It is worth looking too, in Jonah chapter 2, at the prayer Jonah made from the belly of the fish. It reads exactly like a psalm.

The Structure of the Psalter

There are 150 poems in the Book of Psalms – perhaps more if some psalms are the result of combining two poems together, or fewer if one or more longer poems have been divided. To give examples of those oddities, Psalms 14 and 53 are virtually identical, and Psalm 70 can be found as verses 16-21 of Psalm 40.

In most Bibles and Prayer Books the psalms are just numbered. There are, however, headings to the psalms which are printed in some versions of the Psalter, for example, in the Revised Standard Version of the Bible. These headings were added by Jewish scholars and editors in about 200 B.C. They attribute 73 psalms to David, 2 to Solomon, Psalm 90 to Moses, 12 psalms to Asaph, 11 to Korah, Psalm 88 to Heman and Psalm 89 to Ethan. Asaph and Heman are mentioned as musicians involved in the splendid liturgy when the ark was installed in the newly built temple of Solomon, all described in II Chronicles 5.12.

Some of the headings make precise claims about the origin of the psalm. The clearest example is Psalm 51 which says: *To the leader. A Psalm of David, when the prophet Nathan came to him after he had gone in to Bathsheba.* The incident referred to is in 2 Samuel, chapters 11 and 12 and it is a very fitting situation for the penitential tone of the psalm. However it is usually thought that the offering of sacrifices in Jerusalem, mentioned in verses 18 and 19, make it unlikely that David wrote the psalm. David's son, Solomon, built the temple in Jerusalem after David was dead. So the headings are sometimes helpful, sometimes a little confusing.

At about the time that the headings were added, the Psalter was divided into five books. This may have been an attempt to reflect the division of the Torah into its five books (Genesis, Exodus, Leviticus, Numbers and Deuteronomy), thus giving the Psalter added status. The divisions are: Book I, Psalms 1-41; Book II, Psalms 42-72; Book III, Psalms 73-89; Book IV, Psalms 90-106; Book V, Psalms 107-150.

Some special arranging is evident. Each of the first four books ends with a doxology, that is, verses of praise to God. There is no doxology at the end of Book V as the whole book is one long doxology. Other special arrangements have been made such as the placing of Psalm 1 as a fitting introduction to the whole psalter, and Psalm 150 as a suitable and triumphal conclusion.

What Do the Scholars Say?

(This section may seem a little technical and perhaps tedious. Skip it if you wish. But I think there is valuable information which will help understand the original use of many of the psalms and their value for us today.)

In each generation Christian scholars have tried to show how the psalms can deepen and strengthen Christian faith, as they speak to us of our dearest hopes and deepest fears. We have already noted what Martin Luther and John Calvin said about the scope and depth of the psalms, how they constantly address matters which are common to all men and women who have faith in God and who take God, life and themselves seriously.

Christian scholars of the 20th century enquired chiefly into the original setting and purpose of each psalm. To summarise and over-simplify, we can say that Hermann Gunkel suggested that we can place the psalms in several categories: a) *Hymns of Praise,* b) *Laments (both individual and communal),* c) *Thanksgivings (both individual and communal),* d) *Royal Psalms,* e) *Pilgrim Psalms* and f) *Wisdom Psalms.*

Building on Gunkel's work Sigmund Mowinckel believed that many psalms were composed for the New Year Festival in the Second Temple, rebuilt after the return from exile in Babylon. He taught that at the festival the ark was carried in procession and placed in the temple in a ritual enthronement of Yahweh as king of Israel. The festival celebrated Yahweh's kingship and his victory over chaos in the ordering of creation. They believed that the proper keeping of the festival would ensure good harvests and political and military security in the coming year.

Artur Weiser suggested that many psalms were for use at the same New Year Festival but its main purpose, along with the enthronement of Yahweh, was the annual renewal of the Covenant between Yahweh and Israel, so that the Covenant became as real and effective for the worshippers in the temple as it had been when first made at Sinai. A Christian parallel to this might be the annual celebration of Christ's resurrection when a historical event is made present to the worshippers, so that we sing, 'Jesus Christ is risen today'. The Covenant renewal might also remind Christians of the Renewal of Baptismal vows made in the liturgy for Easter Eve. The scholars' various festival theories are not incompatible, and we shall see that these explanations can be wonderfully helpful to us as we try to see how a particular psalm was originally used. The scholars' theories do not and cannot answer all our questions, and so we remain puzzled by the origins and meanings of some psalms.

To imagine a psalm being used in worship after the return from the Babylonian exile, in a liturgy or service in the rebuilt temple in Jerusalem can be very enlightening. We find that sometimes more than one voice is saying or singing different sections of the psalm. Often there is what seems to be a congregational refrain or response rather like a chorus in a Christian hymn.

It is instructive to look at a Christian liturgy, for example, the Anglican Office of Morning Prayer as it stands in the Alternative

Service Book of 1980. If we take away all the rubrics and two or three lines which are specifically Christian, we find ourselves reading something that looks and sounds very much like a psalm.

"If we say we have no sin, we deceive ourselves, and the truth is not in us.
If we confess our sins, God is faithful and just and will forgive us our sins,
and cleanse us from all unrighteousness.
Let us confess our sins to almighty God.
Almighty God, our heavenly Father,
we have sinned against you and against our fellow men,
through negligence, through weakness, through our own deliberate fault.
We are truly sorry and repent of all our sins...
forgive us all that is past;
and grant that we may serve you in newness of life
to the glory of your name. Amen.
Almighty God, who forgives all who truly repent, have mercy upon you,
pardon and deliver you from all your sins,
confirm and strengthen you in all goodness,
and keep you in life eternal... Amen.
O Lord, open our lips;
and our mouth shall proclaim your praise.
Let us worship the Lord.
All praise to his name.
Glory to the Father... as it was in the beginning, is now,
and shall be for ever. Amen."

Of course, what we have here is invitation, confession, absolution, versicle and response and a final burst of praise of God. The invitation is to be spoken by *The Minister. All* say the confession. A *Priest* gives the absolution, and the *Minister* and *People* share the Versicles and Responses and the concluding Gloria. We shall find that many psalms seem to have this sort of mixture in them, and that we miss much of their drama and meaning if we treat them simply as the monologue prayers of an individual.

We can sometimes imagine ourselves joining the temple congregation and taking part in a national celebration such as the enthronement of a king or a royal marriage (Psalm 45). Sometimes, it is a national occasion, a thanksgiving for victory or a lament after defeat. In II Chronicles chapter 5 there is what seems to be the arrangements for the service celebrating the taking of the Ark into the newly built temple of Solomon. It is quite likely to be a reading back into the time of Solomon, the practice current in the Second Temple, when it had been rebuilt and restored under Nehemiah. Verses 12 and 13 read, "and all the Levitical singers, Asaph, Heman, and Jeduthun, their sons and kinsmen, arrayed in fine linen, with cymbals, harps, and lyres, stood east of the altar with a hundred and twenty priests who were trumpeters; and it was the duty of the trumpeters and singers to make themselves heard in unison in praise and thanksgiving to the Lord." It is with good reason that the Psalter has been called *The Hymn Book of the Second Temple.*

Hebrew Wisdom. Wisdom teaching in the Old Testament is complex and varied. To over-simplify, we might say that it seeks to teach people how to lead the good life, life as God intends, based on the teaching of the Law. The careful ordering of the psalms to convey this teaching is seen in its simplest and clearest form in the placing of Psalm 1 to set the tone for the whole collection, and Psalm 150 to conclude in fitting fashion – praising God. In this, what is called 'canonical' way of thinking, the sanctuary, so often mentioned and so precious to the psalmist, is not the temple of Solomon nor the temple rebuilt after the exile under Nehemiah, but Wisdom itself. The whole book seeks to teach people how they should live. In Psalm 119, the quintessential Wisdom psalm, the phrase "teach me your statutes" is constantly repeated, using different synonyms – statutes, law, commandments, word, decrees, judgements, precepts, ordinances.

The Psalter is carefully arranged to press home its vital message about the acts of God in creation and in history, and his requirement, set out in the law, for humans to be just as God is just. Divine justice is seen as the foundation of all existence. God is the guarantor of justice. In the end, however unfair life might seem to be at any given moment, the righteous will be rewarded and the wicked punished. Humans must also be merciful as God is merciful, and like God must care for the poor and needy. The requirement for humans to be just and merciful is as strong in the psalms as it is in the prophets and it is noticeable that throughout the psalter the qualifications for pilgrims to join the worshipping community at festivals are always moral, never ritual. We see this very clearly in Psalms 15 and 24.

Walter Brueggeman in *Israel's Praise* argues that liturgy, whether Jewish or Christian, is drama through which the worshippers 'create' a world, an ideal world, a world as God would have it be. In the psalms the king rules in Jerusalem as God's viceroy. The real king is always Yahweh, and his earthly representative must rule as Yahweh would, with justice and mercy. Key words are 'loving-kindness and truth'. Brueggeman argues that Israel's praise of God springs naturally and spontaneously from their awareness of specific ways in which God had acted on their behalf – freeing them from slavery in Egypt, leading them safely through the Red Sea, providing food and water in the wilderness, giving them unlikely victory in their conquest of Canaan. With their knowledge of God's acts of mercy in the past, they can be confident of his readiness to help in the present, and so they place before him their national and personal needs and complaints. They find that God indeed still acts with justice and mercy and they praise him in song and dance. Looking at Psalm 136, we see numerous specific acts of God's mercy related and the congregation's repeated response, "*for his steadfast love endures for ever.*" Not just for now, but forever. So the past guarantees not only the present but the future as well.

Christians have a similar understanding of liturgy creating a world-as-it-should-be. Such a world, so different from the world that is, can only be created if it is first imagined. In the Eucharist, Christians recall the saving acts of God in Jesus, and having remembered and made them present, we go out to change the world into the vision we have been given. In a closing prayer of the Eucharist we ask God to "send us out into the world in the power of your Spirit to live and work to your praise and glory." That is, we are sent out to live as God requires, trying to establish the Kingdom of God on earth 'as it is in heaven'.

How Are the Various Sorts of Psalms Relevant to Christians?

The detailed work of scholars, many of whom I have not even mentioned, throws light onto many psalms, helping us to see how they might have been used by pilgrims at the great festivals, or how the king's task under God is to rule with justice and mercy. In the end what matters to most Christians is how they can do what the psalmists did, and use the psalms in public worship and private prayer to draw closer to God, to express their thanks to him, and to pour out before him their inmost hopes and fears. We shall look briefly at how the different sorts of psalms might help us as we try to live as Christians.

Laments are the psalms which tell of anguish, pain, distress and despair. Can any adult claim never to have felt the anguish of the author of psalm 130? *Out of the depths I cry to you, O Lord. Lord, hear my voice! Let your ears be attentive to my supplication.* Such a cry from the heart will ring true to many a person grieving the death of a loved one. It will strike a chord with any person wrongly accused or reviled. It will make sense to someone whose long hoped-for and worked-for aims have crumbled into nothing. Those who have lost their faith or are struggling to hold on to it will find echoes of their own misery. They all know what it is to be in the depths.

Sometimes the problems seem to be physical suffering. It comes as no surprise that Jesus had the words of Psalm 22 on his lips as he died on the cross. The psalmist speaks of physical pains: *I am poured out like water, and all my bones are out of joint; my heart is like wax; it is melted within my breast; my mouth is dried up like a potsherd, and my tongue sticks to my jaws; you lay me in the dust of death.*

People who are desperately ill and perhaps fearing the approach of death, or someone finding the weaknesses of old age increasingly burdensome, especially if they fear their condition is the result of their sin, real or imagined, will understand the cry of the writer of psalm 38: *There is no soundness in my flesh because of your indignation; there is no health in my bones because of my sin... My wounds grow foul and fester because of my foolishness; I am utterly bowed down and prostrate.* When the psalmist cries out tastelessly or tactlessly we should understand that the cry arises from real pain, real suffering.

Sometimes the lament is for the nation or for the community of believers. Psalm 44 laments the defeat and humbling of the nation. *You have made us turn back from the foe, and our enemies have taken spoil for themselves. You have made us like sheep for slaughter, and have scattered us among the nations.* Like this psalm, the many psalms with similar themes usually express themselves in general terms. There is no mention of specific enemies, the names of nations or the rulers are not set down. This means that such psalms could be used in any national emergency. This is not dissimilar to the way in which Christian worship often uses the same hymns on, for example, Remembrance Sunday. "O God, our help in ages past...," "Thy kingdom come, O God; thy rule, O Christ begin" and similar hymns are found suitable and appropriate year after year.

Psalms of Praise. In his book *Reflections on the Psalms* C.S. Lewis wrote, "Praise almost seems like inner health made audible." The Hebrew word *Hallel* which means 'praise', is common in the psalms and is used in all its grammatical forms. It has passed into Christian prayers of praise in the plural form with the addition of *Yah* or *Jah,* the name of God, giving us *Hallelujah.* God is praised in the psalms for his power in creation (Psalm 19); for his superiority over other 'gods', which are not real gods at all (Psalm 89. 5-8). He is praised for saving the nation (Psalm 80), for choosing gifted rulers (Psalm 77), for success in war (Psalm 44), for family life (Psalm 127), for bountiful harvests (Psalm 65) and for personal help in all sorts of circumstances (to give just one example, Psalm 7).

Christians often thank God for his care and his blessing in the silence of their private prayers, though some Christians are confident and ready to praise God openly in public worship, as their gratitude overcomes natural reticence and possible embarrassment before their fellow-worshippers. The Psalter clearly intends that the praise of God should be vocal and public. A doxology, a shout of praise, concludes each of the five books of the Psalter and the whole collection builds up to the explosion of universal praise in Psalm 150.

The Royal Psalms remind the king of his duty under God who is the real ruler. In Deuteronomy (17. 18-20) we read that the king is to have a copy of the Torah written out for him so that he will know how he should exercise his power and be unable to claim ignorance as an excuse for failing in his duty. Despite this, the Old Testament records the failings of many rulers, and so there grew an expectation that in time God would send his ideal king, anointed as his adopted son, coming from the house of David, and he would rule the kingdom with justice, loving kindness and truth. Christians believe that Jesus is that ideal king who invites all to join him in the setting up of the kingdom of God.

Pilgrim Psalms. The Christian life is often described as a pilgrimage, and many Christians go on pilgrimage to holy places – Jerusalem, Bethlehem, Nazareth, Rome, Santiago, Walsingham, Canterbury and many other places. In the psalms, we see the pilgrims planning their journey with delight (Psalm 122); we see them struggling through the arid valley of Baca (Psalm 84). We see them processing round Jerusalem and looking with wonder at its great buildings (Psalm 48). We see the pilgrims in the temple and we hear their words of praise and thanksgiving (Psalm 98). Several psalms speak of the worshipper seeking or seeing the face of God (17.15, 24.6, 27.8-9, 67.1).

Psalm 15 sets out the conditions which the pilgrim must fulfil to enter the temple at festival time to seek the presence or face of God. The conditions are strictly ethical – *O Lord, who may abide in your tent? Who may dwell on your holy hill? Those who walk blamelessly, and do what is right, and speak the truth from their heart; who do not slander with their tongue, and do no evil to their friends, nor take up a reproach against their neighbours.* Psalm 24 poses a similar question, *Who shall ascend the hill of the Lord? And who shall stand in his holy place?* It gives the answer, *He who has clean hands and a pure heart, who does not lift up his soul to what is false, and does not swear deceitfully.* That answer leads us directly to the Sermon on the Mount and Jesus' words, *Blessed are the pure in heart for they shall see God.* The vision of God is precisely the reward the psalmist's pilgrim sought.

Being with Christ in the Psalter

Perhaps, the greatest incentive for Christians to read, study and pray the psalms is that Jesus died with the words of Psalm 22 on his lips. The Gospels record that he said the opening words of the psalm, *My God, my God, why have you forsaken me?* That may be like saying that someone sang "O come, all ye faithful." The first line is used as a title and the meaning is that the whole was sung. Perhaps Our Lord prayed the whole of Psalm 22 as he died – and perhaps other psalms too. It would be natural for a devout Jew, unjustly condemned, to pray in that way.

Jesus used the psalms in his teaching. He was called 'Rabbi' both by his disciples and his opponents, and we can be sure that as a devout Jew he would know and use the psalms constantly. The Gospel writers record more than twenty quotations or allusions to the psalms in the teaching of Jesus. He quoted Psalm 91 when fighting temptation in the wilderness (Luke 4.10-11). We have already noted his reference to purity of heart in the Sermon on the Mount, looking back to Psalms 15 and 24. He also used Psalm 48.2 a little later in that collection of teaching. He quoted Psalm 118 and Psalm 110 in controversy with Jewish religious leaders (Luke 13.35 and Matt. 26.64). He quoted Psalm 41.9 at the Last Supper, in anguish that one of his closest friends was to betray him. And Luke, in his narrative of the Passion, records the final words of Jesus as being from Psalm 31.5, "Jesus, crying with a loud voice, said,

Father, into thy hands I commit my spirit. And having said this he breathed his last." (Luke 23.46).

Despite our earlier thoughts about *enemies* in the psalms, can we really imagine Jesus saying *Happy shall they be who take your little ones and dash them against the rock* (Psalm 137.9)? Perhaps we should put this question alongside another apparent puzzle for Christians. Why did sinless Jesus undergo the baptism of repentance at the hands of John the Baptist? Perhaps the answer to both puzzles is that Jesus was identifying himself as fully and deeply as possible with human beings and their frailties. He wanted to know how hurt and angry, how vengeful and irrational people can be. We too can let the Psalms' words of vengeance remind us that, even if our lives are mainly comfortable, we live in a pain-filled world, and we can make the saying of pain-filled psalms an exercise in intercession. We might remember too that in general terms the first half of the psalter is dominated by lament and the second half by praise and thanksgiving, so there is a recognition that though we live in a world of pain and sadness, it is God's world, and pain and sadness can never have the last word. In recognising this pattern, which is that of death and life, in the psalms we again find Christ, crucified and risen.

In some psalms we find our own lives mirrored. Not only as individuals do we share the pain, the guilt and the forgiveness of the psalmists. The Church, just like Israel, often forgets and forsakes God and is faithless. When we return we find him waiting, longing for our return, and forgiving. Sometimes as we struggle in the darkness of life, we can learn from the psalms that the darkness we fear is in fact the shadow of the sheltering hand of God as in Psalm 91.4.

Thomas Merton, in his book *Bread in the Wilderness*, says that sometimes, as we read the psalms, the presence of Christ suddenly flashes upon us and we know he is with us; then he departs. It is like the experience of the disciples in Emmaus in the evening of the first Easter Day (Luke 24, 28-30).

Merton also wrote that we should say the psalms "with a firm hope that we shall find God hidden in His revealed word." We should expect to find Our Lord as we pray the psalms. Of course we should. When speaking to his critics Jesus said, "You search the scriptures because you think in them you have eternal life; and it is they that testify on my behalf." (John 5.39). As we search the psalms for Christ we can be sure that the Holy Spirit which inspired the writers will help us to find him there.

I hope that thinking about the individual psalms, perhaps as a daily discipline for a set period, will show us how similar in many ways are our lives to those of the writers of the psalms. The needs of the poor and down-trodden, and our God-given responsibility towards them, have not changed, nor have the virtues and failings of leaders and rulers. Nor has God changed. The God whom the psalmists seek, whom they adore and praise, to whom they plead and by whom they expect to be judged, never changes. What we learn of the nature of God in the psalms has been displayed for us in the life and teaching of Jesus Christ.

***

What follows are my reflections on the individual psalms. I look at each psalm in turn. I try to explain briefly what the psalmist seems to be saying and, leaning on the work of biblical scholars, what the occasion may have been when the psalm was said or sung. Then I reflect. I think about what the psalm has meant to me. I try to point out the links and connections with other parts of Scripture, and the foreshadowing and influence of the psalms on the life and teaching of Jesus. I ponder what a psalm might be saying to the Church and to individual Christian today. Generally, my own thoughts are set out after looking at the apparent meaning and original purpose of the psalm, though sometimes, it has seemed more appropriate to slot them in the middle of suggestions as to how the psalm may first have been used. Sometimes I consider the meaning of the psalm as a whole; sometimes I concentrate on a verse, a phrase or just a few words.

When reading the comments which follow on each of the psalms it will be helpful to have the text of the psalms before you. I have used the text of the Revised Standard Version of the bible. Other versions will be slightly different in their wording.

***

Thoughts on the Individual Psalms

Psalm 1

This psalm seems to have been deliberately chosen as the opening poem of the whole collection. It is moral exhortation, and things are presented as black or white. A person has to choose.

The poem begins with the word *blessed,* which can mean happy, fortunate, healthy or flourishing. It certainly means that the person enjoys the favour of God. They enjoy that favour because they have avoided the temptations that surround them. They have ignored the advice of the wicked. They do not behave like the wicked, and avoid joining in their scornful mockery of the virtuous (v. 1). Most important, besides avoiding these pitfalls, they have prayerfully pondered God's law, finding it a delight and not a burden (v. 2). This is the way of life which God required from Joshua when he was commissioned to take over the role which Moses had performed as leader of the nation: "Only be strong and very courageous, being careful to do according to all the law which Moses my servant commanded you; turn not from it to the right hand or to the left, that you may have good success wherever you go." We might also note that the whole of Psalm 119 reads like a commentary on or a celebration of verse 2 of this psalm.

In verse 3 the psalmist creates a lovely and vivid simile. The good person is like a tree planted advantageously close to water. Like such a tree he lives, and his life is fruitful, bringing benefit to others. Because he is rooted in God's law everything he does prospers. Such prosperity is by no means simply material. A person prospers when they fulfil the purpose God has for them in life. Jeremiah used a very similar picture when he said, "Blessed is the man who trusts in the Lord… He is like a tree planted by water, that sends out its roots by the stream, and does not fear when the heat comes, for its leaves remain green, and is not anxious in the year of drought, for it does not cease to bear fruit." (Jer. 17.7, 8).

When a person is like a healthy, flourishing tree they bring healing, encouragement and life to others. In Christian terms, we might think that people like Mother Teresa and Martin Luther King have brought such blessings. We each might also think of many unknown, uncelebrated and unselfish Christians known to us personally whose way is undoubtedly *blessed.*

A second vivid simile (v.4) pictures those who do not delight in God's law, who are scornful and care nothing for other people. Unlike the firmly rooted righteous, the wicked have no stability in their lives. They are flimsy, and can be swept about by any breeze of fashion or opinion. Nor do their lives benefit others in any way. They are like the worthless part of a crop, the chaff, good only for being thrown away, blown away or burned.

The final verse of the psalm declares that God is aware of the life of the righteous. He does not need to condemn the wicked. Their way of life is condemnation enough; it brings its own punishment.

In this lovely poem there are many links with the teaching of Jesus. He began his 'Sermon on the Mount' (in Matthew's Gospel, chapters 5,6 and 7) with the word 'Blessed', perhaps knowing or hoping that it would immediately turn his hearers' minds back to this psalm. As we read Jesus' teaching in these three chapters of Matthew's Gospel (or very similar words in Luke chapter 6) we find many echoes of words and thoughts from the psalm.

In the final verse of the psalm, the writer sets before people the two *ways*, one of which they must choose. Again, like the psalmist, Jesus sets before people a choice between two ways. "Enter through the narrow gate; for the gate is wide and the road is easy that leads to destruction, and there are many who take it. For the gate is narrow and the road is hard that leads to life, and there are few who find it." (Matthew 7.13-14). In the Acts of the Apostles the disciples of Jesus are said to 'belong to the Way.' (Acts 9.2, and many other places). In John's Gospel Jesus says, "I am the Way, the Truth and the Life." (14.6).

The psalm rejoices in God's law and those who keep it. Jesus said, again in the Sermon on the Mount, that he came to fulfil the Law and the Prophets, not to destroy them (Matthew 5.17). And later in the same collection of teaching (Matthew 5.44), he said, "I say to you, Love your enemies and pray for those who persecute you." Perhaps when he spoke of enemies he had in mind the many and various enemies we meet in a number of the psalms. When we feel persecuted or undervalued and think that we have an enemy or enemies, we should leave any judgement of them to God. We should try to understand why they act as they do and what their needs are. Our pattern and inspiration might be the first Christian martyr, St.

Stephen. He died, praying, "Lord Jesus, do not hold this sin against them." (Acts 7.60). And, of course, Stephen's pattern and inspiration was Our Lord who, on the cross, prayed "Father, forgive them; for they know not what they do" (Luke 23.34). If we try, in some way, to come closer to those examples, perhaps we shall then experience the blessedness which both the writer of Psalm 1 and our Lord promise.

Psalm 2

This psalm may also have been deliberately placed. It ends as Psalm 1 began with the promise of *blessedness.* The final verse says that this blessedness is available to all who take refuge in God, and the rest of the psalm indicates that it is primarily the king who must take such refuge, rather than relying on his own wisdom, power or virtue.

The psalm moves us from the concerns of individuals which dominate Psalm 1 to the concerns of nations. Many scholars think that this psalm was used at the enthronement of a king of Judah in Jerusalem. Even when the nations of Israel and Judah were united under David and Solomon they were small players on the large international stage occupied by great powers like Egypt, Assyria, Babylon and the Hittites. Nonetheless they were important because they were a buffer state through which the greater powers usually had to pass to attack each other. In the *Books of Kings*, we can read about the constant invasions and the treaties made and broken.

For the psalmist the wars and victories, the ambitions and arrogance of rulers are futile. They strut the stage. They think they are powerful, but in reality all power belongs to God, and in verse 4 the psalmist pictures God laughing at their antics. Then in verse 5 his scorn turns to anger as they dare to threaten the man he has placed on the throne of Judah.

In the political and military affairs of the Middle East, the enthronement of a king, even in a small nation like Judah, would be watched warily. Who could tell what a new ruler might attempt, what gifts he had, what alliances he might make? Well might nations be wary and suspicious. For the psalmist the enthronement ceremony in Jerusalem had a cosmic significance. The king was God's appointment. He was given unparalleled dignity by being adopted as God's son against whom, if God so chose, no earthly power could stand (v. 7). Though it was certainly not obvious, the Davidic king in Jerusalem was more than a petty Middle Eastern ruler. Despite appearances, despite military and political realities, his rule was part of God's plan which had first been declared to Abraham, that through him and his descendants all the families of the earth should be blessed (Genesis 12.3).

This psalm raises the difficult question about God's rule in an apparently Godless world. The chaotic state of the world – the wars, the cruelties, the accidents of nature, the apparent triumph of evil – forces us to ask the question, "Is God really in control?" Not only in the psalms, but throughout the Old Testament the answer is always a resounding 'Yes'. God is in control and he uses nations and their rulers gradually to achieve his beneficent ends despite human wickedness and stupidity. So the defeats and setbacks of his people are punishment for their apostasy. He will accomplish his ends in his own way however strange those ways may seem to mere humans. Therefore he will choose Cyrus of Persia to end the ascendency of Babylon and ensure the return of the Jewish exiles to Judah (Isaiah 45.1-7).

What do we think about it? Is God in control? Is the setting up of his kingdom delayed because he gave human beings free will and, as he will not force us to be good and obedient, has he constantly to adjust his plans?

Christians cannot be indifferent to what goes on in the world. We believe that Jesus inaugurated the kingdom of God, and called people to help him establish the kingdom in its fullness. By our baptism we have been enrolled to help with the task. In our prayers we say, "Thy kingdom come", and by our actions we try to make it a reality. We cannot allow ourselves to be discouraged by the seeming greatness of the task. We may not be able to influence international or even national affairs, but we have our own bit of the garden to care for and make beautiful. We should just get on with it. Mother Teresa said, "What can you do to promote world peace? Go home and love your family."

From the earliest days of the faith, Christians have linked this psalm with Jesus. The words of verse 3, "You are my son, today I have begotten you", were heard from heaven after he had been baptised by John (Mark 1.11). St Paul used them in one of his missionary sermons (Acts 13.34). They are used in the *Letter to the Hebrews* to stress that as God's Son, Jesus ranks far above any other being (Hebrews 1.5 and 5.5). Most striking of all is the fact that the three titles used in this psalm, Anointed One, Son and King, are used against Jesus in his trials (Mark 14.61 and 15.2). The Hebrew of verses 11 and 12 is obscure and its meaning uncertain. We cannot, however, fail to be struck by the words *kiss his feet.* They remind us of the story of the 'woman of the city' who was present at a meal at a Pharisee's house at which Jesus was a guest: "Standing behind him at his feet, weeping, she began to wet his feet with her tears, and wiped them with the hair of her head, and kissed his feet, and anointed them with the ointment." (Luke 7.36-50).

It might seem strange and unrealistic for the psalmist to imagine that the enthronement of a king in little Judah had cosmic significance. But those enthronements foreshadowed a future one. When Pontius Pilate was Procurator of Judaea he oversaw the crucifixion of many Jews. But one of the victims had been heralded, at his baptism by John, as God's son. In his ministry he had proclaimed the coming of God's kingdom and now, helpless, he reigned from his throne, the cross. Christians believe that what seemed to most onlookers to be an everyday cruel but trivial event, was actually of cosmic significance. And the vision of the psalmist – *Ask of me, and I will make the nations your heritage, and the ends of the earth your possession,* is the hope and longing of all Christians, that God's kingdom of justice and love will be established on earth as it is in heaven.

Psalm 3

The heading to this psalm says, *a Psalm of David, when he fled from Absalom his son.* The incident is recorded in 2 Samuel, chapter 15. The words of the psalm are certainly appropriate in the mouth of a ruler against whom are ranged many enemies. Whoever the ruler or king is, his many enemies taunt him and encourage themselves by saying that the God who appointed him and is supposed to guide and protect him is powerless and can do nothing; *there is no help for him in God.*

Despite appearances and the apparently overwhelming power of his enemies, the poet-king declares his trust in God who is his help and shield. He looks back, and from personal experience can say that God has been his shield and his sustainer. His enemies are mistaken; God hears him, listens to him and acts. He finds confidence in his belief that God makes his earthly home on Mount Zion, *his holy hill.* The king is perhaps recalling his own coronation and enthronement and the assurances given in the temple liturgy that he was chosen by God and adopted as God's son, to rule his people. That assurance gives him strength.

Because of this assurance he can sleep soundly and not be troubled by the enormous numbers in the armies ranged against him (v.5). We find a similar assurance hundreds of years later when the

Jews were being oppressed by the armies of Syria. Judas Maccabee encouraged his small army saying, "It is not on the size of the army that victory in battles depends, but strength comes from Heaven. They come against us in great insolence and lawlessness to destroy us and our wives and our children, and to despoil us, but we fight for our lives and our laws." (I Macc. 3.19-22). Similar sentiments and words have inspired and strengthened many who have gone into battle believing their cause was also the cause of God.

The psalm draws to a close with a prayer for God's help and deliverance. The defeat of his enemies will not be the king's own doing. It is God who will smite the enemy and the victory will be God's, not the king's. The final words ask for God's blessing on the nation, God's chosen people.

Should Christians follow the psalmist's example and pray for victory in war? Whether we should or not, we do. It seems to be the most natural thing even if we know that our enemy is uttering the same prayer to the same God. Things have changed greatly from the psalmist's day when wars were conducted with swords and spears and bows. He could never have imagined the destructive power of modern weapons. What do Christians think? Some, for example the Friends or Quakers, are pacifists while others believe that war is, in some circumstances, the lesser evil.

Each year Christians are forced to consider their attitude to war as they gather to pray on Remembrance Sunday. Along with the quite proper gratitude and remembrance of those who died in armed conflicts, there always lurks the temptation to glorify war. That can never be right. Whether we are pacifists or would simply like to be able to be pacifists, we should remind ourselves that though Jesus never gave clear teaching on the matter, he behaved as a pacifist. Despite having a Canaanaean, or Zealot, as a disciple (Mark 3.18), he seemed to distance himself from any nationalist group. When arrested, he complained that they had come after him as if he were a military Messiah (Mark 14.48). The word used in that verse and traditionally translated as 'robber' was commonly used to mean a militant nationalist. Jesus then refused to defend himself in court, and told Pilate that if he were the kind of Messiah who was set on driving out the Roman invaders, his followers would have fought for him (John 18.36).

It seems to be the most natural of human reactions to oppose force with force. We should remember that that was not the way of Christ. His way is the costly, painful way of the cross. The atheist, George Bernard Shaw, is reputed to have said, "It's not that

Christianity has been tried and found wanting. It's that it's been found difficult and not tried."

The psalm teaches trust in God. The poet-king had experienced the help of God in the past and he finds that help continuing in the present. Because of that he could also look with confidence to the future. When we feel despondent, fearful or despairing it is good to look back over our life and recall a time or times when we were aware of God's help and guidance. Then, like the psalmist, we can assure ourselves that he will be with us now, our shield and the lifter of our head.

Psalm 4

This psalm has traditionally been used at the late evening service Compline because of the final verse in which the psalmist says he can go to his bed in complete tranquillity because he trusts that God will keep him safe.

Trust in God is the theme of the psalm. It begins with an almost peremptory cry to God to listen to the prayer that is being offered. He is praying with confidence because he has experienced God's care in the past when he has been in distress.

In verses 2 and 3 he turns to those who have told lies about him, and tells them that God will always help the faithful, among whom he counts himself. He goes on to say that though their anger can be understood and accepted, their deliberate wrong-doing cannot. He advises them to examine their lives, to look into their consciences. Then they will see where they have gone wrong. They will fall silent; their lies and their false accusations will cease. They should then formally seal their repentance by the offering of sacrifice.

The psalmist knows that many people find life a struggle. They long for something good to come along – *who will show us any good?* (v. 6). He then prays for them in words very similar to part of the Aaronic blessing, beautiful words which are often used in Christian worship: "The Lord bless you and keep you; the Lord make his face to shine upon you and be gracious to you; the Lord lift up his countenance upon you, and give you peace." (Numbers 6.24-26). Perhaps, the psalmist intends that his brief allusion to the blessing will help people to invoke the whole blessing on themselves.

He goes on to say that for him God's blessing brings joy greater than that felt when the fields yield a rich harvest. With that assurance of God's care and blessing he can lie down, certain of a good night's sleep.

35

Few people escape the occasional night made sleepless with worry. The causes might be perfectly understandable; worries about health (one's own, or more likely, that of family or friend). It might be worry about children or parents, about money or jobs. What we all know is that such worry rarely helps. We also know that things are always far worse at 3.00 a.m. than at 8.00 a.m. It is the unnecessary anticipation of disasters which may never materialise that is destructive. Jesus told us to live a day at a time, "So do not worry about tomorrow, for tomorrow will bring worries of its own. Today's trouble is enough for today." (Matt. 6.34).

The psalmist gives good advice. The searching of our conscience before we sleep; a prayer for God's forgiveness, and perhaps, the repeating of the psalm's closing words might bring us the calm and assurance which the psalmist found. *In peace, I will both lie down and sleep; for thou alone, O Lord, makest me dwell in safety.*

Psalm 5

After the evening setting of psalm 4 we come to one that may have been composed for use at the morning sacrifice. (This order should not surprise us. Remember that the Sabbath, and indeed every day, begins at dusk.) In the first two verses, the poet pleads with God to listen to him, using three separate words or phrases, *give ear, give heed* and *hearken.* He desperately wants to unburden himself and asks that not just his words, but his thoughts also should be considered by God.

Like most people who pray, he is aware of how quickly his mind wanders, how easily he is distracted, and he fears that he is not worthy to be noticed by God. He tries to do the right thing, praying and offering sacrifice. He uses the word *watch* in verse 3, so perhaps, he had kept vigil through the night, watching, praying and waiting on God in silence.

In verses 5 and 6 he begins to unburden himself. He knows that the wicked do not qualify to take part in the festival liturgy and acknowledges, in verse 7, that he enters the temple, not because of his own goodness, but because of God's mercy and loving-kindness. We are reminded of the centurion's words to Jesus, words which are sometimes used just before we receive Communion, "Lord... I am not worthy to have you come under my roof." (Matthew 8.8). Our dependence on God's mercy and forgiveness rather than on our own virtues finds its place in the Anglican liturgy in the Prayer of Humble Access: "We do not presume to come to this your table, merciful Lord, trusting in our own righteousness, but in your manifold and great mercies…"

The psalmist's life is complex and difficult. He cannot see clearly what he ought to do. If the speaker is the king or some other person with authority and responsibility, as many scholars think, he has the worries and needs of the nation on his mind, not just his own concerns. And so, in verse 8, he pours out his greatest need in prayer, *Lead me, Lord.* If only that were a regular and sincere prayer of all those in authority!

It is the psalmist's awareness of his own weaknesses that lifts him above his enemies. They flatter, they lie. His description of their *throat,* their speaking, as *an open sepulchre,* a gaping tomb, reminds us that Jesus called some of the Pharisees *white-washed tombs,* because they appeared bright and clean at first glance but on closer inspection could be seen to be full of corruption (Matt. 23.27). We should never judge people purely by appearances – nor expect ourselves to be so judged.

In verse 10 he asks God to call his enemies to account. There is no shying away from the seriousness of wickedness, of lives which are a rebellion, not just against the psalmist or other people, but also against God. But the psalmist is content, as we should be, to leave judgement in the hands of God.

In verse 11, there is an interesting and significant change. Up to this point he has been concerned with his own prayers, his part in the festival liturgy, his enemies, his conscience and God's mercy to him. He has been at the centre of it all. But now he prays that all who take refuge in God may rejoice and sing for joy. He has left the wicked to the judgement and mercy of God, and now feels himself part of the family of believers. He is confident that God will bless all the righteous.

At one time, it was difficult for Christians of one denomination to bless those of another denomination and count them as righteous. Generally speaking, we are now a little better, a little more charitable when we think of our fellow-Christians. We can forgive what appear to be their oddities and we can count them righteous. What about the righteous of other faiths? The rise of militant Islam and the growth of fundamentalism in other religions, not excluding Christianity, can make us forget or overlook the righteous among Hindus, Buddhists, and Sikhs, among Jews and Muslims. And what about righteous atheists? Unlike fashionable clothing, it's not the label that counts, it's the way of life. Jesus was asked, "Lord, will those who are saved be few?" He gave what must have been a surprising but very clear answer. He says, "You will weep and gnash your teeth, when you see Abraham and Isaac and Jacob and all the prophets in the kingdom of God and you yourselves thrust out. And men will come from east and west, and from north and south, and sit at table in the kingdom of God." (Luke 13. 28, 29). He also said, "Not everyone who says to me, 'Lord, Lord,' shall enter the kingdom of heaven, but he who does the will of my Father who is in heaven." We might imagine God smiling with pleasure as he welcomes the righteous of all faiths (and of none) along with the saints and martyrs whom we would expect to find in his company. Our business is to try to ensure that we are there too.

Psalm 6

This psalm is regarded as the first of the seven Penitential Psalms. The others are Psalms 32, 38, 51, 102, 130 and 143.

The psalmist comes before God asking for mercy. The precise nature of his sin is not described or mentioned, but he clearly feels that God's anger and punishment would be just. The result of his sin is pain and anguish in both body and mind (v.2). His situation is long-standing and his prayer has often been repeated, and so he asks, *How long?* (v. 3).

In verses 4 and 5 we see that he shares the common belief of the time that a relationship with God was possible only for the living. If God does not relieve his suffering and he dies, he will no longer be able to praise God, and praising God is the purpose of human life.

His suffering is so intense that he cannot keep it out of his thoughts and prayers (vv. 6, 7). He cannot sleep because of his feelings of guilt and he is afraid *because of my foes.* Who or what the foes are we cannot tell. They may be people or they may be the temptations which seem to attack him violently, and which he has not been able to overcome.

In verse 8 there is a change of mood. It has been suggested that what the psalmist has said so far has been a form of confession – perhaps in an act of public worship. If so, it might have been followed by an absolution, words of forgiveness and reassurance spoken by a priest or other leader of worship which have not found their way into the text of the psalm. Sure of having received forgiveness, he is confident that his prayer has been heard (vv. 8, 9).

He can end his poem dismissing his enemies, the *workers of evil.* From the tone of the whole psalm it seems probable that his enemies are indeed his fears, his feelings of guilt and perhaps his ill-health.

Because his confidence in God's care and mercy has been renewed he knows that those enemies can be overcome.

This psalm reminds us of the efficacy of confession, whether in public worship or in private. The use of a set form of confession in a service can be liberating or it can count for very little. St. Paul wrote, "Let a man examine himself and so eat the bread and drink the cup." (I Cor.11.28). The set form of General Confession in a service assumes that we have already looked into our lives and our consciences so that we are not merely going through a routine. It is when we really mean what we say in a confession that we feel the warmth of God's mercy; burdens are shed and a new start is possible.

The psalmist became sure of God's forgiveness. How much more reason have Christians to share that confidence. Constantly in the Gospels we read of Jesus forgiving, sometimes, at the same time as healing (Mark 2.5). In the remarkable story in John 8, 1-12, we see how Jesus dealt with a woman accused of adultery. Having pierced the consciences of those who accused her so that, ashamed, they all went away Jesus said to her, "Woman, where are they? Has no one condemned you?" She said, "No one, Lord." And Jesus said, "Neither do I condemn you; go and do not sin again." He not only spoke about forgiveness; he practised it. Who can forget that as he was nailed to the cross he prayed, "Father, forgive them; for they know not what they do." (Luke 23.34).

In the Lord's Prayer we say, "Forgive us our trespasses as we forgive those who trespass against us." In Mark 11.25 Jesus utters very challenging words on forgiveness: "And whenever you stand praying, forgive, if you have anything against anyone; so that your Father also who is in heaven may forgive you, your trespasses." It firmly places the responsibility on us. He seems to be saying that if we are unforgiving we prevent God forgiving us. It is almost as if God's forgiveness pours down constantly and copiously, like rain from the clouds. However, we have the umbrella of unforgiving-ness. We can put up that umbrella by failing to forgive those who offend us. If we do, we harden ourselves and prevent God's forgiveness reaching us and washing away our sins. God's forgiveness is unlimited, it is real and it is liberating and health-giving, but is not cheap.

Psalm 7

Time and again, as we read this psalm, we meet the poet's sure confidence that God is just. It is for this divine justice that the psalmist prays, believing that God will protect and care for him.

So fierce is the attack that is being made on him that he feels like the victim of a wild animal (v.2). He recounts the things he is accused of, but claims that they are all slanders; he has done none of them. Confident in his innocence he invites God to let his enemies triumph over him if he is guilty (vv 5, 6).

He pictures the court of heaven, rather as in the first chapter of Job, with God as the supreme judge surrounded by other, lesser, heavenly beings. God knows all the facts and his judgement is therefore fair. Again the psalmist claims the innocence which will ensure his vindication (v.7).

Both good and bad will receive justice (v. 9). The wicked will be dealt with severely.

He ends thanking and praising God for his justice, and promising to sing the praises of the righteous God. Perhaps, he intends taking part in an act of public worship in the temple and so joining in the singing of God's praise.

The idea of divine justice and of God's *wrath* which is mentioned so often in the Old Testament, and is by no means absent from the New Testament, should not be misunderstood. The picture of God with clipboard in hand, noting down our every mistake and sin and then thinking out a suitable punishment – rather like Gilbert and Sullivan's Mikado – is not helpful. God created the world with physical laws. If you drop a cup it will fall. If the floor is hard the cup will break. We expect such an outcome. It is the law of gravity and without it, life as we know it would be impossible because it would be unpredictable. The Bible teaches that there are similar moral laws in God's creation. Wickedness does not go unpunished because, like the dropped cup, it brings destruction upon itself.

In his book, *The Go-Between God*, John Taylor wrote, "the wrath of God is only another name for the divine dissatisfaction. The unfulfilled, the spoiled, the second-best must be exposed to a clear, unambiguous disapproval." Christians believe that were it not for the mercy of God, revealed in the Bible and demonstrated in the life, teaching, death and resurrection of Jesus, we should all, cup-like, clatter to the floor. We have good reason to share the psalmist's belief in and praise of God's justice. We also have great reason to praise the patience and mercy of God.

Psalm 8

This is a wonderful hymn of praise to the Creator. It begins and ends with an exclamation of wonder at the majesty of the Lord, Yahweh, the God of Israel. Yahweh is no tribal god, no mere agricultural god like the baals of Canaan. He is the sole creator of all.

The poet grandly interprets the random, inarticulate cries of babies and small infants as words of praise glorifying God. Perhaps he is thinking too of the instinctive awe with which children observe the wonders of nature (v. 2). It reminds us that Jesus told his disciples that they must become like little children if they are to enter God's kingdom; they too must be open to the wonder and majesty of God and of his creation (Mark 10.15).

The poet's observation of the night sky fills him with wonder. It is difficult now for most people to see the night sky in its full glory because of the artificial light we provide to keep our villages, towns and cities safe at night. I recall two occasions in my life, one in mid-Wales and one in Turkey when, far from urban life, I was awe-struck by the night sky. Looking at the sheer abundance of stars, I became aware how vivid and extravagant was God's promise to Abraham that his descendants would be as numerous as the stars of heaven (Genesis 15.5).

His star-gazing convinces the psalmist of the greatness of God. That leads him on to realise that in comparison humans are very feeble. He is filled with wonder (in verse 4) that the great God is not only aware of the human race, but actually cares for it.

Despite man's lowly standing, God has set him in authority over the rest of creation. In verses 3-8 he follows the theme of the first creation story in Genesis chapter 1, in which man is given authority and responsibility.

The human race seems always to have assumed its authority quite readily, and down the centuries has used animals and plants for food and comfort. Those who live close to nature have traditionally been sensitive in their contacts with the natural world. They have known and recognised the burden of human responsibility. Modern urban life in a consumer society tends to put nature at a distance, and we can easily take it for granted, use it and assume our authority over it. Thankfully our responsibility for God's creation has been recognised more fully in recent years. Not all those who care for the creation would accept that it is God's creation and that he gave humans the responsibility they readily shoulder. Happily, regardless of their motive, what they do glorifies God and we should be grateful for all who recognise and take up this task, which we believe is God-given.

Psalms 9 and 10

We look at these two psalms together for a number of reasons. The most compelling is that in the Greek version of the Hebrew Bible, known as the Septuagint, the two are one psalm. Also there is no title to Psalm 10 separating it from Psalm 9. And despite the text being rather jumbled (what is known as 'corrupt'), there is some evidence that the opening words of each verse of the psalms were arranged in alphabetical order. So we look at the two psalms together.

In the opening verses the psalmist seems to be looking back to some military triumph. The words were perhaps said by the king in a formal service of thanksgiving in the temple. We notice that victory is attributed not to the king's leadership or strength, but to God. *Thou hast rebuked the nations, thou hast destroyed the wicked.*

The psalm goes on to assert that God orders the fortunes of nations from his heavenly throne (vv. 7, 8), and that he always cares for the downtrodden and oppressed (vv. 9, 10). The psalmist then calls others to praise God, perhaps inviting a congregational response.

Having declared his faith he goes on to make his own plea, *be gracious to me, O Lord.* The prayer is made in faith and he hopes to be able to give thanks again in the congregation of worshippers (v.14).

Once again wrong-doing is believed to carry within it the seeds of its own destruction (vv.15-17) whereas the needy will always be remembered by God. He ends with a plea that God should act decisively and put hubristic man in his proper place (vv.19, 20).

(Psalm 10). The poet now turns to his personal needs. He feels that God is distant and unconcerned about his sufferings. Because God's presence in the world is not obvious, the wicked oppress the poor and boast that God does not respond to his worshippers because *there is no God.* He goes on to detail the unjust acts of the wicked – lies, cursing, deceit, violence, murder. It is godlessness that makes the wicked man act as he does for he argues that even if God exists, *he will never see it (*v.11).

The poet returns to the cry which ended Psalm 9, *arise, O Lord.* He recalls that God has acted in the past (v.14) and he calls on him to act again. He reiterates his faith in the supreme power of God, even over nations which do not acknowledge him (v.16).

The psalm ends with a statement that God will help *the meek, the fatherless and the oppressed,* and arrogant humans will be put in their place.

We have probably all at some time made a similar prayer, the passionate prayer of a believer who fears that God is not listening. "Arise, O Lord," said the psalmist. How often have we prayed that prayer, though probably in different words? "Do something, God, please." When a loved-one is ill, when marriages break up, when jobs cannot be found, when we read of suffering, injustice, starvation, we sometimes move from the frustrated prayer of faith and think the thoughts of the arrogant or the crushed – *God has forgotten, he has hidden his face, he will never see it* (Ps.10.11).

In many of the psalms the poets plead with God not to hide his face, not to turn away and ignore their plea. Christians often feel the same; that our prayers go nowhere or are not answered. The great mystics write of the 'dark night of the soul', their experience of blankness when God seems to be absent. What should we do? We must keep on praying however hard it is. When we feel we are achieving nothing, we should remember that someone, to whom we should be very grateful, said, "If you are trying to pray, you are praying." Some Christians used to talk about 'storming the gates of heaven,' meaning, praying and praying, asking and asking, and going on asking. We might not like the expression, but its sentiment is sound and in accordance with Isaiah chapter 62, verses 6 and 7: "You who put the Lord in remembrance, take no rest, and give him no rest until he establishes Jerusalem."

Like the psalmist, we have to go on praying, refusing to despair and believing with Lady Julian of Norwich that because God is loving and merciful, "all shall be well, and all manner of things shall be well."

Psalm 11

The first verse tells us that the psalmist's situation is so dangerous that his friends have advised him to flee and take refuge in the mountains. But even before he mentions this advice he proclaims that his safety lies in Yahweh, the God of Israel. Nevertheless he feels as if he is being hunted by an assailant he cannot see (v.2). He believes that the attacks made on him are the symptom of a malaise which will undermine and destroy society, leaving the righteous unable to influence the nation for good (v.3).

He then reminds himself and his hearers that things are not what they seem. However chaotic and unjust things seem to be, God rules, not only in heaven but on earth too. Perhaps this psalm was used in a temple liturgy celebrating God's kingship over the nation. Yahweh rules, not only over the nation of Israel, but over all nations. He sees and knows everything.

Testing and adversity come to good and bad alike; *God tests the righteous and the wicked.* And it is the response to the testing that determines who are the righteous and who are the wicked (v.5).

It then seems a strange contradiction that having said, in v.5, that God hates those who indulge in violence, he goes on in v.6, to predict that God will punish them violently. The punishment specified is akin to that poured out on Sodom and Gomorrah (Genesis 19.24), and so perhaps the words are poetic, metaphorical, not meant to be taken literally.

The psalm ends asserting that God will reward the righteous. Many would question that statement, standing with Job and saying that all too often the righteous suffer and suffer unjustly. In the Old Testament the received belief is that God favours the righteous and punishes the wicked. Thus when the righteous and prosperous Job is stricken with poverty, bereavement and sickness his friends, the 'Comforters' can only say that he must have done something wrong even if he can't remember what it was (for example, Job 4.7). Job cannot accept their simplistic explanation of his misery, and is only satisfied when God forces him to realise that his point of view is very personal and limited: he does not and cannot understand the mind and actions of God (Job 38-42).

It is often said that it is not what happens to us in life that determines the sort of person we are, but how we deal with what happens. Christians know that suffering can be redemptive, and the supreme example of the innocent suffering is Jesus. So we learn that not all suffering is futile, and St Paul can even say that his own sufferings go to make up what is lacking in the sufferings of Jesus (Colossians 1.24).

The psalmist's categories of righteous and wicked are stark, black and white, mutually exclusive. Most of us are aware that we are a mixture of the two, tending now one way, now the other. So we pray for God's grace to help us move gradually towards the righteous end of the balance.

We should note how the psalm ends. *The Lord is righteous, he loves righteous deeds.* The reward for those who do such deeds is not wealth or popularity, not health or long life. It is the vision of God: *the upright shall behold his face.* That vision was sought by the psalmist and it is sought by us. "It will be the reward," said Jesus, "for the pure in heart." (Matt. 5.8).

Psalm 12

The poet calls for God's help. He fears that he and others who are faithful to God and God's laws are powerless. Society is dominated by clever talkers, using words to achieve their ends, even if the words are lies. They will say anything to achieve their ends (v.1, 2). They know that they deceive people, and they glory in their cleverness; *with our tongue we will prevail, our lips are with us; who is our master?* (v. 4). The psalmist prays that God will put an end to their power and their influence (v.3).

In verse 5 there is a change of voice. It becomes the voice of God. Perhaps the words were spoken by a priest. They state that God is waiting to help. It is the plight of the poor and needy that moves God to act. Here again we find the theme repeated, not just throughout the psalter, but in the prophets too, that God cares for the poor and needy. For just three examples in the prophetic writings, we might look at Ezekiel 34.3,4, Amos 5.12, and Micah 6.8.

In stark contrast to the lying words of the ungodly, God's words are utterly trustworthy. Throughout Israel's history God's words and God's faithfulness have been tested many times, and have been found as pure and valuable as refined silver (v.6).

The psalm ends very realistically, expecting corruption to continue among rulers. Not only that, among the ruling elite dishonesty is expected and admired; *On every side the wicked prowl, as vileness is exalted among the sons of men (*v.8). So his prayer returns to the *help* of verse 1, asking *Do thou, O Lord, protect us.*

It is impossible not to make comparisons with politics today, or probably at any time since and before the psalmist wrote. Many, perhaps all, who put themselves forward to serve as our representatives and find themselves in positions of power and influence genuinely want the opportunity to do good for society. However, power corrupts and there is evidence that some fall from the highest standards of behaviour. As in the psalmist's day, the power of the word is triumphant. 'Spin doctors' are used to present matters cleverly, though not necessarily honestly. *With our tongues we will prevail* could be the motto of any political party. No one will dare to be a Jeremiah and speak the truth regardless of an unpleasant outcome for himself. If the example is set by people of influence and power it will be followed, and people will assume that half-truths or untruths are acceptable in our dealings with each other. What a comment that is on any society!

Like the psalmist we need to ask for God's protection from deceitful words. We need also to realise that we have far, far more power than did the ordinary citizen in the psalmist's day. We should demand integrity from people in public life. More important, we should set such standards in our own day-to-day contacts with people. Eventually, those who lead might learn to follow.

Psalm 13

This is the prayer of a deeply troubled man. It has a simple structure moving from lament to song of praise.

His agony, whether it is physical, mental or spiritual, or all three, is poured out in the thrice repeated *how long?* It seems to the psalmist that he has been asking for God's help for a very long time, and God has still not answered. It is the spiritual pain that troubles him most deeply, and he mentions it first. Has God forgotten him, or worse, is God hiding from him? He speaks of pain in his soul and sorrow in his heart. His deepest suffering is his separation from God. In the first two verses, whatever it is that is separating him from God is the *enemy.*

In the second section of the psalm, verses 3 and 4, he seems to be speaking of physical pain and even fears that he might die. Again the enemy may be the problem he is wrestling with, or it may be critics and detractors who would delight to be able to say that his faith in God has been shaken.

Verse 5 begins with a resounding *But.* It now appears that his plea *How long?* and his prayer *consider and answer me* have been heard. God has not forgotten him; their relationship has been restored and God has been *bountiful* in bestowing *steadfast love* and *salvation.* The joy with which he is now filled leads him to sing God's praises.

This little gem of a psalm is wonderful to turn to and ponder when we feel dispirited and alone. One of the great benefits of the psalms is that they match all our moods and needs. In the Introduction, we read of Luther's and Calvin's eloquent testimony to this. When we are tempted to despair of God or of fellow humans, when we feel isolated and think that no one suffers as we suffer and that no one understands us, by reading the psalms we are reminded that others have felt the same. By perseverance in prayer and steadfastness in faith they have come through with prayers answered and faith strengthened.

We find Our Lord in this psalm. He felt that God had deserted him and on the cross he prayed, "My God, my God, why have you forsaken me?" The clouds had started to gather over Jesus in the Garden of Gethsemane when he feared that the suffering he saw ahead would be too much for him. All three Synoptic Gospels record how he prayed, "Father, all things are possible to thee; remove this cup from me." All three record that, strengthened somehow, Jesus continued, "Yet not what I will, but what thou wilt." St. Luke alone records that at that moment an angel strengthened him (Luke 22.43).

When we doubt our strength and faithfulness we should try to remember that in similar circumstances Our Lord received help from God. How much more do we need that help and, having been there himself, how ready Our Lord is to strengthen us?

Psalm 14

The psalmist looks at the nation and sees corruption everywhere (v.1). He believes that the cause of the decay in society is atheism. In the Old Testament world virtually everyone believed in God or gods. Atheism was not so much an intellectual theory, as it is today, it was a practical matter. It meant behaving as if there were no God. In the psalmist's opinion, it is such people who lead and influence society, causing its foundations to totter.

The poet pictures God looking down from heaven on those in authority in the nation, and vainly searching for a good person, a person who cares for those in need as God cares for them. He cannot find one that *does good.* The logic of the atheists is inexorable. If there is no God, or if we discount his reality, then we can do as we please. Ordinary people are the victims of practical atheism. The powerful are like gluttons. In their lust for wealth and power, it is as if they gobble up people, counting them cheap, of no more account than a loaf of bread. It is a pitiful picture of the psalmist's society.

In verses 5 and 6 the psalmist says that God cares for the very people who are despised and ill-used by the wicked. This insistence that God cares for the poor and needy we find repeated time and again in the psalms as in the prophets. This bias to the poor is seen, not only in the clear teaching of Jesus, but even in the stories surrounding his birth. Poor shepherds are the first to be told the good news and to visit and worship the Christ-child. Kings or Wise Men, the powerful and the clever, come later.

Verse 7 prays that the nation might be delivered from its corrupt leaders and that, beginning from the temple in Jerusalem, God's ways will radiate throughout the nation creating or restoring a just and healthy society.

How important it is that we pray for all in positions of influence, authority and responsibility in society. How important too that Christians put themselves forward to serve in such positions.

Christian involvement in politics is vital. Those who say that religion's business is saving souls and preparing people for heaven, and it should stick to that, have not read or have failed to understand the core teaching of both Old and New Testaments. Both are about seeking to establish God's kingdom 'on earth as it is in heaven'. We are called to transform the world, not to ignore it.

Psalm 15

This psalm sounds as if it might have been used as a form of preparation for involvement in a great festival liturgy. In verse 1, the speaker asks who is worthy to approach God in his sacred place, the temple, on the holy hill of Zion. A formal setting is made more likely by the use of the word *tabernacle,* rather than temple. It takes the worshippers thoughts back to the days of the wilderness wanderings of Israel when a moveable tent, a tabernacle, was the place where Moses would meet with God 'face to face.' (Exodus 33.7-11). The pilgrim worshippers in the temple also hoped to meet with God.

After the question in verse 1, the answer, perhaps delivered by a priest, takes up the rest of the psalm. It is noticeable and important that there are no ritual requirements; nothing about ritual purity or ceremonial actions. All the requirements are moral ones. First comes the positive one: a blameless life is required, not only avoiding sin but actually doing good. Then come the negatives. Just as in the Ten Commandments, prohibitions are listed. All are concerned with the sustaining of a just and peaceful society. Thus good people will not speak evil of others; they will be loyal friends and good neighbours; they will avoid bad and seek good company. They will always speak the truth even if it is to their disadvantage. They will not make money from usury. They will be totally incorruptible.

At this point in the psalm, it is likely that we have a clear picture of what makes the ideal citizen and we have forgotten that the point was to discover who was fit to approach and worship God. It is salutary to be reminded that God wants just and generous living rather than overt piety and the cultivation of our own inner life. The final words of the psalm say that one who fulfils all the standards laid down *shall never be moved.* Perhaps, that means that their awareness of God's presence will be constant.

A Christian would probably say that it is right for us to strive to attain high standards in our lives, but that in fact we never achieve it. St. Paul gave the classic expression of this realistic look at ourselves in Romans 7.19; "For I do not do the good I want, but the evil I do not want is what I do." Very properly, as we come close to God in the Eucharist, just before we receive the sacrament, we say "We do not presume to come to this your table, merciful Lord, trusting in our own righteousness, but in your manifold and great mercies."

When, like the psalmist, we approach the holy God, we try to be worthy and to live according to his laws. But we know that, in the end, we rely not on our own achievements but on God's mercy and grace.

Psalm 16

The text of this psalm is very 'corrupt' and translators have had to make educated guesses at the meaning of some of the verses.

In the first verse the psalmist prays that God will protect him, and in verse 2 we understand that he has received such protection in the past. In verse 3 he speaks of how important is fellowship or membership in a faith community. His delight is to be in the company of his fellow-worshippers, *the saints.* The word does not mean morally flawless, but 'dedicated' or 'set apart' for God. St. Paul regularly describes the Christian communities to whom he writes as 'saints' (for example, II Cor. 1.1 and Philippians 1.1), or 'called to be saints' (Romans 1.7 and I Cor. 1.2). We are reminded that membership and fellowship are vital to our faith. Someone once said, "There is no such thing as a solitary Christian." The most remote anchorite is a vital part of the Body of Christ. He prays for his fellow-Christians whom he never sees and for the world which he has left, and his prayers and membership are as vital to the life of the Church as the blood which courses unseen around our bodies is vital for our physical life. Each Christian has a role to play, important for the well-being of all other members, as St. Paul spells out in Romans chapter 12. How good it is that we now share the Peace in Communion services, acknowledging that we are in communion with each other as well as with God. Indeed we cannot be in communion with God if we are not in communion with each other (I John 4.20).

Verse 4 records the psalmist's abhorrence of other gods and their cults. As indicated in the Introduction, the lure of other gods was a constant problem throughout the history of Israel. Some of the practices of these cults were barbaric. The psalmist says he will not be part of the pouring of blood as a sacrifice. He is probably thinking of human sacrifice because sacrifices in the temple are regularly mentioned and there seems to have been a ritual of the sprinkling of blood in the Passover liturgy in the temple (II Chron. 35.11). This probably continued the practice recorded in Exodus 24.3-8. It is a vivid scene as Moses seals the covenant made with God by pouring half of the blood of sacrificed oxen on the altar and pouring or sprinkling the other half on the people. The psalmist is distancing himself from the foreign cults which were adopted by some people in Israel and Judah, and which required the sacrifice of children (II Kings 16.3). Human sacrifice had long been removed from the religion of Yahweh. The story of how God prevented Abraham from sacrificing Isaac presses that home (Genesis 22).

Verses 5-8 speak of the happiness the psalmist enjoys because of his closeness to God. Like Christians today, he drinks the cultic cup of wine and places his life in God's hands. He feels guided by God and perhaps, as elsewhere in both Old and New Testaments, dreams are seen as one of the ways in which God communicates with men (Some of the many examples of this belief are found in the Joseph stories in Genesis 37.3, and chapters 40 and 41 and, in the New Testament, in Matthew 1.20 and chapter 2.12,13 and19). Because God has a place in the psalmist's life, and is always in his thoughts when he is making decisions, his life is calm and steadfast. It is noticeable that though he mentions in verse 4, those who worship other gods, there is no diatribe against them, no longing for their punishment.

The psalm ends with two verses of rejoicing and hope. He is happy in *heart, soul and body* and has no fear that death will suddenly overtake him and therefore exclude him from God's presence. The early church found in the words of verse 10 a foreshadowing of the resurrection of Jesus. In his sermon in the synagogue in Antioch in Pisidia, St. Paul said, "And as for the fact that he raised him from the dead… he says in another psalm, 'Thou wilt not let thy Holy One see corruption.'"

Verse 11 is beautiful. God guides the poet on the *path of life* and in communion with God he finds *fullness of joy.* We are reminded of Jesus saying that he came as the Good Shepherd so that his sheep, his followers, "may have life and have it abundantly." (John 10.10). There is no naïve attempt by the psalmist to spell out what *pleasure for evermore* might be. That can safely be left to God.

Psalm 17

This psalm may have been part of a temple liturgy in which was enacted God's judgement, his separating of the righteous from the wicked. The picture is very similar to that painted by Jesus in his parable of the sheep and the goats (Matt. 25.31-46). Naturally the psalmist sees himself as one of the righteous, and in the first 5 verses he claims his innocence before God.

In verses 6-9 he affirms his confidence that his prayer will be heard. His plea is that God will protect him from his *deadly* enemies, who surround him and seek to destroy him. Violence seems to be threatened. Verse 8 has the lovely lines which are used as a versicle and response in the evening service of Compline, asking God for protection. *Keep me as the apple of the eye; hide me in the shadow of thy wings.* Generally we do not welcome any shadow or darkness in life; we prefer the broad, sunlit uplands of happiness and contentment. The psalm reminds us that what might seem like darkness may be the gentle overshadowing of God's hand or, picturing God as a mother bird, the shelter of her wings. Francis Thompson felt this, and in his poem *The Hound of Heaven* wrote, "Is my gloom after all, Shade of his hand, outstretched, caressingly?"

The psalmist's opponents are described: pitiless, arrogant, relentless, savage (vv. 10-12). He asks God to intervene and defeat them. Because of the uncertainty of the text it is difficult to know precisely what verse 14 means. It almost sounds as if he is asking God to destroy them by poison which will affect two or perhaps three generations. While we might be surprised or repelled, if that is indeed the meaning, it does remind us that people do harbour feelings of hatred and violence for all sorts of reasons – for being wrongfully accused, for being made redundant, for being bullied, overlooked, deceived, cheated. We can all extend the list. From praying with this psalm we can perhaps learn not to judge those who seem to oppress us. We cannot fully know their reasons. And we can learn not to demand vengeance, but to follow our Lord and put all things into the hands of God. On the cross, he might well have prayed this psalm as well as Psalm 22, pleading his innocence and the injustice of his plight.

The psalmist, having exhausted his incoherent anger (v.15) and having asked God to take care of things, expresses his deepest longing, that he will see God. *When I awake* suggests that he might be following the practice of vigil (sometimes called 'incubation'), spending a night in the temple in prayer in the hope that he will receive some message or guidance from God. He hopes to see the face of God, which is either something that happens in the temple liturgy which was understood as a revelation of God, a moment of ecstatic fervour for the congregation, or perhaps he means a more general but constant sense of the presence of God and his overshadowing love.

Psalm 18

The psalm's heading says, *A Psalm of David the servant of the Lord, who addressed the words of this song to the Lord on the day when the Lord delivered him from the hands of all his enemies, and from the hand of Saul.* It is interesting that II Samuel chapter 22 contains the whole of the psalm (apart from the first verse) in exactly that setting. If we hesitate to place it as precisely as that, it certainly seems to be a song of thanksgiving for victory, spoken or sung by a king.

It begins (vv.1-2) with a positive avalanche of words celebrating God's support and protection, his encouragement and his faithfulness. In verse 3 he begins his narrative, telling how God responded to his pleas for help. Then, in the next few verses he tells us how critical his situation was. He was close to death and beyond human aid; only God could help. He pictures his prayers reaching the temple in Jerusalem, and God hearing and responding (v.6).

In verses 7-15 he describes in traditional terms the coming of God into the situation. Perhaps he is picturing a dramatic moment in the temple liturgy which assures worshippers of God's presence, or he is using descriptive language similar to that used in Exodus 19. 16-19, when God comes down on Mount Sinai. The fearsome power of the creator is to be seen in the wonders of the natural world.

In verses 16-19 he speaks of how God *delivered* him. Perhaps he sees his salvation, *he drew me out of many waters,* as similar to and as decisive as that enacted by God for the nation at the Red Sea.

He claims (vv. 20-24) that God has helped him because he has ruled as God required, with *clean hands,* avoiding the company of the wicked and observing God's ordinances and statutes.

Verses 25-30 are addressed by the king to God who rewards the righteous and appropriately punishes the wicked, making the king confident that with the help of God he can achieve anything.

The king's personal thanksgiving begins in verse 30. He details some of the ways in which God has helped and inspired him. It is God who has made him a mighty warrior, equipping him with speed and strength. He has been able to pursue and overthrow his enemies and reduce their threat to nothing, mere *dust before the wind (*v.42). He has received the surrender of his enemies (v. 44). He then blesses and thanks God for all the help he has received. With an almost missionary zeal he says that he will use his hard-won power and influence to extol God among the nations – the Gentiles. Finally, the help God has given is seen as God's faithfulness to the covenant made with his *anointed* king, the current representative of the house of David (II Samuel 7.16).

Christians believe that Jesus, whose title *the Christ,* literally means 'the anointed one', is the ruler of the kingdom of God, which he began to establish on earth during his ministry. The task of completing Christ's work when, as the psalmist hoped, all nations will acknowledge his kingship, is given to each generation of Christians to carry forward.

This psalm has a very personal significance for me. Shortly before I was ordained deacon in the Michaelmas Ordinations of 1959, I was feeling, as many do, doubts about my vocation. Was God really calling me to the priesthood? Was I fit to be a priest? It must have been the 3rd September because as I said the Office of Evening Prayer using the Book of Common Prayer, I found that Psalm 18 was the set psalm. As I read the opening verse of the psalm I found reassurance that it didn't matter very much whether I was up to it. In that Prayer Book version I read, "I will love thee, O Lord, my strength; the Lord is my stony rock, and my defence: my Saviour, my God, and my might, in whom I will trust, my buckler, the horn also of my salvation, and my refuge." With that deluge of support and assurance I was able to set my doubts aside or at least live with them.

Psalm 19

Many scholars think that this psalm is made up of two originally separate poems; verses 1-6 in praise of God the creator, and verses 7-14 in praise of God's Law, the Torah. That may well be the case, but those who joined the two parts together did so for a reason, and that reason may become clear as we look at the psalm.

We begin (vv 1-4) with a hymn of praise for the glory of God revealed in his creation (We might notice that this is like Psalm 8 vv 1-3). In verse 1 we feel that the poet must be looking at the glory of the night sky. He finds its magnificent silence eloquent with the praise of God. The unfailing regularity of day and night speaks to him of how, in the act of creation, God imposed order on chaos, just as we read in Genesis chapter 1. We learn that nature is one of the ways by which God communicates with humans.

The greatest glory of the created world is the sun, which in the regularity of its movements reflects God's careful planning. The sun was, of course, regarded as a deity by many in the ancient world and it may well be that verses 4b, 5, 6 are based on a Babylonian hymn to the sun. The daily progress of the sun, and its unavoidable effects on man and nature, is compared to the striding forth of a champion, unconquerable and confident, challenging his puny opponents. (The not very commendable biblical example of such a warrior is Goliath of Gath. (I Samuel 17). The poet is aware that the sun is absolutely regular and inescapable. In a pre-scientific world he seems to know instinctively that it is vital for human life. It gives light and warmth and *there is nothing hid from its heat.*

It is not surprising, therefore, that in verse 7 he turns to the Torah, God's Law. Like the sun, it is ever-present, unchangeable and necessary for life. To the believer it gives light and warmth, and no one can hide from it. Then verse by verse he records properties of the Law followed by the consequences if a Law is observed. Thus the perfect Law revives the soul; its sure testimony makes the simple wise; its right precepts make the heart rejoice. The golden beams of the sun which warm the earth and enable growth are perhaps in the mind of the psalmist when he compares the *ordinances of the Lord* to fine gold and honey, rich and golden.

In the last three verses of the psalm the poet turns to self-examination. He is worried lest he has unwittingly sinned. In verse 12 he foreshadows the words Our Lord told us to use in our prayers, "lead us not into temptation." His morality is severe. He is not concerned with "not doing anybody any harm." He seeks to be perfect, *blameless and innocent of the great transgression* (v.13). We are led to consider that Our Lord must have meditated much on this psalm because he ends an important section of his Sermon on the Mount with the words, *You therefore, must be perfect, as your heavenly Father is perfect.* (Matthew 5.48).

The closing verse of the psalm is often used by preachers before they start their sermon. After much thought and long preparation, using all the resources of a lifetime of study and pastoral experience, the preacher asks that what he or she says may not be tainted with human pride and weakness, but may be acceptable to God; may indeed be the words which God would have them speak.

Psalm 20

This psalm is in the form of an intercession for the king, perhaps on the eve of a battle. The prayer is that God will ensure that the king's battle plans are successful, and that the king himself receives God's protection. God's response is seen as coming from the temple in Jerusalem (v.2), where this prayer is being offered and where the king has personally offered the appropriate sacrifice (v.3). The prayer for victory is made *in the name of our God*. It is probable that the name was *Yahweh Sabaoth,* Lord of hosts, literally Lord of armies, as in II Samuel 7.27, I Kings 18.15 and II Kings 19.31 and many other places.

There is a distinct change of mood in verse 6. It may be that there has been some response by a priest or other liturgical leader in words or action in the liturgy, assuring the worshippers that God will answer their prayers and fulfil their desires. So the psalm continues by affirming with full confidence that God will indeed support his anointed king and make him victorious.

Verse 7 reminds us that the fearsome weaponry of the enemy, horses and chariots, seem to have been rarely used by the army of Israel. Only kings or leaders occasionally fight from a chariot. (II Sam. 8.4, II Sam. 15.1 and I Kings 10.26). The fact that Israel fights with feebler weaponry serves to prove that their victories were attributable only to the help of God. Verse 8 recalls past victories won against the odds.

The final verse reads like a congregational response after an individual has made fairly lengthy biddings, rather like the "Lord, in your mercy: hear our prayer" of Christian liturgy. Here, after the prayer for God's help and protection for the king in the perilous situation which confronts him and his army, the congregation roars out, *Give victory to the king, O Lord.*

I recall a Eucharist in the Anglican cathedral in Hong Kong. We had been in the city for three weeks and at no time had there been any indication whatsoever that we were in a Communist country. Then, in the intercessions at the Eucharist we were called to pray for the *President of the Chinese Republic.* I felt so pleased and proud that Christians always pray for the head of state, for rulers and statesmen, whoever they may be and whatever their politics or religion might be. It is an acknowledgement that they all need God's help, even if they do not acknowledge his existence. Our prayers for rulers and governors are a vital part of our working for the establishment of God's kingdom, on earth as it is in heaven. So how good it is that the final verse of this psalm has made its way into the daily Offices of Morning and Evening Prayer as the second versicle and response of the Lesser Litany. The Prayer Book's faithful rendering was "O Lord, save the Queen: and let our cry come unto thee." In present forms of the services it now reads, "O Lord, save the Queen: and teach her counsellors wisdom." All leaders and rulers need our prayers.

Psalm 21

The anointing and coronation of a king in Jerusalem seems a possible setting for this psalm. As so often in psalms which are urgent prayers about practical matters such as politics or warfare, the first concern of the psalmist is not the practical matters, but God. So the first 7 verses are addressed to God. Verse 2 records that God has answered the king's prayers, both spoken, *the request of his lips,* and unspoken, *his heart's desire.*

Even if the ritual actions are performed by priests, there is no question that it is God who is the king-maker (v.3). The crowning is the sign of the renewal of the covenant that God made with the house of David. (I Kings 9.4-7). The king is therefore under the protection of God and no one should raise a hand against the Lord's anointed (see I Sam. 24.11 and II Sam. 1.14). Because of God's protection the king's reign will be long. This was a traditional divine gift. When Solomon asked for wisdom, 'an understanding heart', the request pleased God, and Solomon received what he did not ask for, "riches, honour and a long life." (I Kings 3.10-14).

In verses 5 and 6 it is acknowledged that all that the king will accomplish will be due to the blessings of God, not to his own abilities or virtues. Verse 7 reads rather like a congregational response to the hymn of praise now ended, the people replying, *For the king trusts in the Lord; and through the steadfast love of the Most High he shall not be moved.*

In verses 8-12 the psalmist addresses the newly anointed king. In optimistic terms success is predicted. These few verses remind us how complex and risky was foreign policy in Judah. As a buffer state between the super-powers of the time, Egypt, Assyria, Babylon and Persia they were constantly being invaded and constantly making and breaking treaties. These verses idealise the role and success of the king, under the protection of God. Perhaps we can also detect a touch of morale-boosting at a critical time for the nation.

The psalm ends as it began, rejoicing, not in king or country, but in God.

Once again this psalm reminds us of the violent and conflict-ridden world in which we live, and how difficult is the role of those who rule. We might also ask how Our Lord would regard this psalm. Perhaps he pitied those with power. His parents had probably told him how, shortly after he was born, they had to flee from the murderous intentions of Herod the Great. Jesus certainly had a shrewd opinion of Herod the Great's son, Antipas, whom he called 'that fox.' (Luke 13.32).

In St John's account of the Passion it sometimes appears that it was Pilate who was on trial and Jesus who was judge – as in reality he was. Denis Potter's play, *Son of Man*, brilliantly emphasised this reversal of roles. In the royal family of Judah in Jesus' day the father was a killer (and not just of the children of Bethlehem), the son was sly. The examples of kingship in Judah in the time of Jesus had little to commend them. No wonder that when Pilate asked, "Are you the king of the Jews?" Jesus said, "My kingship is not of this world." He accepted the title and transformed the reality. In St John's gospel (12. 24) Jesus says, "I shall draw all men to myself, when I am lifted up from the earth." He was certainly 'lifted up' when he was crucified, and the cross was his only throne.

Psalm 22

Of all the psalms this is the one which a Christian cannot read unmoved. It is the passionate prayer of one who feels abandoned by God. It is full of wonderful imagery and graphic descriptions of a believer's sufferings. The Passion narratives in the gospels quote it and allude to it constantly.

Verses 1-21 are a heartfelt lament, and the sufferer asks the question which all who suffer ask God, *Why? Why me? Why my wife? Why my child? Why such terrible suffering? Why?* Behind all the physical sufferings and fears which he mentions later, the deepest suffering is caused by his apparent abandonment by God. He has cried to God day and night, and still God does not answer (vv. 1, 2).

In verses 3-5 he looks back over the nation's history and recalls that in the days of their ancestors God heard their cries and helped them; *in thee they trusted and were not disappointed.*

But then he looks at himself and feels that the failure of God to respond must be due to his own unworthiness. *I am a worm, and no man; scorned by men, and despised by the people.* Like a worm he is in the dust, unnoticed and trampled underfoot by the scorn of those who mock his trust in God (vv. 7, 8). The self-loathing which the psalmist feels may tell us of his depression or despair. But he pulls himself back from the brink by reminding himself that he has been in God's hands from birth. Now, in another perilous situation, he pleads that God will be with him again and will this time deliver him by assuring him of his presence. Only God can help (v.11).

Verses 12-21 relate in vivid metaphors how perilous his situation is. Verses 14 and 15 seem to describe the sort of physical reactions which accompany extreme fear. He feels hunted. His enemies surround him, circling as savage dogs might surround their wounded and dying prey. As we move through this part of the psalm we find his fears escalating, and lions join the dogs to describe the fierceness and deadliness of the situation, and his terrible fear.

In the Greek and Syriac versions of the psalm, the second part of verse 21 reads *thou hast answered me from the horns of the wild oxen.* It is a puzzle. The *horns of the wild oxen* might refer to some object in the temple. If so, it could be a liturgical response, perhaps a priest assuring the supplicant that God has heard and answered his prayer. If that is the case, it would happily explain the distinct change of mood which begins in verse 22 and continues to the end of the psalm. In these concluding verses there is an ever-growing feeling of relief and thanksgiving. His earlier fears were unfounded. God has not deserted him; *for he has not despised or abhorred the affliction of the afflicted; and he has not hid his face from him, but has heard, when he cried to him* (v. 24). His questions have been answered and his fears abolished. God is present and caring.

He goes on to promise a public thanksgiving (v.25) and a gift of food to the needy as a token of his gratitude (v.26). His thankfulness is as overwhelming as his lament has been, and he imagines the company of those praising God growing from himself to all Israel (v. 23) including the worshipping congregation of which he is a part (v.26). But that is not enough; the ends of the earth, all nations, will join in the praise (v.27). Even the dead who, in the religion of Judah at this time, were usually thought of as being beyond the reach of God, shall bow to him (v.29). God's wonderful mercy shall be taught to future generations, that they too may join in the song of praise (vv. 30, 31).

From the opening words of this psalm a Christian's thoughts are taken to Calvary. In the Introduction (p.10) I explained how recording that Jesus said, *My God, my God, why has thou forsaken me?* may be like saying that someone sang *O come, all ye faithful,* meaning, of course, that they sang the whole hymn. Jesus may well have recited this and other psalms as he died on the cross, as so many Christian martyrs have died saying the Lord's Prayer or indeed psalms. The evangelists certainly had this psalm in the forefront of their minds as they composed their Passion narratives.

Thinking of what the psalmist says in verse 2 we might note that Jesus would have spent a sleepless night after his arrest in the Garden of Gethsemane. He was taken for an informal examination in the High Priest's house (Mark 14.53-65) before the very early, and probably illegal, meeting of the Sanhedrin (Mark 15.1).

Like the psalmist, Jesus was mocked because he trusted in God (vv 7-8); (Matthew 27.8-44). The physical weakness the psalmist describes in verses 14 and 15 foreshadow the weakness of Jesus – sleepless, ill-treated, scourged and thirsty (John 19.28). *They have pierced my hands and my feet* (v.16) is rather puzzling as a description of the psalmist's suffering, but nothing could be more appropriate in the case of a man being crucified. (John 20.25).

The hope of a growing and spreading response of praise in the closing verses of the psalm reminds us of the spread of the Christian gospel. It began with one man, Jesus. Around him he gathered the Three – Peter, James and John. Then there was the Twelve (Mark 3.14), and the Seventy, or Seventy-Two. (Luke 10.1). After Pentecost the spread of the gospel followed the pattern Jesus laid down (Acts 1.8), from Jerusalem, into Judaea, on to Samaria and away to the end of the earth. That Christ-imposed task is still the work of the Church. When it is accomplished it will fulfil the psalmist's hope that all people will join in joyful praise of God.

Psalm 23

This best known of all the psalms speaks to people in many differing circumstances. That is why it is chosen as often at weddings as at funerals. This is no new practice. In his novel *Salvation,* about Chasidic Judaism in Poland in the early 19th century, Sholem Asch pictures a scene at a party celebrating the birth of a child at which Psalm 23 is sung to a polka tune brought from a nearby village. The psalm is found suitable for all sorts of occasions because it is a calm prayer of faith uttered by someone at peace with himself and with God.

The image of the shepherd conveys meanings of protector, guide and leader. The mention of anointing in verse 5 might suggest that these words are spoken by the king. That would be fitting because, as we read in Ezekiel 34. 11-16, *the shepherds of Israel* were the leaders of the nation who, in Ezekiel's day, were not carrying out their task of caring for their flock, feeding them and keeping them safe. Again in Isaiah, we read that God will come to rule, and his rule will be one of mercy; "he will feed his flock like a shepherd, he will gather the lambs in his arms, he will carry them in his bosom, and gently lead those that are with young." (Is. 40.11).

So the psalmist gives the earthly king of Judah words which seem to mean, "I might be the king, the shepherd of the nation, but Yahweh, the Lord, is my shepherd."

God's guiding hand has placed him in a pleasant situation, with good pasture and water. He has guided him to do the right thing *for his name's sake.* This suggests that the psalmist or the king, left to his own devices, might well have chosen otherwise. Like a good shepherd God protects him when danger or death threatens. He uses rod and staff; the rod to beat off predators, and the staff to guide the flock.

In verse 5 the image of the shepherd is laid aside, and God is seen as a generous host. He prepares a meal for his guest, welcomes him with anointing (in contrast see Luke 7. 36-50), and ensures that the guest's cup is always full. Such is the generosity of God's love. The psalmist is sure that God's care will be sustained throughout his life.

His final longing to *dwell in the house of the Lord for ever* is not so much a desire to be always in the temple building as to be assured that he is continually in the presence of God.

Of course Our Lord knew what had been said about shepherds in Isaiah and Ezekiel as mentioned above, and also in Jeremiah 23.1, and Psalm 80, verse 1 as well as in this psalm. He took the word and its associations to new heights; "I am the good shepherd. The good shepherd lays down his life for the sheep." (John 10.11). All the qualities required in a shepherd are found in Jesus – his rule as king (John 18.36); his care for the weak (Matt. 25.31-46); his seeking for the lost (Luke 15. 2-7). He is also the generous host at the table prepared for his sheep. We eat the bread which is his body and we drink the wine which is his blood, shed for us and for many. (Matt. 26. 26-28). A few hours after speaking those words, the good shepherd laid down his life for the sheep.

Psalm 24

This psalm may well have been used at a great festival as the procession bearing the ark reached the temple.

The first two verses celebrate God's grandeur as creator. It seems that the procession reaches the temple gates, and the congregation asks who will be allowed to enter the sacred building (v.3). Verse 4 sounds like a formal priestly response to the question, reminding people that the requirements are moral – purity of heart and truthfulness. Those whose lives conform to this requirement will not only be allowed to enter the temple, they will also receive God's blessing.

The procession, bearing the ark, the symbol of God's presence, stands at the gates and demands entry for the King of glory. The gate-keepers, probably Levites, respond by asking, *Who is the King of glory?* The procession replies that it is Yahweh who, throughout the history of Israel, had shown himself mighty in battle. It is he who demands entry. The gates are still not opened and so the demand is made again. The gate-keepers are still not satisfied and repeat their question. This time the answer is more precise. It is Yahweh Sabaoth, Yahweh of armies, of the armies of heaven and of the armies of Israel; he is the King of glory. The right answer has been given and we know the gates will be opened.

We can see in our mind's eye, as we say or sing this psalm, a grand liturgical occasion with procession, choir, congregation, questions and responses, all carefully rehearsed and carried out with magnificence – all to the glory of God. Carefully prepared worship is a wonderful and uplifting experience, and the fact that it has been planned and rehearsed, far from making it mechanical and contrived, enables the worshippers to concentrate their hearts and minds on the meaning of what they are saying and doing.

As we sing this psalm, we may be led to think of Jesus entering Jerusalem on Palm Sunday and going straight to the temple, repeating the actions of the pilgrims. (Mark 11.11).

Holman Hunt's painting of Christ standing outside a closed door and knocking, inspired by the words in Revelation 3.20, famously shows that there is no handle on the outside of the door. It can only be opened from the inside. Our Lord is always knocking, always asking us to open our hearts and let him in. This psalm might inspire us to open the gates of our hearts, knowing that if we do the King of glory will come in.

Psalm 25

This is an acrostic poem, each verse (with a few exceptions which are probably due to copying errors) beginning with successive letter of the Hebrew alphabet. Keeping to this pattern has in no way lessened the sensitivity of the poem. It is a series of pleas or laments uttered by a worried and lonely man. It can therefore be of help to others who are similarly afflicted.

The opening three verses make it clear that only God can help the psalmist. Verses 4 and 5 could fit very comfortably into Psalm 119, as he asks God to help him to live righteously by the keeping of God's law.

He recalls sins in his past life and asks forgiveness (vv.7, 11). God's nature is goodness, and the law teaches that men should copy God's *steadfast love and faithfulness.* If a man follows God's way, he will live in prosperity (v.13), but the most valuable reward will be not material prosperity but the friendship of God.

He ends the psalm mentioning his *foes.* We cannot be certain if these foes are people or his feelings of guilt and inadequacy. Whoever or whatever they are, he knows that only God can help him withstand them. He prays that he might be upright and honest and so deserving of God's help. He knows that he has no right to demand help, and so he humbly asks for it, and is ready to wait; *I wait for thee* (v.21).

Verse 22 is probably an addition. It is not in the alphabetical scheme of the psalm and it widens what has been an intensely personal prayer into a much wider one for all Israel. Perhaps, someone's marginal note has been incorporated into the text.

Despite the constraints imposed by the alphabetical pattern, the psalm is very true to life. When we feel isolated and are burdened by our past sins, we cannot order our thoughts clearly or logically. We jump ahead, asking God to help, and then return to the feelings which preoccupy us. And in the midst of all our self-concern we keep trying to lead or force our thoughts back to God and our need for his forgiveness. Most, perhaps all, people who try to pray are familiar with this inability to control our thoughts. We have to be patient with ourselves, gently bringing our thoughts back to God.

It is helpful to know that even famous Christians have struggled with similar difficulties. John Donne, Dean of St. Paul's and famous preacher and poet, said in Sermon 80. "I neglect God and his angels for the noise of a fly, for the rattling of a coach, for the whining of a door; I talk on, in the same posture of praying; eyes lifted up; knees bowed down; as though I prayed to God; and if God or his angels should ask me when I last thought of God in that prayer, I cannot tell; sometimes I find that I had forgot what I was about, but when I began to forget it, I cannot tell. A memory of yesterday's pleasures, a fear of tomorrow's danger, a straw under my knee, a noise in mine ear, a light in mine eye, an anything, a nothing, a fancy, a chimera in my brain, troubles me in my prayer. So certainly is there nothing, nothing in spiritual things, perfect in this world." Isn't it comforting to read that!

So when we find our mind wandering as we pray, we need not be despondent. We need to bring ourselves gently back to where we should be. Sometimes it helps to use a familiar set form of prayer, like the Lord's Prayer. Or we might use a psalm. Whatever we do we should try to reassure ourselves that God understands and values our struggle and hears and accepts our prayers. Like the psalmist we do our best. We offer our prayers to God and say, *I wait for thee.*

Psalm 26

In a style reminiscent of Psalm 7 the poet protests his innocence before God. We seem to have not so much the impassioned private prayer of a believer, but a formal declaration over which he is willing to be tested (v.2). The psalmist has confidence in God's mercy and steadfast love as well as in his own faithfulness (v.3). He then lists the offences with which he seems to have been charged, and again declares his innocence (vv. 4, 5).

Verse 6 seems to refer to a ritual act of cleansing as preparation for participating in the procession which will move around the altar. The psalmist's innocence has been accepted and, ritually cleansed, he can join in singing the praises of God, recalling God's wonderful acts in caring for the nation in the past (v.7). This ritual cleansing might remind us of a priest washing his hands at the Offertory in a Communion service and perhaps repeating words from this psalm. It might also remind us of the ritual ablutions of Muslims before they worship, and the rows of taps and bowls for the purpose outside the mosque.

In verses 8-10 he declares his love for the temple, God's dwelling-place on earth, and pleads that he might not be counted among those who break the covenant and indulge in violence. He makes a final vow that he will conduct his life with integrity, but realises that in the end it will not be his striving but God's graciousness that will put his life on a firm foundation (v.12), enabling him to play his part in the praise of God uttered by the *great congregation* in the temple.

So often the writers of the psalms reveal their awareness that human striving will always be just that – striving. No one achieves perfection; all require God's grace and mercy. The Torah lays down very clearly what believers should do or not do. The Ten Commandments, though central, are but a small part of the Law. It is quite wrong to draw a sharp contrast, as some Christian writers and preachers once did, between Judaism as a religion of law and Christianity as a religion of grace. It is the Old Testament that tells us that Yahweh is "A God merciful and gracious, slow to anger and abounding in steadfast love and faithfulness." (Exodus 34.6). Or to take one example from the prophets, Jeremiah has God say, "let him who glories glory in this, that he understands and knows me, that I am the Lord who practise steadfast love, justice and righteousness in the earth; for in these things I delight," (Jeremiah 9.24). Or we may simply look at Psalm 136 and see that the second half of every verse says, *for his steadfast love endures for ever.* It is this Old Testament God, full of loving kindness, mercy and truth, who became human in Jesus.

Psalm 27

This psalm begins, not as a prayer, but as a declaration. Like Psalm 2 it makes statements about Yahweh, the Lord. They are the statements of a person with a firm faith. He speaks of what Yahweh is to him – his light and his salvation. His experience in the past and what he is experiencing in the present (vv.1, 2) lead him to trust confidently that the Lord's protection will be there in the future too. He need not fear though his enemies are many and may oppose him in war (v.3).

He longs to be part of the faithful community worshipping God in the temple in Jerusalem. There he will be able to meditate on the beauty of God's perfection, and offer prayers in that holy place (v.4). He will feel secure in the temple, *set upon a high rock.* Then he will offer a sacrifice as a sign of his thanksgiving, and join in the joyful praise of God in the temple liturgy (v.6).

In verse 7 there is a change of tone. Perhaps it is the psalmist's knowledge of himself, that even when he feels most secure and closest to God, he can still fail. This might remind us of St. Paul's words of warning to the Christians of Corinth, and indeed to all Christians: "Therefore let anyone who thinks that he stands take heed lest he fall." (I Cor. 10.12). The psalmist knows that he needs God's help and mercy and so he prays, *be gracious to me and answer me* (v.7).

Many times in the psalms and in other parts of the Old Testament we read that the believer seeks God's face. Or he asks God not to hide his face from him. (Pss. 17.15; 24.6; 67.1; Ezek. 7.22; II Chron. 30.9). To be 'before someone's face' simply means to be in their presence, and there are too many examples of this in the Old Testament to start listing them. So, in most cases to see God's face or to be before his face means to be aware of his presence, and this might be experienced anywhere. In the psalms it seems sometimes to refer to a particular moment in the temple liturgy when, somehow, the people are assured that they are in the presence of God. This may remind Christians of the moment of the elevation of the sacrament in the Eucharist when the 'real presence' of Christ is acknowledged; his 'real' presence which is believed by some worshippers to be physical in the bread and wine, and by others to be a 'real' though spiritual presence.

In verse 10 the psalmist returns to the confidence of the early verses. He says that human help, even family ties, may fail him, but God will not. He asks that God will show him how he ought to live, setting his life on a firm foundation (v.11).

He has been falsely accused, and his enemies intend violence against him (v.12). Despite this threat he declares that he has confidence that God, in his goodness, will preserve his life (v.13).

He ends by exhorting himself, and perhaps others who feel similarly vulnerable, to show trust in God by being courageous and patient. He knows that prayers are not always answered immediately or in the way expected, so *wait for the Lord.* Such waiting is proof of faith.

In many psalms, for example Psalms 18, 27, 28, 31, 42, 61 and 62, God is called a rock, and in others he is said to place the person with faith on a rock, giving their life a firm foundation. In this psalm, in speaking of being in the temple in Jerusalem (vv.4, 5) the poet says that God will set him on a rock. This is not simply a metaphor. The Dome of the Rock mosque stands on the Temple Mount. Inside the building the great rock can be seen rising, jutting, out of the ground. In his book *Jerusalem: The Biography* Simon Sebag Montefiore tells of the building of the Dome of the Rock mosque in the years 691/2 by Abd al Malik, the Muslim Commander of Jerusalem. He writes, "The Rock was the site of Adam's paradise, Abraham's altar, the place where David and Solomon planned the temple and which was later visited by Muhamad on his Night Journey." It is a rock with a history.

We might also be reminded of St. Paul's words referring to the Jewish tradition, based on Numbers 20.10,11 and 21.16, that a water-producing rock accompanied the Israelites on their journey through the wilderness. 'That rock', says St. Paul, 'was Christ'. (I Cor. 10.4). The assurance the psalmist found in the rock, real or metaphorical, on which God set him, Christians find in Jesus. A. M. Toplady's hymn *Rock of Ages* is a stern Victorian meditation on Jesus as our rock, the firm foundation of our faith and our only hope of salvation.

Psalm 28

In the service of Holy Communion, Confession is followed, naturally, by Absolution. Then, in its newly forgiven state, the congregation breaks into a joyful hymn of praise, "Glory to God in the Highest." This psalm has a similar pattern.

Verses 1-5 are a plea for deliverance from death and from sharing the punishment of the wicked. In the first verse the psalmist asks God to be his rock, that word linking this psalm to the previous one. He shares the common view of his day that death puts an end to any relationship with God. Therefore, if God does not hear or respond, the psalmist is as good as dead. We learn in verse 2 that he is in the temple, and the lifting of his hands towards the sanctuary may be a ritual gesture, re-enforcing his verbal plea. The wicked are deceitful, feigning friendship while plotting mischief. He prays that God will deal with them as they deserve. The root of their wickedness is their failure to recognise the hand of God in human affairs (vv.3, 4, 5).

Between verse 5 and verse 6 we might imagine some liturgical absolution, an assurance, perhaps uttered by a priest, that God does hear and will act. If that is so, then the words and tone of verse 6 are the joyful response, *Blessed be the Lord, for he has heard the voice of my supplication.* These words too, like the *Gloria* in the Eucharist, might be a part of a temple liturgy, and many other worshippers might be saying or singing the words with the psalmist.

After the joy over God's care and protection for the individual in verses 6 and 7, the next two verses widen the thanksgiving to embrace the nation and in particular the king; *he is the saving refuge of his anointed.* This prayer for the king, appointed and anointed by God to be the ruler and shepherd of the nation, seems to remind the poet that in reality it is God himself who is their shepherd and he will care for them for ever.

Verse 9 found its way into the great Christian hymn of praise, Te Deum. It is most clearly discernible in the Book of Common Prayer version. The Te Deum has an interesting tradition attached to it. It is said to have been composed at the baptism of St. Augustine by St. Ambrose, the two saints alternately improvising the verses. It's a delightful legend. Later scholarship believes the hymn was composed by Niceta, a bishop in Dacia (more or less modern Romania) towards the end of the 4th century. In the English Prayer Book of 1549 it was ordered to be said at Mattins throughout the year except during Lent when it was replaced by the Benedicite. Since then, it has appeared in all revisions of the Prayer Book as a canticle which can be said at Morning Prayer.

We can suppose that Bishop Niceta had no idea that his words would become so widely known and used. The author of Psalm 28 might be even more surprised to find his words being so readily and regularly used by Christians.

Psalm 29

This psalm, full of vivid imagery, is a wonderful hymn praising Yahweh as the creator and controller of nature. The poet begins by calling on the members of the court of heaven to praise God. These beings were regarded as intermediaries between God and humans; indeed the word *angel* means *messenger*. If this psalm was written for use in a temple liturgy, as verses 9 and 10 suggest, the cherubim, whose wings formed a canopy over the ark, the symbol of God's presence, are called to join in the worship. This reminds us of Isaiah's vision in which the prophet sees the cherubim (they are actually called 'seraphim' in Isaiah) and hears their song of praise. (Isaiah 6.1-8). This joining of heavenly and earthly praise is continued in the Christian Eucharist when the worshippers join 'with angels and archangels and with all the company of heaven...'

In verses 3-8 the psalmist describes the terrifying power of God in nature. He pictures a storm gathering over the sea. There is thunder and lightning as *the voice of the Lord flashes forth flames of fire*. Thunder is here regarded as the voice of God, or perhaps a symbol of the voice of God, as it is in John 12.27-30. The storm is also on land, shattering trees and shaking the earth. The translation of verse 9a is uncertain. It may mean, as in the RSV, *The voice of the Lord makes the oaks to whirl,* which fits very nicely with the mention of the cedars in verse 5. The other possible meaning, as in the Book of Common Prayer, is *the voice of the Lord makes the hinds calve.* The idea of animals bringing their young to birth early because of storm-induced terror is attractive because it moves the consequences of God's power in nature from the inanimate to the animate. Then, in the second half of verse 9 he declares that humans too, seeing and reflecting on God's power, exclaim *Glory.*

The final two verses give us another glimpse of temple worship. Besides the six-winged cherubim pictured by Isaiah, the poet says that Yahweh is *enthroned over the flood.* This might refer to God's power over the watery chaos out of which he created the world (Genesis 1.1-2), or it might be another reference to the furniture of the temple. In I Kings 7.23 it says that Solomon made 'the bronze sea'. It is described as a grand water-filled circular bowl, some 16 or 17 feet in diameter and elaborately decorated and mounted. Perhaps this is the Psalmist's 'flood'.

In the temple, the most holy place, God's people glorify him and the psalmist says that God will always strengthen his people and bless them, not with prosperity or power, but with peace.

Sacred places are important to people of faith. Many who do not join in the regular worship of their local church speak of the peace they experience when they enter a church and find themselves alone in the quietness. It is often said that a building that has been prayed in for many years acquires an atmosphere, perhaps a sanctity, that communicates itself to receptive minds and hearts. We should cherish our sacred places, our places of worship, however grand or humble they might be. We should care for their fabric – though it is difficult when ancient buildings are being cared for by a very limited number of people. A well-tended building is a sign that people care, that they believe that God is to be found in the building by anyone who respects the sacred place. A quiet, empty church which is beautifully kept is also a sign that those who worship regularly in that place love and glorify God when they are not in church and not singing hymns or saying prayers.

Verse 2 of this psalm, in the wording of the Authorised Version, inspired the writing of the hymn "O worship the Lord in the beauty of holiness." It is a beautiful hymn and we can sing it as a prayer. It is worth noting that Evelyn Underhill wrote that "To worship the Lord in the beauty of holiness does not mean the unbridled enthusiasm of the dervish, but the quiet and steadfast loyalty of the saint."

Psalm 30

The psalm has the title, *A Psalm of David. A Song at the Dedication of the Temple.* That is confusing. It might be either but it can't be both. The temple was built after the death of David by his son Solomon.

It is a prayer of thanksgiving for God's help. The first verse sums up the purpose of the psalm, and verses 2 and 3 suggest that the author has been healed of a dangerous illness which had brought him close to death. If physical death was not the danger, he had perhaps reached a point at which, in the depths of depression and despair, he felt that life was not worth living.

In verse 4 he calls on the congregation to join him in thanksgiving, reminding them of God's unchanging love and care. He reflects that we sometimes think that God is punishing us, but eventually we realise that God's love never ceases. And though we may feel sunk in darkness, every night is followed by a dawn (v.5).

John Keble's lovely hymn, "New every morning is the love our waking and uprising prove," captures the feeling of verse 5 perfectly.

The psalmist goes on to recall how he had prospered in life (v. 6) and unthinkingly assumed that it was his own cleverness that had achieved it. But in fact it was God's kindness that had helped him, and when he tried to be self-sufficient he realised how much he owed to God (v. 7).

Stricken by the realisation of his own obtuseness he cries to God, suggesting rather petulantly that if he should die he would not be able to continue to praise God (vv.8, 9). But he has realised how puny are his own efforts and he prays again in verse 10 for God's help and grace. As we saw in considering Psalm 27, St. Paul echoes the thought of the psalmist as he comes to accept that he is not as self-sufficient and invulnerable as he once thought. Paul writes to his friends in Corinth, warning of over-confidence, "Therefore let anyone who thinks he stands take heed lest he fall." (I Cor. 10.12).

The two final verses are a song of joy and thanksgiving. He has been brought back from the brink of the grave. He can dance for joy and, instead of sackcloth, wear a smile. He promises that he will not forget God's goodness and that his thanksgiving will continue for the rest of his life.

It seems as if much of the psalmist's life had been successful and happy, free from any serious problems. He had unthinkingly accepted the good things of life as if they were his due. It was only when the hard times came that he realised how fragile was his happiness and his life. He gives us pictures of himself thinking that he was at the point of death, worrying through the night only to find that in the morning all his fears had been exaggerated and were largely unnecessary. Many people share that experience.

But even when he has acknowledged that it was God who had blessed him and given him a good life, he still blames God when things go wrong. It wasn't so much his own shortcomings, it was because God had hidden his face (v.7). In despair it is very hard, perhaps impossible, to feel the love of God or the kindness of human friends. When, at last, the breakthrough comes it is like a bright new day; *joy comes with the morning (v.5)*.

Psalm 31

There is a realism in the pattern of this psalm. Pleading for God's help, the poet cannot concentrate on just one of his problems but finds his mind constantly rushing on to the next which he also wants to place before God. This is an experience which most people who pray will recognise.

Verses 1-8 are a prolonged cry for help. Though he feels like a hunted animal fearful of a hidden net, he recognises that God is his rock and fortress. He fears that death is close at hand and commits himself to God; *into thy hands I commit my spirit.* They are words of trust, of a faith that in the end God is the only refuge. Our Lord used them as he died (Luke 23.46) and Martin Luther, no doubt with the death of Christ in his mind, used them on his death bed. Also some forms of the late evening service, Compline, use verses 1-5 of this psalm, as the worshippers prepare themselves for a night's sleep – a little death.

In verses 6-8 he thanks God that he is a part of the community of believers and has not been drawn away to the worship of the gods of other nations. He believes that God has recognised both his suffering and his faithfulness and has given him comfort and relief (v.8).

In verse 9 he begins to describe his sufferings, the causes of which are mental and spiritual. He is overwhelmed by grief and sorrow; his body weakens, his sight deteriorates.

Verses 9 and 10 remind us that human nature does not alter much over the years. The psalmist's abject condition attracts not compassion but derision. His enemies taunt him, and his acquaintances do not want to know him. It is as if he were dead and, indeed, he is aware of the whisperings of those who are saying that his death would be the best outcome for everyone (vv. 12, 13).

Our society has made great steps in care and consideration for the helpless and handicapped, and we know that often it is embarrassment rather than cruelty that leads to people ignoring or misjudging the handicapped. It is always easier to talk to the person pushing the wheel-chair than to the person sitting in it. And it will always be difficult for non-sufferers to understand that someone may not be awkward or difficult or noisy or distasteful on purpose. In verses 14-18 the psalmist reaffirms his trust in God. His enemies, whoever or whatever they are, are still there, but he recognises that *my times are in thy hand;* everything, his health, his reputation, his life and his death are ultimately in God's keeping.

There are then two exclamations of faith in God; *O how abundant is thy goodness,* (v.19), and *Blessed be the Lord* (v.21). In these verses he says that his problems and suffering are not removed, but he can live through them because he knows that God is with him in his troubles.

Finally, in verses 23 and 24, on the basis of personal experience of God being with him in his sufferings, he calls on all to share his faith and confidence in God.

There is the lovely story of someone being shown the record of their life in footsteps in the sand. Most of the time there are two sets of prints, their own and God's, because God was walking with them throughout their life. When they complain that at the most difficult times in their life there is only one set of prints, they are gently told, "That is when I was carrying you." When we feel oppressed with problems we might be helped by considering remarks by two eminent Christians. Evelyn Underhill wrote, "All must suffer; the lesson of Christianity is what can be done with suffering, when it is met with self-oblivious courage and love." We put alongside that comment words written by Dietrich Bonhoeffer in the mid-1930s in Hitler's Germany. He wrote, "Jesus asks nothing of us without giving us the strength to perform it." Bonhoeffer was executed in a concentration camp in 1945, shortly before the war ended.

Psalm 32

This psalm celebrates the joy of being forgiven. It is counted as the second of the Penitential Psalms and is said to have been St. Augustine's favourite psalm.

So great is the psalmist's feeling of release that in verse after verse he cries out how wonderful it is that God forgives, and having forgiven, does not accuse. He does not consider himself free of wrong-doing. His sins brought him misery and made him ill. He is certainly a sinner, but a forgiven sinner. In verse 5 he recounts how he finally decided to open his heart to God, confessing all his sins. He found that God forgave him. It is a psalm full of encouragement to all who know themselves to be sinners; *I acknowledged my sin to thee, and I did not hide my iniquity; I said, "I will confess my transgressions to the Lord; then thou did'st forgive the guilt of my sin"* (v.5).

In verse 6 he shows the zeal of the convert. The wonderful release he has experienced is there for everyone. Confession and forgiveness will keep us secure through the storms of life. *Thou dost encompass me with deliverance* (v.7) puts one in mind of the frightened child being wrapped tenderly in its mother's or father's arms and there finding comfort and safety. In verses 8-10 we cannot tell whether it is the poet speaking to his fellow worshippers or if he is imagining words which God addresses to him and his fellows. Whichever it is, the message is to accept, without delay, the teaching given so far. If they do not, they are stupid, obstinate, mule-like, having to be coerced to do the right thing. Bits and bridles are not comfortable things. Everyone has a choice. Each person has to make their choice and then live with the consequences (v.10). Verse 11 is a classic piece of parallelism, each half of the verse saying the same thing in beautifully varied words.

When a paralysed man was brought to Jesus by his very determined friends (Mark 2.1-11), Jesus said to him, "My son, your sins are forgiven." Scribes who were present questioned his right to forgive. Jesus said that it was easy to forgive sins because no one could prove that he hadn't done it. But if he were to do the harder, because verifiable, act, then they must believe that he had done the easier. He told the man to pick up his stretcher and go home, which he did. Was the man paralysed because of guilt feelings? We do not know, though doubtless Jesus did. Guilt can have a devastating effect on a person's life. There may be physical consequences or, more likely, damage to spiritual and social life. The psalmist had tried to hide or bury his guilt within himself and found the consequences destructive: *When I declared not my sin, my body wasted away* (v.3). This psalm reminds us how unfortunate is the person who cannot open their heart to God, and who therefore cannot discover the joy or blessedness of forgiveness as the psalmist did. *Blessed is he whose transgression is forgiven, whose sin is covered* (v.1).

John V. Taylor wrote delightfully about forgiveness in *The Go Between God*: "my Father is not going to be any more pleased with me when I am good than he is now when I am bad. He accepts me and delights in me as I am. It is ridiculous of him, but that is how it is between us. In consequence I want to show my love for him fully and continuously, and I can do that best by insisting on my freedom to push into his presence, grubby and outrageous, without having first to wash my hands and comb my hair…" Later in the same book John Taylor reminds us that "we are citizens of a forgiven universe."

Psalm 33

Many Christian hymns call the faithful to praise God, and give them the words with which to do so: "O praise ye the Lord…," "Come, ye faithful, raise the anthem…" "Rejoice, the Lord is King…" are just some of them. This psalm begins in a similar way; *Rejoice in the Lord, O you righteous.* The mention of musical instruments to accompany the *new song* suggests that the psalm might have been composed specially for a thanksgiving festival in the temple.

Verses 4 and 5 state important facts about the life of faith. First, that God is just and faithful. Second, that God loves righteousness and justice, and he expects men to practise those virtues. And third, that the steadfast love of God is built into his creation.

In verses 6 and 7 God's work in creation is celebrated. Using traditions which are found also in the creation stories in Genesis, it is the effortlessness of God's creativity which is noted. "God said, Let there be light; and there was light." (Genesis 1.3). Creation was by God's word, by the mere breath of his mouth. It was God's breath again which gave life to Adam. (Genesis 2.7).

W.H. Vanstone, in his book *"Love's Endeavour: Love's Expense,"* suggests that God's creative work could not have been so effortless and painless. God's love is always given without limit, and we see the real cost of God's creative activity when we look at the cross. Authentic love, says Vanstone, is always limitless, precarious and vulnerable. He gives, as a suggested illustration of what the creative acts cost God, the true story of a surgeon performing a most complicated operation which lasted for many hours. When the work was successfully completed the surgeon had to be lead from the theatre by the hand, so total was his exhaustion. Those provoking thoughts need to be set against the picture of God creating effortlessly, by simply uttering a word. Vanstone makes us think, and helps us to have a deeper understanding of the nature of God and of his love.

The psalmist goes on to say that God did not, as it were, wind up his creation and then leave it to get on by itself. He is the Lord of history as well as of creation, and all men's plans are futile if they do not take God into account. Israel is fortunate, blessed, to be the nation which God has chosen to forward his purpose of bringing blessing to all people (vv. 10-12).

The psalmist pictures God watching the antics of men as they think they control events (vv.13, 15). But earthly power, mighty armies and the latest weapons are no guarantee of success (vv.16, 17). Nevertheless, when God looks down he sees not only vainglorious posturing and futile war-making, he sees also those who honour and respect (*fear*) God and live in hope of his steadfast love. For those people God will care (vv.18, 19).

The final verses, 20-22, are a declaration of faith, a faith that will wait patiently and confidently for God's grace.

The words *the fear of God* or *the fear of the Lord* appear many times in the psalms and elsewhere in both Old and New Testaments. Sometimes, no doubt, *fear* in the sense of *terror* is what is meant. But often that is not the best translation. *Reverence, astonishment, awe, honour* – often one of those words will give a more accurate understanding of the passage. Verse 8 of this psalm, in a classic example of poetic parallelism, shows that *fear* and *awe* in this context mean the same thing.

Returning to the creative power of God's word in verses 6 and 9, Christians are very familiar with the Christmas Gospel reading, "In the beginning was the Word, and the Word was with God, and the Word was God. He was in the beginning with God. All things came into being through him…" (John 1.1, 2). The climax of the passage is in verse 14; "And the Word became flesh and lived among us…" John's stately and sonorous Prologue introduces the Word made flesh, Jesus. We affirm our belief in the pre-existence and the creative work of the Second Person of the Trinity every time we say in the Creed that he was "eternally begotten of the Father… through him all things were made." It was this divine power and glory that Jesus laid aside in the incarnation. The early Christian hymn, composed or quoted by St. Paul, says that Jesus emptied himself of his divine attributes. "Let the same mind be in you that was in Christ Jesus,

> Who, though he was in the form of God,
> Did not regard equality with God as something to be grasped,
> But emptied himself, taking the form of a servant,
> Being born in the likeness of men.
> And being found in human form, he humbled himself
> And became obedient unto death, even death on a cross."
> (Philippians 2.5-8).

The linking of the creative power and the suffering love of God is vividly and poetically expressed in lines in a hymn by Graham Kendrick:

> "Come see his hands and his feet,
> The scars that speak of sacrifice,
> Hands that threw stars into space,
> To cruel nails surrendered."

Psalm 34

As we read this psalm its thoughts seem disjointed with no clearly discernible thread linking them. This is probably because each verse begins with successive letters of the Hebrew alphabet – it is an acrostic, an aid to memory, and adhering to the pattern may have hampered the author as he sought to order his thoughts.

In the first three verses the psalmist *blesses, praises, boasts in, magnifies and exalts* God. He not only sings God's praises but invites others to join him. He then begins to relate his own experience of God. Verse 4 tells us what happened to him. He sought God and God answered. So uplifted is he by his experience that he encourages others to look to God and to share a joy and freedom so great that it will shine through their faces (v.5). Looking back on how he felt before throwing himself on God's mercy, he calls himself *this poor man* (v.6). He pictures God's loving care rather as a guardian angel keeping watch over him (v.7).

He invites others to share his experience of God, an experience so powerful that he must describe it in physical terms. It is as if he says, "Don't take my word for it. Try it yourselves;" *taste and see that the Lord is good.* In another vivid metaphor he says that lions have to stalk and hunt to eat, and are not always successful, but God readily satisfies spiritual hunger, and fulfils the longings of anyone who seeks him (v.10).

In verse 11 there is a change of direction. The psalm becomes a vehicle for the teaching of Wisdom. It is like much in the Books of Proverbs, Ecclesiastes and many psalms (Psalm 25.12 and especially Psalm 119). The teaching is presented as the words of a wise elder instructing young men. *Come, O sons, listen to me, I will teach you the fear of the Lord.* What the fear of the Lord is emerges in the verses which follow. It is a good life, full and long, characterised by the keeping of God's law. We note that there is no mention of luxury, power, wealth, reputation or influence. To achieve a good life a person must avoid gossip and lying. Positive good is required. Virtue and peace must actively be sought (vv.13, 14).

Verses 15 and 16 are a good example of a contrasting parallelism. *The eyes of the Lord are towards the righteous,* looking on them with favour; but *the face of the Lord is against evil doers.* Usually, in the psalms, *the face of the Lord* is sought by devout worshippers as a sign of his favour, the assurance that he watches over them, knows their needs and welcomes their worship. But here the guilty secrets of the wicked are not hidden or overlooked; they are clearly seen by God. There is no escape from God's omniscience and judgement. We are reminded of the chilling words in the Epistle to the Hebrews; "It is a fearful thing to fall into the hands of the living God." (Heb.10.31).

Verse 18 reminds us that the desolate and despairing are God's special care. We do not have to wait for the New Testament to learn of God's compassion and his requirement that humans should be his instruments of care for the weaker members of society. Jesus lived out what the Law, the Prophets and the Writings taught, and he vividly and memorably illustrated it in his own teaching. (For example the Parable of the Sheep and the Goats (Matthew 25.31-46) and the Parables of the Lost Sheep, the Lost Coin and the Prodigal Son. (Luke 15).

The psalmist acknowledges that the righteous have their share of troubles, but they know that God is aware of their distress and that he will help them (v.19).

Verse 20 takes us straight to the Passion story. St. John (19.36) used this verse as a comment on the death of Jesus, seeing it as prophecy fulfilled. The practice at crucifixion was to nail and tie the victim's hands (or wrists) and feet (or heels). Often there was a peg or ledge beneath the feet so that some of the body weight could be taken on it. Hanging on the cross the victim would relieve the pain in his hands by taking weight on his feet and then, as that became unbearable, the weight would be transferred back to the hands. If the victim did not die quickly enough (which would probably mean within the period of duty of the soldiers overseeing the execution) his legs would be broken with a blow from the shaft of a spear. The breaking of the legs would cause the body to drop suddenly and the victim would quickly die of suffocation. St. John relates how when a soldier, presumably sensing that Jesus was dead, forced a spear into his side, blood and then fluid came out, indicating that the heart had stopped beating and that he was dead. There was no need to break his legs and so *he keeps all his bones; not one of them is broken.*

The psalm ends with a statement about God's justice. People have been told how they should live and what God expects of them. It does not say that God will slay the wicked; it will be the evil they have chosen that will destroy them (v.21). Those who try to serve God by their way of life and who turn to God, will find his help and salvation awaiting them.

Psalm 35

This is the desperate prayer of a man who feels unjustly accused and wrongfully persecuted. His anguish is relieved only by shafts of light in verses 9, 18, 27 and 28 in which he looks forward to being able to thank and praise God for the help he has received. We may be reading a psalm which reveals the inner feelings of a king or some other person of public status. To others he may look safe and successful. People turn to him for help. He can only turn to God. We often hear or read of the wrong-doings of people in the public eye. We ought also to be sensitive to the burdens which they bear.

Life is a struggle for the psalmist and in the opening verses he thinks of his situation as warfare. He asks God to fight on his side. The heading of the Psalm is *A Psalm of David.* If we were to look for a situation that might be appropriate to the psalm we might think of Saul's unrelenting and jealousy-fuelled pursuit of David related in I Samuel chapters 20-30.

The psalmist prays that his enemies may be shamed and scattered (vv.4-6) and that they may fall into the very traps they have set for him.

In verse 9, one of the glimpses of light, he speaks as if he expects God to do as he asks, and then he will be able praise God who is known to care for the weak. Verse 10, with its reversals of fortune, voices sentiments similar to those found in the prayer of Hannah (I Sam. 2.1-10) and repeated in the Song of Mary, the Magnificat: "He has put down the mighty from their thrones, and exalted those of low degree; he has filled the hungry with good things, and the rich he has sent away empty." (Luke 1. 52, 53).

After this brief ray of hope he returns to his troubles and in particular to those whose malicious lies not only hurt and damage him, but are the ungrateful response to the concern he showed for them when they were in difficulties. He had treated them with the consideration he would give to a family member or a close friend (v.13, 14). His misery contrasts starkly with the *glee* his enemies show as they see his troubles. Even the lowest in society jeer at him (vv. 15, 16).

How long, O Lord? is a recurring prayer of the psalmists. Here the poet prays that God's response will not be too long delayed, and he looks forward to joining in the communal praise of God, being part of *the mighty throng,* presumably in the temple.

He returns to his woes caused by the men whose deceit destroys not only his life but undermines the peace and stability of society (v.20).

He makes a series of impassioned pleas to God – *be not silent; be not far away (v.22); Bestir thyself (v.22); Vindicate me (v.24)*. We could say that verse 24 sums up the whole psalm. He asks God to help, not because he deserves it, but because it is God's nature to be just.

Finally he reveals that he has not been quite as alone and friendless as the psalm has so far suggested. He calls on all who support him and wish him to be helped and declared innocent to join his thanksgiving and say, *Great is the Lord (v.27)*.

This psalm reminds us of the conflicts and hardships that inevitably arise as people live together in society. There is always a wide range of opinion about what things are important and how things should be done. We need little reminding that dishonesty, cynicism and corruption eat away at society. The psalmist tells us that men had been set up, and presumably paid, to make lying accusations against him (v.11). We may recall the false witnesses set up against Naboth by Queen Jezebel in order to get her own way. She instructed them in the lies they had to tell and it resulted, as was intended, in the death of an innocent man. (I Kings 21). False witnesses were also set up at the trial of Jesus (Mark 14.56, 57), and despite the fact that their stories were inconsistent and their evidence did not stand up, another innocent man died. Too often, in our society, we hear of eminent and influential people lying or cheating. They set an example, as they are supposed to do, but it is sometimes the wrong example. If we want compassion, integrity and justice in life, we cannot wait for others. Christians, from the lowliest to the greatest, must try to live as selflessly, blamelessly and generously as they can.

Psalm 36

The psalm falls into three parts: verses 1-4 which describe the wicked, verses 5-9 which speak of God's generous love and mercy, and verses 10-12, a prayer that God will care for the righteous and that the psalmist himself will not be tempted into the company of the wicked.

It may be that when he speaks of the wicked in the opening verses he is thinking of people whose lives are brazenly wicked. He starts by saying that sin *speaks* or perhaps better, *whispers* to them. How does he know? Familiar with our own inner lives, we can assume that he has heard the insidious voice of temptation himself. The thread that runs through the whole of the psalm is the psalmist's awareness of his own weakness. He knows how vulnerable he is when sin whispers. The writer of the story of the 'Fall' in Genesis 3, has evil, in the form of a serpent, speaking to Eve, planting a seed of self-will, of rebellion against God. Everyone who tries to lead a good life knows what we might call the Eve moment, when good intentions weaken, the besetting sin whispers or hisses, telling us that it is not all that serious, it doesn't really matter, and perhaps God won't notice (v.2). The psalmist knows this struggle within his own conscience. He remembers nights when he has lain awake going over insults, real or imagined, bearing grudges and plotting revenge (v.4), revenge which in the morning will seem ridiculous and unnecessary, just as the worries of the anxious melt away with the coming of light.

He manages to put the fear of his own weakness on one side as he contemplates the goodness of God. It is as if he manages to remind himself that however weak he is, and however strong the temptations that assail him, God's love is greater. It *extends to the heavens,* it is as great and firm as a mountain range, as fathomless as the ocean. It embraces both humans and animals (v.6).

Verses 7-9 contain a wealth of striking pictures of God's loving care. It is like a mother bird sheltering her young (v.7). It is like a generous host, unstinting in his provision of food and drink for his welcome guests (v.8). It is like a flowing stream (v.8), a fountain that sparkles with living water. It is light, like the light of the sun, giving light and life to all things (v.9).

The poem draws to a close with a prayer that the grace and love of God, so ecstatically described, will continue to be felt by those who seek God (v.10). Never completely confident of his own righteousness, he prays that he may be kept humble. He is aware of his own weakness and the attractions of the way of life of those who do not try to honour God (v.11). He strengthens himself with an imagined glimpse of Sheol, the place of the dead. *There the evildoers lie prostrate, they are thrust down, unable to rise.* He doesn't want that to happen to him.

Psalm 37

As we read this psalm we find ourselves saying, from time to time, "that's not always the case", or "he's said that already." Part of the reason for this is a rough alphabetic pattern for the first letter of the verses as an aid to memory. This psalm has the style and content of Hebrew Wisdom teaching such as is found in Proverbs, Ecclesiastes and several other psalms, notably Psalm 119. In verse 25 the teacher claims to speak from long experience, and throughout he is trying to teach the young to keep faith in God, despite the fact that they are surrounded by the temptations of the wealth (v.16) and reputation (v.35) of the wicked.

In the first 8 verses, the exhortation *fret not yourselves* is used three times. Like any good teacher he is making his point in a variety of ways, and the lesson is that they should not upset themselves with envy of their contemporaries who have chosen to pursue worldly success rather than follow God. He points out what, in the end, is perfectly true, but hard for young people on the threshold of life to accept, that all things and all people perish. He makes this point in verse 2.

But he does not simply warn against the choice of a worldly way of life. His positive message is that if they seek God they will discover that the finding of him is the prize above all else. God will give them the *desires of your heart* (v.4). The righteous have the incomparable solace of being able to lay their problems before God. Patient stillness before God will prevent envy of the wicked growing into a practical following of their ways (vv.7, 8). Waiting for the Lord will also result in possession of *the land* (v.9).

In this psalm *the land* figures prominently, being mentioned no less than six times, in verses 3, 9, 11, 22, 29 and 34. It must be important. The Land—the Promised Land and now for Jews, Christians and Muslims, a Holy Land—is an important part of the Covenant between God and Abraham, that through him and his descendants, God's blessing would come upon all people. Abraham's people were given the task of bringing the knowledge of the one God to all people, and they were given a land as the base for their task. We read of God's promise to Abraham in, for example, Genesis 12.7 and 17.8. The covenant is renewed with Jacob in Genesis 28.15 and 35.12. It was then passed on to Joseph by the dying Jacob in Genesis 48.3,4. The promise was renewed with Moses in his experience of God at the Burning Bush (Exodus 3.8), and the books of Numbers, Joshua and Judges tell the story of the painful wilderness wanderings, and the sometimes brutal process of settlement in the land that they believed was theirs by God's gift.

Of course, it wasn't an empty land. Any land 'flowing with milk and honey' would never lack inhabitants, so the Israelites had to conquer, drive off or co-exist with the various Canaanite people whose home it was. Eventually David made Jerusalem the capital, and Solomon built the temple there to be the earthly dwelling place of God. Incursions into the land by foreign forces were looked upon not only as military and political matters, they were also affronts to God.

Some or all of that lies behind the psalmist's repeated promise that the land would be the reward for righteousness. We can also see that it is behind the territorial disputes which continue in our time – Palestinians (Muslim and Christian) looking for a homeland, and Jews, particularly Zionists, wanting to live in the land given, or given back, to them after their inhuman treatment in the 20th century. For Zionists it is not only a matter of a national territory; it is the wish to see the fulfilment of prophecies such as Isaiah 604, 5, Jeremiah 32.37,38 and Ezekiel 34. 12, 13, which speak of the restoration of Israel, a final return from every exile.

Time and again the psalmist-teacher tells his pupils that what seem to be the advantages of the selfish life are short-lived. They can be confident of this because it is the natural consequence of God's justice which is unfailing and unavoidable.

In verses 14 and 15 he uses military metaphors to teach that evil deeds have within them the seeds of their own destruction; *their sword shall enter their own heart, and their bows shall be broken.* Other exhortations of the psalm do not lose their power or relevance, as when generosity is praised in verses 21 and 26.

In verse after verse he teaches that God cares for the righteous. That is not always self-evident and many people would stand alongside Job and say that all too often the righteous suffer unjustly. If we could speak with him, the Wisdom teacher-psalmist would point us to the final chapter of the Book of Job where his wealth and family are greater than at the beginning. But his seven sons and three daughters who died in chapter 1 cannot be so easily set aside. It is probably better biblical scholarship to set aside the book's prose conclusion (Job 42. 7-end) and, like Job, continue to wrestle with the ever-valid problems which the book considers.

In the way of a good teacher, the psalmist uses his own experience of life to press home his message (vv. 35, 36). His picture of the downfall of a wicked man as a tree withering away reminds us of Jesus and the fruitless fig tree, a story recounted in Mark 11.12-14 and 20-25. The psalmist then moves to his conclusion with a contrasting picture of the ideal person, the sort of person on whom his pupils might model their lives. Such a person will be *blameless, upright and peaceable* (v.37). Finally, he assures his pupils that God will always be their refuge and protect them against the ever-tempting snares of evil.

We might feel that some of the teaching in the psalm is simply unrealistic. Most people have seen wealthy and corrupt people prospering and the good suffering. But this is only one piece of teaching, and as every preacher knows, you cannot preach the whole gospel in one sermon. In this psalm the teacher is seeking to portray the righteous life as one that reasonable people should follow. He presses home this teaching single-mindedly and leaves other issues, such as how to deal with the calamities of life, *the evil times* (v.19), for another occasion.

The Authorised Version of verses 4 and 7 counselling patience in waiting for God's help, are placed, beautifully and movingly, in Mendelssohn's oratorio, 'Elijah'. They are wonderfully comforting and uplifting and, sung by Kathleen Ferrier, are achingly beautiful.

Psalm 38

This psalm, full of anguish, is regarded as the Third Penitential Psalm. Who can this poor soul be? He believes that his sufferings are the result of his sin (v.3). This is the response of someone with a very tender conscience who has been taught (we might wish to say conditioned), to believe that any misfortune must be the consequence of and the punishment for sin. Sin often brings unpleasant consequences. On the other hand, if the concept of sin means nothing to people, they are more likely to respond to calamity by saying, *Why me? What have I done to deserve this?* There are, however, still many people of faith or without faith who are like the psalmist, and suffer too readily from a guilty conscience, having been schooled in guilt without that teaching having been balanced by vital teaching about the never-failing grace and forgiveness of God.

The symptoms described – acute pain, wounds which *grow foul and fester,* weakness, a high temperature, concern about his heart, problems with his eyes and probably with his ears, along with his being shunned by family and friends (v.11) suggest something like leprosy. Job's symptoms seem to have been similar. He could not remain at home nor in normal society. He took himself to the town rubbish dump and sat there scraping and scratching his erupting skin with bits of broken pottery. (Job 2. 7, 8). The psalmist tells us that his pains feel like God's *arrows,* piercing and punishing him.

His enemies take advantage of his weakness to plot against him, making careful plans (v.12). He laments that he is quite unable to defend himself. He cannot really hear their accusations and certainly cannot say anything in his own defence. Verses 13 and 14 may remind us of Our Lord's silence before the High Priest (Mark 14.61) and Pilate (Mark 15.5). The psalmist has come utterly to the end of his own resources and can only throw himself on the mercy of God, praying that he will sustain and protect him. Realising that he can do no more to help himself, he confesses simply but comprehensively, *I confess my iniquity, I am sorry for my sin (v.*18).

He remarks again on the power of his enemies and claims that he is the target of their malice because he leads a good life (vv. 19, 20). The psalm closes with a final plea to God for help, and to help quickly. The number of times he pleads for God's help and forgiveness remind us of Jesus' parable of the importunate or nagging widow, who would not give up pleading with a judge who didn't want to be bothered. Jesus ends his story by saying, "And will not God vindicate his elect, who cry to him day and night? Will he delay long over them? I tell you he will vindicate them speedily." (Luke 18.1-8).

Christians believe in God's unconditional love for all people, demonstrated in the life, teaching, death and resurrection of Jesus. It has been said that God forgives us, not when we confess our sin, not when we commit the sin, but even before we sin. In the words of the First Letter of John, "We have an advocate with the Father, Jesus Christ the righteous; and he is the expiation for our sins, and not for ours only but also for the sins of the whole world." (I John 2. 1, 2). Our sin can never be more powerful than God's grace. Our confession and our attempts at amendment of life are not the condition of our forgiveness, but a response to God's unconquerable love. Peter must have discovered the truth of that when he met Jesus after the resurrection. The subject of his running away in the Garden of Gethsemane, and his denial in the courtyard of the High Priest's house are not even mentioned. Jesus moves on and gives Peter a job to do: "feed my lambs." (John 21.15-19). What job is God asking you to do?

It is good to be honest with ourselves, to know our strengths and our weaknesses. It is good to strive to live a Christ-like life. It is good to be able to leave the past behind, confident in God's forgiveness surrounding us, behind and before. It is not good to be so absorbed with ourselves, with our own sins and feelings of guilt that we allow them to obscure God's forgiveness, demonstrated so clearly and in so costly a manner on the cross.

Psalm 39

At the beginning of this psalm, we are again led to think of Our Lord's silence before his accusers, and we ask ourselves, "Why is the psalmist not speaking?" In the first verse he fears that if he speaks he will, in some way, *sin with his tongue*. Is he questioning in his heart the goodness and justice of God, but keeping his thoughts to himself lest the godless seize on his words as a vindication of their way of life? Whatever the reason for his silence, it has caused him great distress and eventually, he can hold back no longer, and words, like a smouldering fire suddenly fed with air, burst forth (v.3).

What seems to be troubling him is his own mortality. How much longer does he have to live? He reflects that compared with the eternity of God, all human life is negligible, *a mere breath* (v. 5). All that a man achieves, all that he strives for, is left behind and he cannot tell what becomes of it (v.6).

He wants his relationship with God to be right before he dies, and in verse 7, he asks himself why he is waiting for his own death. He realises that it is a pointless speculation. His hope rests on God, and he asks to be forgiven for whatever he has done wrong (v.8). Having done that, there is no more to be said, and he returns to his former dumbness. This time, however, his words suggest that his silence is not so much his own choice as God's punishment, one of God's *strokes, blows* chastening him. He wilts under God's punishment, reflecting again how ephemeral is human life (v.11).

In verse 12 he asks God to listen to his plea and, more than that, to look at him and notice the tears which tell of his distress. He asks God not to ignore them. He has little time left and will soon go the way of his ancestors. Then in a sudden change of mind he asks God not to look at him. He cannot bear the eye of the righteous God to be on him, looking deep into him and knowing him through and through. His confusion comes out in his words. Before he dies he wants a little joy in his life, to have a little *gladness,* without his conscience disturbing him by telling him that his past life has displeased God.

This psalmist is a worrier. He is uncomfortable with himself. He is aware that his life has been sullied with sin, and though his deeply held faith tells him that God's forgiveness is his only hope if he is to have some happiness and contentment in his last days, he cannot decide what he should do. He cannot decide whether to voice his troubles and his hopes or whether to keep silent. He cannot decide whether he wants God to be close to him or not.

We might wonder if his silence is not entirely something he has chosen. Ezekiel is told by God that he will be dumb for a time (Ezek. 3.26), as is Zechariah, the father of John the Baptist (Luke1.20). In these cases the dumbness seems to be the result of an overwhelming spiritual experience, and in time speech returned. Today such attacks of temporary dumbness would be attributed to hysteria or perhaps to a stroke, neither of which necessarily rules out their being genuine religious experiences. Verse 9 would support this sort of interpretation of what happened to the psalmist, and would fit well with his distraught and confused state of mind.

Many people suffer anxiety about their death. They may be worried about how a loved one will cope without them. If they are people of faith they may be uneasy about facing their Maker, about any judgement that might take place. Even people of life-long and profound faith are sometimes deeply worried by the approach of death. The knowledge that Jesus will be our judge, when he returns "to judge the living and dead," is not always as comforting as it should be. We believe that it is Christ's nature to forgive, and that his death was a sacrifice for the sins of the whole world, offered once for all. So for the Christian, there should be no need to fear what will happen after death.

Some people, including some Christians, hold the Platonic view that at death our immortal soul is released from the burdensome shell of the body. Christian belief is that there will be a resurrection of 'the body', like the resurrection of Jesus, and that there will be final judgement of all people. However, most people in our society have no belief in any sort of life beyond the grave. They think that as they die all their thoughts, words, deeds and memories die with them. They will live on only in their descendants and in the memory of those who knew them, and perhaps in the work they did or the reputation they established.

A much greater worry for most people is one that the psalmist did not mention. It is the manner of death, not its date. Will I die in pain? Will I die at home? Will my family care for me? Will the state care for me? Can I choose when I die and how I die? As people live longer these questions become more pressing; they are our generation's version of the psalmist's worry. Much has been done in recent times to try to help people prepare for death and to make the whole process more dignified and pain free. The homes inspired and founded by the war hero, Leonard Cheshire, for the care of younger people suffering from incurable diseases, and the hospice movement, led and inspired by Dame Cecily Saunders, have helped and are helping many people.

All the questions in the last paragraph have medical and ethical implications, and they will go on being debated. So we find the psalmist's worries have their close equivalent in our generation. We should pray for those approaching death, those who care for them, those who will miss them. We should also confidently commend those who have died to God's care and keeping. They live on in God's presence and there is no reason why we should not continue to pray for them, and believe that they, as part of the vast Communion of Saints, are praying for us.

Psalm 40

It is good to have this prayer of a confident believer after the anxiety and uncertainty of Psalm 39.

The psalmist's life has not been totally care free. He has had his share of troubles. He has been in *the desolate pit,* the depths of despair. He had felt as if his life had no firm foundation, as though he was walking through a *miry bog* (v.2). But he is now free of those problems. He had called on God and God had set his life on a firm foundation, a rock, and has so changed things that instead of words of despair he can sing a song of praise. Knowing that God has helped him, he wants others to follow his example and *wait patiently for the Lord* (vv. 1-4).

It is his experience that blessedness, fullness of life, can only be found by those who worship Yahweh, the one true God. Other so-called gods simply lead their worshippers astray. The examples of Yahweh's wonderful deeds are innumerable (v.5).

If this psalm is being said or sung as part of a public liturgy, as the mention of *the great congregation* in verse 9 suggests, the psalmist might look around at the temple's ritual objects, the cherubim with outspread wings sheltering the ark, the throne, the sea of bronze and the altar. However awe-inspiring the setting and the liturgy of the temple may have been, the psalmist has the confidence to speak out and to say that sacrifice is not what God really wants from men. He wants them to do his will which, as we know from many psalms as well as from the prophets, is to care for the poor and needy.

He rejoices that he has made a full public testimony and stresses how he tried to ensure that his message was not ignored: *I have told...; I have not restrained my lips...; I have not hid...; I have spoken...; I have not concealed...* Having received God's help and deliverance he intends that all should be aware of it (vv.9, 10).

In verses 11 and 12 he again turns to God in prayer, asking for God's continuing mercy and steadfast love. His life is still full of difficulties, *evils without number* press on him and destroy his health.

(We now need to note that verses 13-17 replicate the words of Psalm 70 apart from a few words in verse 17.)

Asking again for God's help, he says that he has opponents who would like to see him dead or at least dishonoured. The psalmist does not pray for the destruction of his opponents; he simply asks that their plots and their bitterness against him might be nullified. We are reminded of Jeremiah and how unpopular he was with some of the religious establishment. (Jer. 20. 1-2). The earlier references to *the desolate pit* and *the miry bog* also make us recall how Jeremiah was put in a muddy well, and would have been left there to die had not the kindness of one man saved him (Jer. 38. 6-13).

Verse 16 sounds like an instruction or invitation to the congregation, those who are loyal to Yahweh, that they praise God in their worship with the shout *Great is the Lord.*

Finally he returns to his own situation. No matter how outwardly confident he may be, when he thinks of himself as a man before his God, he admits that he is *poor and needy;* he still needs the help of God, and hopes that he will not have to wait too long for it; *do not tarry, O my God.*

This psalm shows us a man doing what we should all do more readily. He speaks openly of his faith and of what God has done for him. He is clearly important enough to have enemies in the religious hierarchy and he speaks of the low points in his life to which his opponents have brought him. But he speaks readily of how God lifted him up. How wise he is that in the end he still thinks of himself apart from God as *poor and needy.* He is one of those, not necessarily poor in the material things of life, for whom God has a special care. He has found the treasure of realising that in God's eyes he is a beloved child.

Psalm 41

The word *blessed* begins both the first and last verses of this psalm. The beginning of verse 1 comes very close to Jesus' first Beatitude, especially in St. Luke's version, *blessed are you poor.* (Luke 6.20). Concern for the poor is a recurring theme in the Psalter: God's sets the example and men must follow. If people care for the poor, God will care for them (v.2). The outworking of the blessedness of caring for others was neatly and appropriately illustrated when the Dalai Lama was asked what was the secret of happiness. He replied, "Be kind."

Having made the general point, the psalmist turns to his own experience (vv.4-9). He has been seriously ill and believes it was punishment for sin. His illness was welcomed by his enemies who hoped that he would die. He had visitors when he was ill, but they were about as useful as Job's 'Comforters'. Indeed, they were worse because, having been to see him, they gossiped about his condition, enjoying their morbid imaginings. Verse 8 sounds like the unpleasant satisfaction of the habitual pessimist, shaking his head and saying, "he's not long for this world." Sadly, also, a close friend had turned against him. We are not told why. He ends his reminiscing in verse 10. He has become embittered, and prays that God will help him to be revenged on his enemies.

It may be that after verse 10 some sort of absolution has been given. That would account for the change of mood in verse 11. Now he is confident that his enemies have not triumphed, and that his prayer for forgiveness has been answered. He claims that he retained his integrity, his dependence on God, throughout his suffering and that, as a result, God has vindicated him. He feels as though he is again in God's presence. This may mean that he is in the temple or it may be a more general feeling of utter trust that God is close to him (v.12).

Verse 13, a blessing on God, may have been inserted as an appropriate ending to the first book of the Psalter. Alternatively, the psalm may have been chosen to conclude Book I because of its final verse.

When we read the second half of verse 10, *raise me up that I may requite them,* we may think, "What an unworthy sentiment." We should be slow to judge. We have to accept that those were the psalmist's feelings at that time. We do not know how far he had been provoked. We do not know if he misjudged or exaggerated what his enemies said and did. Certainly his hurt was deep enough to make him utter such thoughts.

Vengeance still plays a significant and insidious part in human affairs at a personal and at an international level. Rupert Shortt, in his book *Christianophobia*, records a remarkable and heart-warming story about one Christian man's thoughts of vengeance, and how he dealt with them. The setting is Nigeria in the late 1990's when persecution of Christians was common and violent. He writes about Pastor James Wuye who, as a young man led a Christian militia dedicated to protecting churches from Islamist-inspired violence. He justified his conduct by saying that "We've been beaten on both cheeks, there's no other cheek to turn." However, despite having his right arm cut off by a machete, he overcame thoughts of vengeance, and he and a Muslim cleric, Muhammad Ashafa, are now dedicated to community bridge-building in the very violent city of Kaduna. They are an example to all people of faith. Thoughts of vengeance have been overcome and set aside.

Psalms 42 and 43

This beautiful poem marks the beginning of Book II of the Psalter. We look at Psalms 42 and 43 together because they are both a part of a single poem. Psalm 42 contains two strophes of the poem and Psalm 43 one. The fact that there is no heading to Psalm 43 also suggests the two were originally one. There is also a similar refrain in verses 5 and 11 of Psalm 42 and in verse 5 of Psalm 43.

The psalms record the poet's longing to return to Jerusalem and to join in the worship in the temple. It seems as if, at one time, he had an important liturgical office to perform. He *led them in procession to the house of God.* (42.4). Perhaps he is a Levite and in earlier days was a temple musician or singer (43.4). Whatever his role, he misses it grievously. He seems to live far away from Jerusalem. *The land of Jordan and of Hermon, from Mount Mizar* seems to have been in the neighbourhood of what later became Caesarea Philippi, more than a hundred miles north of Jerusalem – in those days a foreign land. The words of verse 5, *My soul is cast down within me* remind us of Jesus' words in the Garden of Gethsemane. He said to his disciples, "My soul is very sorrowful, even to death."

(Psalm 42) Verses 1-5 form the first section of the poem. It begins with a lovely simile of his soul's thirst for God being like that of a deer desperately searching for water in the parching heat of a desert land. Living far from Jerusalem, his longing for God and for Jerusalem is mocked by his neighbours. *Where is your God?* they say. Perhaps their allegiance was to other gods and they think that the poet is too far from Jerusalem for his God to be able to reach him. Or it may be that they have images of their god, whereas Yahweh, God of Israel, was unseen and, for true believers, no attempt could be made to represent him. The question may be a straightforward, puzzled enquiry. Disdain for and mockery of the other gods and their worshippers is widespread in the psalms and in the prophets. Isaiah of Babylon derides the images of foreign gods and the naïve understanding of the reality of God which they reveal. (Isaiah 40. 18-20).

The first section of the psalm ends with the psalmist reprimanding himself for his lack of faith. He may feel *cast down* at the moment but, he tells himself, *Hope in God; for I shall again praise him, my help and my God.*

He fails to restore his own confidence and is still *cast down.* Distance seems to be the problem, and the difficulties of living among people to whom Yahweh, the God of Israel, means nothing. He knows that returning to Jerusalem and joining in the worship of the temple would give him great joy. It would slake his spiritual thirst. But at this time it seems impossible that he should ever return. After lack of water in verse 1, he now feels as if he were drowning in misery, floundering and in danger of losing his life (v. 7). Even in his deep unhappiness, he continues his prayers night and day (v.8). This is perhaps a deliberate act of discipline like a priest who, going through a time of doubt about his faith and his vocation, faithfully fulfils his duty of saying the daily Offices of Morning and Evening Prayer.

The psalmist knows that God is his only hope, the rock on which he can stand secure while the storm and torrents mentioned in verse 7 crash around him. He holds to his faith despite the attacks and taunts of his enemies or detractors; still they ask, *Where is your God?* Again, in the refrain, he encourages himself. There is no need to be *cast down* and *disquieted,* because God gives him hope that he will again worship God in Jerusalem (v.11).

(Psalm 43) Again he tells us that he lives among *ungodly people* (v.1). To them he is an alien with an alien religion. They have little time or sympathy for him. In this unfriendly situation, he fears that God has forsaken him. Perhaps he again wonders if he is too far from Jerusalem for God's grace to reach him. This 'territorial' aspect of religion is well illustrated in the story of the Syrian general, Naaman, whom Elisha healed of leprosy. When he returned to his own country he took with him a cart-load of soil from Israel so that he could worship Yahweh although he was in Syria. (II Kings 5. 17, 18). Or we might recall Psalm 137 in which the exile asks the question *How shall we sing the Lord's song in a foreign land?*

In verse 3 he prays for God's light to reach him and lead him to Jerusalem. It is as if, living in spiritual darkness, he hopes to follow the light shining out from Jerusalem, leading him *to thy holy hill and to thy dwelling.* He imagines himself back in Jerusalem, taking part

90

once again in the joyful liturgy of the temple. This time the refrain has the final word. He is convinced that his thirst for God will be satisfied. He will return. His soul now has no reason to be cast down.

The psalmist longed to go to Jerusalem to be near God, to find God. It was one of the lessons learnt in the Babylonian exile that God is not limited by space as humans are. The exile taught them that God can be found and worshipped anywhere. Jesus, passing through Samaria and talking to a Samaritan woman about the fact that Jews and Samaritans believed that different mountains were sacred, said, "Woman, believe me, the hour is coming when neither on this mountain, nor in Jerusalem will you worship the Father… God is spirit, and those who worship him must worship in spirit and truth." (John 4.21-23). William Cowper's hymn sets out the Christian belief that God is present everywhere, especially when Christians worship together:

"Jesus, where'ere thy people meet, There they behold thy mercy seat; Where'ere they seek thee, thou art found, And every place is hallowed ground."

Psalm 44

This psalm appears to be spoken by the king at a formal liturgy in the temple. As we shall see, the words may not be his own but a prepared prayer spoken on behalf of the nation. The occasion seems to be after a military defeat resulting in a prolonged period of subjugation by a foreign power. Artur Weiser suggests that the occasion would be the annual service marking the Renewal of the Covenant.

The psalm begins with the recalling of God's mighty acts in the past, concentrating particularly on the remarkable campaign for the occupation of Canaan. It is acknowledged that the Israelites, weary from forty years of wandering in the wilderness, could hardly have expected to achieve victories like that at Jericho. Therefore, it must have been by God's help: *Not by their own sword did they win the land, nor did their own arm give them victory; but thy right hand and the light of thy countenance* (v.3). In a wonderful phrase, Weiser describes their success as due to 'the incomprehensible miracle of his love'. In verses 4-8 the king records his own role and responsibilities. He is king, but only as viceroy for Yahweh who is, and always has been, the nation's real king. So victories in the king's reign are attributed to God, and thanks are given.

But all that is in the past. In the present, it seems as if God is no longer fighting on Israel's behalf. God has *not gone out with our armies.* Retreats and defeats have been the result, with death, exile and slavery their fate. Now they are scorned by neighbouring peoples. *Thou hast made us a byword among the nations, a laughingstock among the peoples.* And there can only be one cause – the action or inaction of Yahweh. It is not by accident that they suffer; it is Yahweh's doing. *Thou hast cast us off… Thou hast made us turn back.* Verse after verse accuses Yahweh of causing the suffering (vv.9-16).

Verse 17 sounds like the petulant cry of a spoiled child. *We have not forgotten thee… Our heart has not turned back.* The king claims that he and his people have not been unfaithful to Yahweh; they have kept the Covenant (v.17). Surely any disloyalty would be known to Yahweh (v.21).

What can explain their terrible misfortunes? There is no hint that their claim to be faithful to the Covenant might be exaggerated. In the Books of Samuel and Kings we read that under the monarchy there were numerous examples of apostasy and unfaithfulness. The prophets warn and rail against it constantly. The necessity for the reforms of King Josiah make the true situation very clear. (II Kings 23).

While the reason for their sufferings remains unknown or unacknowledged, their reality cannot be avoided, and in verse 22 it seems that they must simply be accepted. Then in the final four verses of the psalm there is an impassioned plea to Yahweh to come to their aid. They have accepted that they can do nothing in their own strength; they are utterly powerless. They need God to look on them again and lift them to their feet. We can perhaps imagine the final four verses as a congregational response to the king's outpouring of woe, with the whole temple congregation imploring, *Rouse thyself! Rise up, come to our help! Deliver us!*

We might consider whether this psalm might be rather like the Queen's Speech at the opening of Parliament. It is delivered by the monarch, but has been prepared and written by politicians or, in this case, priests. If so, here we have the king reading his script, some of which he might prefer not to say. The stages in the speech are clearly defined. First there is a reminder to everyone (including God) of how, in the past, Yahweh had protected them and made them victorious. The king then very properly says that all his success, all his military prowess, is the result of God's help. God is the cause of everything. Therefore he must be the cause of defeat as well as of victory. No blame is laid on the people who might have been disloyal to the Covenant. The nation is presented in its ideal form.

The closing congregational cry, *Rouse thyself!* reminds us of Elijah's taunting of the prophets of baal when their god fails to answer them. (I Kings 18.25-29). He suggests that their god might be on a journey or asleep and needs rousing. Christians believe that it was God's long-term plan for the human race that he would indeed rouse himself in a way which the psalmist and others in the congregation in Jerusalem could not have imagined. He roused himself by entering human life in Jesus, sharing that life with all its successes and its failures, its pleasures and its pains. In Jesus, God roused himself, not to remove human problems and suffering, but to share them.

Psalm 45

This is a psalm written for a very important royal occasion, probably a royal marriage. The psalmist begins by telling us how moved and inspired he is to be writing this poem or prayer. Poetry and music specially commissioned for and performed at royal weddings are things we are used to in Great Britain.

He proclaims how noble is the royal groom; blessed by God with good looks and gracious speech (v.2). The primary responsibility of the king will be the protection of his people. He will therefore have to be a warrior. He will certainly win victories (v. 5), but his strength is not for self-aggrandisement, power-seeking or land-grabbing; it is to further *the cause of truth and to defend the right (v.4).*

He reigns because he has been chosen by God; his throne is therefore *divine.* God's choice is declared by the ceremony of anointing – a practice continued in the Coronation liturgy of the Anglican Church. It is fitting that the wedding of a divinely appointed king should be an occasion of great magnificence. We are treated (vv.8, 9) to a picture of the royal group. Their robes are magnificent. The most expensive perfumes have been used. Music adds to the occasion and the company is made up of the most distinguished guests.

In verse 10 the poet begins to set out the responsibilities of the royal bride. She was probably a very young woman, a girl. She is advised to forget her home and family. She is now to be at her husband's disposal; *he is your lord.* Comfort is offered: she will receive so much honour and so many gifts that she will soon overcome her homesickness. In her private quarters, she is dressed by the companions who wait on her so that she is fit for a king (vv. 14, 15). There is no mystery about her primary purpose. She is to bear children to ensure the continuing of the royal line, the chosen house of David. For fulfilling her role and ensuring the nation's future she will be remembered for ever (vv.16, 17). Some translations insert the words 'O king' in verse 16. The words are not present in the Hebrew and seem to weaken the thought that the royal bride's first duty is to bear a son and so ensure the continuation of the Davidic dynasty.

Great state occasions always present the nation, its leaders and its people in an ideal way. It is an opportunity for the nation to imagine itself as it ought to be, rather than as it is. This is a legitimate function of a royal occasion. If the ideal were never put before people they would never know to what they should aspire.

It is interesting that despite the importance of the bride in this psalm, in the historical books of the Old Testament queens are of very little significance, apart perhaps, from Bathsheba who rather irregularly fulfilled her purpose by bearing Solomon who would succeed his father David. Other queens are remembered more for bringing with them at marriage their own foreign god or gods, and thereby polluting the pure religion of Yahweh. The best example of this is Jezebel who not only vigorously promoted her own baal worship, but seems also to have been a very nasty and vindictive woman. (I Kings 21).

Sometimes this psalm has been allegorised and the bride has been looked upon as a foreshadowing of the Blessed Virgin Mary, bearer of the royal Son of God, making this a Messianic psalm.

The writer of the Book of Revelation seems to have had this psalm in his mind when he described his vision of the consummation of all things. He sees "the holy city, new Jerusalem, coming down from God as a bride adorned for her husband." (Rev. 21.2). This is the ideal Church, the Communion of Saints, "the Bride, the wife of the Lamb." (Rev. 21.9). Like the ideal of the nation presented in the psalm, Christian worship reminds us that we are the Body of Christ and presents us with the ideal of the Church which we must strive to make a reality.

Psalm 46

This is a hymn in praise of God's power and his desire for peace and justice among men. It takes us from a conflict-torn past and present to the hope of a future in which evil has been defeated and war abolished.

The opening three verses celebrate God's care and protection of Israel. He is their *refuge and strength.* Even if cataclysmic upheavals in nature should occur, apparently reversing the order God imposed on chaos in his act of creation – even then he will prove to be faithful. (For the proper balance of the poem the refrain in verses 7 and 11 should also have followed verse 3).

The holy city is watered and made *glad* by a river with many tributaries; it can be free from fear of drought (v.4). Jerusalem is God's habitation on earth and therefore, the psalmist believes, the city can never fall. If she is threatened by enemies *she shall not be moved; God will help her.* The belief in Jerusalem's inviolability is found in Isaiah's words of encouragement to King Hezekiah when the Assyrian army led by King Sennacherib threatened the city. Isaiah, speaking what he believed was the word of the Lord, said, "He shall not come into this city, or shoot an arrow there, or come before it with a shield, or cast up a siege mound against it… For I will defend this city and save it, for my own sake and for the sake of my servant David." (Isaiah 37. 33-35).

Jeremiah thought and taught otherwise. He was caught up in a conflict about whether God would always protect Jerusalem. His opponents repeated "this is the temple of the Lord," as if it were a magical formula ensuring the city's and therefore their own safety. Jeremiah told them that their faithlessness would be the cause of God abandoning the city and its subsequent destruction. He says, "Do not trust these deceptive words." (Jer. 7.1-4). In much the same way, when Jesus' disciples marvelled at the seemingly immoveable mass of Herod's temple, he said, "Do you see these great buildings? There will not be left here one stone upon another." (Mark 13.2).

Fears of destruction are not simply from the fevered imagination of the psalmist; the world is in tumult: *the nations rage, the kingdoms totter (v.6)*. Nevertheless, he is confident that God's care for Israel remains unchanged (v.7).

Verses 8 and 9 look ahead to a time when God will have defeated all Israel's enemies. Weapons of war will be destroyed, and Isaiah's and Micah's dream of nations beating 'their swords into ploughshares and their spears into pruning hooks' will be accomplished. (Isaiah 2.2-4 and Micah 4.1-4). Israel will then be free to fulfil her God-given task of bringing blessing on all nations in accordance with the promise made to Abraham. (Gen. 12.2, 3).

In verse 10 we hear the voice of God, the words perhaps spoken by a priest. He calls all nations to acknowledge his just and gentle rule. Earthly rulers may rejoice in their imagined power. We might say they are like so many Canutes, fondly believing that their actions can make a difference, quite unable to see their own powerlessness.

The psalmist reminds us that everyone needs to learn that only Yahweh controls the world's destinies. The psalm ends with its confident and comforting refrain, *The Lord of Hosts is with us; the God of Jacob is our refuge.*

The psalm builds up to the hope of universal peace. The mention of the river in verse 4 seems to draw on a tradition in which Jerusalem, city of peace, is like a fresh spring out of which pours healing water giving life and bringing healing to all nations. A river flowing from the temple appears in Ezekiel's vision of Jerusalem. It brings life wherever it flows, even to the Dead Sea. On its banks grow all sorts of trees; "their leaves will not wither nor their fruit fail, but they will bear fresh fruit every month because the water for them flows from the sanctuary. Their fruit will be for food, and their leaves for healing." (Ezek. 47). The vision of the writer of the Book of Revelation draws on the same tradition. He sees the wondrous river; "on either side of the river, the tree of life with its twelve kinds of fruit, yielding its fruit each month; and the leaves of the tree were for the healing of the nations." (Rev. 22.1, 2).

Little changes in the world. Politicians still strut the world stage, imagining, indeed hoping, usually with the best of intentions, that their decisions will make a difference. Over the years, few human interventions seem to be wholly beneficial. Once again we learn that hope for the world depends on those with power seeking guidance from God and trying to rule as God's representatives. Grace flows from God, like a life-giving river. We must pray that world leaders learn that God's gifts are lavish and, if they are used aright, they will be for the healing of the nations. We need to pray too that gifted and able Christians in all nations will be willing to take on the unenviable tasks of political leadership.

Psalm 47

This psalm along with Psalms 93 and 96-99, celebrates the universal rule of Yahweh. He is no local godling, like those of the surrounding peoples, he is *a great king over all the earth (v. 2).*

Verse 5 seems to describe a formal liturgy with procession, music and clapping. So verse 1, (and the same applies to verse 6), may be an invitation to the congregation to start to praise God. Such an instruction might be given by a priest or other liturgical official. On the other hand it could be a part of the people's praise, rather like a church congregation addressing and encouraging itself in singing a hymn such as, "Come, let us join our cheerful songs with angels round the throne."

If the service is the New Year festival, with the enthronement of Yahweh in the temple and the renewing of the covenant, this psalm lifts the concept of the kingship of Yahweh from his being Israel's king, with the nation's earthly ruler his viceroy, to his being Lord of all nations. The evidence for his lordship over other nations is seen in the way he has given victory in war to Israel. It was God who enabled them to overcome the peoples of Canaan as they invaded and settled in the Promised Land (v.3). God's choosing of Israel as his special people is a cause for pride (v. 4), and it is noticeable that there is no recognition here of the responsibilities attached to that choice.

Verses 5 to 8 describe something of the splendid ritual marking the occasion. God's *going up* (v.5) is probably the procession bearing the ark, the symbol of God's presence, and its being set in its accustomed place under the canopy of the wings of the cherubim. Once the ark is in position it can be said that *God reigns over the nations; God sits on his holy throne (v.8).*

The important members of the congregation are noticed; foreign notables as well as eminent Judaeans (v.9). We might wonder what the foreign guests made of this exalting of Yahweh as universal king and God. They were probably unmoved. They would be politicians and high-ranking military men. They would know how to behave even if they disagreed and disapproved of the belittling of their own god or gods. They might be quietly noting the strengths and weaknesses of Jerusalem with a view to future campaigns.

The universal rule of Yahweh is an inescapable belief once he is regarded as the only God. It sometimes seems difficult to see evidence of his rule in the world. The end of warfare, multilateral disarmament, as pictured in Psalm 46, is slow in coming. God's desire that all people should live in harmony seems as far away now as it has ever been. The establishing of God's kingdom 'on earth as it is in heaven' is an ongoing and slow work, requiring the cooperation of all people with God. It is the task of every Christian, a task taken on at baptism, to work steadily to build God's kingdom. We are often tempted to say or think, *But what can I do?* The answer is 'keep trying'. It is better to light one candle than to curse the darkness.

Psalm 48

This psalm reads like a hymn for the congregation of pilgrims gathered in the temple in Jerusalem. Perhaps verses 1 to 3 were to be sung by all. They celebrate the greatness of Yahweh and how his presence sanctifies the city and its magnificent buildings, its *citadels*. The mention, in verse 2, of *Mount Zion, in the far north* links with similar references in Isaiah 14.13, Job 37.22 and Psalm 75.6. Perhaps the clearest reference this tradition about the north is found in Ezekiel's account of his vision of God: "As I looked, behold, a stormy wind came out of the north, and a great cloud, with brightness round about it, and fire flashing forth continually, and in the midst of the fire, as it were gleaming bronze…" (Ezekiel 1.4). In each of these cases it seems as if there is some ancient and deep-rooted tradition that God was inaccessible, somewhere far away in the north. So here, speaking of Zion as *the far north* means that Zion is where God is to be found.

Verses 4-7 recall Israel's salvation history, remembering the kings of neighbouring peoples who had, over the years, made war on them. Sihon of Ammon, Og of Bashan, (both of whom are mentioned in Psalms 135 and 136), Agag of Amalek, Ben Hadad of Syria, Mesha of Moab were the kings of some of the lesser nations who are mentioned in the historical books. The psalm tells us that as they marched on Jerusalem, expecting to overthrow the city, their alliances foundered as they saw its magnificence. The very sight of the city threw them into disarray like a storm-endangered fleet (v.7).

The pilgrims now share the initial experience of the foreign kings; they see the holy city. But for them, it creates not terror, but delight, because it is the place where God's steadfast love and his victorious goodness are concentrated. The pilgrims now stand in that holy place where they recall God's mighty acts on Israel's behalf, possibly hearing a liturgical recitation of the salvation history. This causes them to rejoice and praise God (vv. 9-11).

The pilgrimage is almost over. The pilgrims are told to commit to memory the sight of all the wonderful buildings, so that when they return to their far-flung homes they can tell their children of their experiences (vv.12, 13). It is still the case that pilgrimage to Jerusalem, and to other holy places, fills pilgrims with memories which they treasure and which they cannot keep to themselves. Many a solid church-goer has returned from the Holy Land filled with a new enthusiasm and a need to share the riches of their pilgrim experience. They might be, for a period, a 'Jerusalem bore'.

Finally, in verse 14 God's eternal love and care is celebrated. It may be that the psalmist has raised his view beyond the commonly accepted belief that death, descent into Sheol, separates people from God; *The dead do not praise the Lord, nor do any that go down into silence* (Psalm 115.17). Here he insists that *this is our God, our God for ever and ever. He will be our guide for ever.* Perhaps, however, his confidence is that God will be the nation's guide for as long as it exists, rather than a belief in "the resurrection of the dead and life of the world to come" which Christians proclaim. The psalmist's words may betray an instinctive longing for such a faith.

Psalm 49

This psalm is a piece of Wisdom teaching. It is in the form of a hymn to be sung accompanied by the lyre (v.4). The poet is a teacher of Wisdom and he calls all to hear him, as what he will say has universal significance. He speaks to all, *both low and high, rich and poor together.* Verses 3 and 4 contain common but important words in Wisdom teaching – *understanding, proverb, riddle.*

The poet has suffered at the hands of the rich (vv. 5, 6) and he knows that it is not an uncommon experience. So, for himself, and for his hearers he asks why the wealthy can act so cruelly and unjustly, and apparently get away with it. The unspoken question is 'does God not care'?

He sees death as the answer. Even the wealthiest cannot escape death and no one is rich enough to be able to buy himself back from death (vv. 7-9). He acknowledges that even the wise, like himself, cannot avoid death. In death the wise and the foolish, the rich and the poor are equal. In verses 12 and 20 there is a refrain, comparing humans to cattle; both can only expect to live the usual life-span of their sort. He reflects that the rich have been accustomed to having their own way, buying whatever and whomever they want (v.13). But he imagines death as a shepherd, herding them all into Sheol. His picture of people being herded into the pit was a common theme in medieval Christian art, painted on the walls of churches to encourage or frighten people into righteousness. Each such painting is appropriately known as a 'Doom'. Several survive, mainly in ancient parish churches. They are now carefully restored and preserved.

Having set the scene, the psalmist in verse 16, begins to give his considered answer. It is that those who wish to follow the way of righteousness must not envy the rich. However successful and powerful they become, however exalted their reputation, they cannot take their wealth with them into Sheol. In death they are separated from God; they are no better than animals (vv.18-20). The lesson is *do not envy the rich.*

What a hard lesson it is! Envy, covetousness, and jealousy seem to have a history as long as the human race. Cain was jealous because God deemed his brother Abel's sacrifice more acceptable, more valuable than his own (Genesis 4.1-18). The story of the Tower of Babel is about human dissatisfaction at being human and therefore limited. The builders of the tower are jealous of God because he is in heaven and they can see no reason why they should not also be there. (Gen.11). Sarah envied the ability of Hagar to bear a son for Abraham. (Gen. 21.9, 10). Joseph's brothers were jealous because of his favoured treatment by their father; his coat with long sleeves indicating that he was not expected to do any manual work (Gen. 37.3, 4). The examples are numerous and it is not surprising that *Thou shalt not covet* is one of the Ten Commandments.

The very poor, the destitute, those who have never known any kind of luxury, the people in Third World countries who live from year to year with drought or flood, famine or terror, do not and cannot envy the rich because they cannot imagine what wealth or luxury is. What they want is not wealth but a cup of water, the next meal or some medication. Envy is more likely to be found among those who have quite a lot but want still more. They are rich enough, but they want to be very rich. The advertising industry feeds on the instinct to envy, creating a desire to have more or better mobile phones, cars, push-chairs, houses, spouses…

A distinction needs to be made between envy and the desire to improve life for oneself and one's family. Aspiration is the word often used. Aspiration and hard work have raised standards for many people but it is a hazardously thin line between justifiable aspiration and unjustifiable envy.

The Psalmist-Sage's answer, *Do not envy the rich,* is certainly a wise answer. St. Paul took up the theme in his letter to Timothy. Contrasting a proper Christian attitude with the desire for wealth, he wrote, "There is great gain in godliness with contentment; for we brought nothing into the world, and we cannot take anything out of the world; but if we have food and clothing, with these we shall be content." (I Timothy 6.6-8). It is still true. Contentment is great wealth. It means that we do not have to try to keep up with the Joneses either materially or spiritually, because we know that each of us is of infinite value in the sight of God.

Psalm 50

This psalm seems to be part of the liturgy for the Festival of Covenant Renewal (v.5). The first six verses announce the coming of God, perfect in beauty, accompanied by fire and tempest. These are the natural phenomena said to have accompanied the coming of God on Mount Sinai at the inception of the Covenant. (Exodus 19. 16-20). There may have been some action in the temple liturgy— perhaps drums and flashes of light – which represented the powers of nature veiling the actual presence of God. With his presence thus assured, God is then imagined as calling his people together to renew the covenant (v.5). The first half of verses 7 and 16 sound like a spoken rubric, perhaps a Levite or other liturgical officiant, telling the congregation that the voice which they will now hear is speaking as the voice of God. And again the words which follow would probably be spoken or sung by a priest or Levite.

God speaks first to *my faithful ones* (v.5) and *my people* (v.7). They are called to gather in the presence of God to hear his judgements. *I am God, your God* echoes the first of the Ten Commandments (Exodus 20. 2, 3) and would be a reminder of the rest of the Covenant into which Israel had entered and promised to keep.

God says that they have certainly observed the externals of the Covenant. Their sacrifices and burnt offerings are continually before him (v.8). But God does not need them nor want them. He is no human; he does not share their needs. If he wanted food or drink he has all animals, wild and domesticated, as well as the birds, at his disposal (vv. 12, 13). That is not what he wants from humans. From his Covenant partner he requires an offering, not of blood, but of thanksgiving. He invites them to call on him when they are in trouble. He will help them and they will thank him.

In verse 16 we begin to hear what God says to the wicked. The wicked are also members of the Covenant community gathered in the temple. They say the same words as everyone else, but for all their outward appearance and profession, they do not keep the Covenant. They cannot discipline themselves and so they ignore the Covenant's demands. In verse 18 they are accused of conniving at theft and adultery, both expressly forbidden in the Decalogue. They gossip slanderously (v.19) and are disloyal (v.20). To justify their crimes and sins of omission they have, in effect, created a god in their own image. Their god, like them, will turn a blind eye to wrong-doing. But though God has kept silence so far, he will now bring charges against them.

The two closing verses of the psalm have words of warning for those who disregard the Covenant, and words of encouragement for those who keep it. Verse 22 is stern, addressed to *you who forget*

God. But they are warned, not condemned. There is still time for them to change their way of life. Those who express their gratitude to God honour him, and salvation awaits *him who orders his way aright.*

There is no mystery about the meaning of 'ordering his way aright'. The outward trappings of religion are not wrong but they are not the kernel of Covenant living. As we read verses 8-13 we are reminded of very similar passages in the prophets as they declare 'the word of the Lord'. It is clearly teaching of major significance. "What to me is the multitude of your sacrifices? says the Lord; I have had enough of burnt offerings of rams and the fat of fed beasts; I do not delight in the blood of bulls, or of lambs, or of he-goats... Wash yourselves; make yourselves clean; remove the evil of your doings from before my eyes; cease to do evil, learn to do good; seek justice, correct oppression, defend the fatherless, plead for the widow." (Isaiah 1.16, 17).

Amos takes up the theme. "I despise your feasts... even though you offer me your burnt offerings and cereal offerings, I will not accept them... but let justice roll down like waters, and righteousness like an ever-flowing stream." (Amos 5.21, 22, 24).

Micah adds his voice. "Will the Lord be pleased with thousands of rams, with ten thousands of rivers of oil? Shall I give my first-born for my transgression, the fruit of my body for the sin of my soul? He has showed you, O man, what is good; and what does the Lord require of you but to do justice, and to love kindness, and to walk humbly with your God." (Micah 5.8).

Throughout the Old Testament justice, mercy, kindness and care for those in need are the building blocks of God's kingdom. The same is true in the New Testament, and Jesus, in his teaching and in his actions showed that the Kingdom of God which he was ushering in would be built with the same materials. He also saw the outward trappings of religion as a snare. Mere words do not count. In the Sermon on the Mount he said, "Not everyone who says to me, 'Lord, Lord' will enter the kingdom of heaven, but he who does the will of my Father who is in heaven." (Matt. 7.21). He criticised the scribes and Pharisees because some of them paid strict attention to the exterior practices of religion, robes and ritual actions, to the exclusion of the things which God really requires. "Woe to you, scribes and Pharisees, hypocrites! for you tithe mint and cummin, and have neglected the weightier matters of the law, justice and mercy and faith; these you ought to have done, without neglecting the others." (Matt. 22.23).

The externals of religion can be very attractive, and while generally harmless can sometimes be a distraction from the 'weightier matters of the law'. It is important that when we worship God, things are done reverently and properly – as St. Paul told the Christians of Corinth (I Cor. 14.40), "decently and in order"—but justice, kindness and mercy are far more important than the correct liturgical colour. Kindness to all whom we meet, a thoughtful and proper disposal of our charitable giving, a concern for the needy of our own society and for the needs of the wider world – these things are not optional, they are the duty of every Christian. Our Lord gathered up the wisdom of the Old Testament, added to it, and passed it on to us, illustrating his teaching unforgettably in his parable of the Sheep and the Goats.

Psalm 51

This is the fourth, and arguably the most important of the Penitential Psalms. The heading states that these are David's words of penitence when the court prophet, Nathan, had convinced him of his guilt over his adultery with Bathsheba and the subsequent murder of her husband, Uriah, in an attempt to cover up their guilt. (II Samuel 11.1-12.15). The anguish expressed would certainly be appropriate to that occasion, but the words of verse 18 suggest that it was composed during the rebuilding of the temple under the direction of Nehemiah after the return from exile in Babylon. However, if the final two verses are a later addition we may indeed be reading David's words of sorrow over his sin.

The poet plunges straight into his need for forgiveness. He expresses his confidence in God's *steadfast love* and abundant mercy before confessing his guilt. He feels the contamination of sin; he is stained by his wrong-doing and needs cleansing (vv.1, 2).

Unlike the authors of many of the psalms he makes no claim to righteousness. He knows and admits his guilt. We are not told what the sin is, but the heading referring to David and the urgent need for cleansing which comes out in the psalm suggest something secret and shaming. He acknowledges that in the end all sin is against God because it is a marring of the image of God in which humans are created. (Genesis 1.27). We should probably interpret verse 5 as meaning that he was born with the heritage of imperfection shared by all people, though the words could have been written or spoken by Solomon with complete appropriateness as he was the child of David and Bathsheba's adultery.

The psalmist believes that God wants a person to be totally honest – *truth in the inward being* – honest with himself, with God and with other people (v.6). He asks that he might be cleansed with hyssop. The plant, also called marjoram, was traditionally used in the 'cleansing' of a leper. (Leviticus 14.1-9). It was also used to cleanse someone who had been in contact with a corpse. (Numbers 19.18). (The sprig of hyssop would be dipped in the water or other cleansing liquid, and shaken over the person). It is possible that the poet is submitting himself to a formal rite of cleansing. He fully expects it to change his life, taking away his guilt and filling him with *joy and gladness.*

In verse 10 he looks to the future and, in order to make his cleansing permanent, asks God to fill him with his spirit and to give him a new heart. The gift of the spirit is clearly important as it is defined by three adjectives, *right* (or steadfast), *holy* and *willing.* In the second creation story in Genesis man only became *a living being* after God had breathed his spirit into him. (Gen. 2.7).

The psalmist also asks for a new heart, holding the belief that the heart was the seat of the will and the passions. Jeremiah looked for the day when God's law would be written on men's hearts, an internal rather than an external covenant. (Jer. 1.31). Ezekiel records the word of the Lord that a renewed Israel will consist of people such as the psalmist wishes to be; "I will give them one heart, and put a new spirit within them; I will take the stony heart out of their flesh and give them a heart of flesh." (Ezek. 11.19).

The poet promises that if God hears his plea and forgives him he will proclaim publicly the way of reconciliation that he has experienced. He will *sing aloud of thy deliverance* (vv.13-15). Many people will be familiar with the words of verse 15 as, changed from the singular into the plural, they are used as the opening versicle and response in both Morning and Evening Prayer; "O Lord, open thou our lips: and our mouth shall show forth thy praise."

The poet shares the prophetic view of sacrifice. (See comments on Psalm 50. 8-15). What God wants is not the externals of religion but a penitent heart. He ends his poem with heartfelt words, wrung from his own painful experience; *a broken and contrite heart, O God, thou wilt not despise.*

Verses 18 and 19 seem to be an addition to the original poem. It is as if an official in the rebuilt temple is rather embarrassed by the psalmist's words on sacrifice. The rebuilding of the temple was perhaps complete. The fortifications of the city were being finished. This was a heroic piece of work, the builders working with one hand while in the other they held a weapon. (Nehemiah 4.17). Whoever added the last two verses is anxious that this moving psalm (in particular verse 16) should not in any way seem critical of the immense efforts that had been made and were being made to re-establish the worship of Yahweh in Jerusalem. He looks forward to the day when the sacrifices offered in the temple will be *right sacrifices,* symbolic of the sacrifice of heart and spirit.

In a parish where I served, one of the most moving moments of the whole liturgical year was at the end of the Maundy Thursday Eucharist, at which the Last Supper was recalled, and the feet of some of the congregation were washed, in obedience to Christ's instruction (John 13.14). When the Eucharist was ended the church fell silent and the choir sang this psalm. During the solemn singing, the altar and the sanctuary were stripped of their usual clothing— the Communion vessels were removed as were the altar cloths, the banners set in the corners of the sanctuary and all other moveable items. The sanctuary was laid bare and the lights were switched off with the exception of one lamp which picked out the plain cross on the bare altar. One lady, a visitor, a church-goer for the best part of ninety years, who had never before witnessed the practice, said that it was the most moving service she had ever attended.

Psalm 52

There is a bitterness in the words of this psalm suggesting that the poet has been deeply hurt. He speaks of harm done to those who trust and worship God, the faithful community, and it not until verse 8 that his personal concerns are directly mentioned. We learn in verse 7 that those who make the attacks on believers are wealthy and they think that their wealth can acquire for them anything they desire. The attacks they have made are verbal – lies, treachery, *words that devour.* So cuttingly painful are their words that he compares their tongue to a razor. Perhaps St. James, when writing his letter, had this psalm in mind. He reminds his readers how powerful and potentially destructive is the tongue, how easily used for good or ill. (James 3.1-12).

The psalmist believes that their malicious behaviour will inevitably bring God's judgement and punishment on the perpetrators. In the end death will be their punishment as they are separated for ever from God, because God will tear his spirit from their bodies, the tents in which the divine spirit lives (v.5). Then the righteous will celebrate the downfall, relieved that, despite appearances, wealth does not exempt a person from God's justice.

Having spoken on behalf of the community, he now declares that in contrast to the wealthy, who have no assurance of a happy future, he is flourishing like a healthy tree, nourished by the *steadfast love* of God. (This may well remind us of Psalm 1 where the righteous person is compared to a flourishing tree). Aware of God's goodness, he promises to make a public declaration of his faith in a formal liturgy, *in the presence of the godly.*

It is salutary to realise that the people of the Bible were very much like us. We might be tempted to think that apart from the obvious villains, (who are rarely of the people of Israel but almost always those of another nation who worship another god), the people of the Bible were rather more religious than we are and without the failings and temptations that occur in our urbanised and acquisitive society. The psalmists tell us that there were plenty of acquisitive people in their day. There were plenty of jealous people, plenty of violent people, plenty of people in prominent positions in society who were untrustworthy. We see also that the response of those who strove for higher standards was not always without bitterness and vindictiveness. Happily the psalmists also teach us to retain our trust in God and to wait for his response even when the waiting is wearisome. Like Christians who know and value the strength which comes from belonging to a community of faith, the psalmist looks forward to the joy of declaring his faith in the presence of fellow believers.

Psalm 53 (See Psalm 14)

Psalm 54

There are three parts to this psalm. In the first part, verses 1-3, we hear the lament of someone who believes that he is being maliciously attacked. Legal measures may have been taken against him as he asks God to hear and vindicate him. His opponents are *insolent* and *ruthless;* however flimsy their arguments against him, they will press them vigorously. His plea in verse 2 will sound familiar to many Christian worshippers. Intercessions are often punctuated by, "Lord, hear our prayer: and let our cry come unto thee."

In verses 4 and 5 he expresses his confidence that God will help. It is confidence built on past experience: *God is my helper; He will requite my enemies.*

In verse 6 he is sure of his vindication and promises a sacrifice as a public token of his thanks to God. Finally he rejoices at having been proved right and guilt-free.

Twice, in verses 1 and 6, he mentions the 'name' of God. Generally, in the Old Testament a person's name reveals their character or their nature. Abraham, Sarah and Jacob are given new names at significant moments in their lives. (Genesis 17.5, 17.15, 32.28). No human can comprehend the nature of God; therefore God's name must, like his nature, remain a mystery. In the story of the Burning Bush in Exodus (3.14) Moses asks God to reveal his name. The answer is "I am," or "I am who I am." This seems to mean that God is a mystery, and all that can be said of him with certainty is that he is who he is and that further speculation is useless. If God says his name is "I am," then naturally when any human says God's name it becomes "He is." In Hebrew that is very close to 'Yahweh', which is the name now printed in the Jerusalem Bible and some other versions of the Bible. Usually the four Hebrew letters making up the divine name are translated 'Lord'. When reading the Scriptures a Jew will avoid having to pronounce the name, but will say either 'HaShem' which means 'the Name', or 'Adonai' which means 'My Lord'.

Often in the psalms we hear that the people of other nations derided the people of Israel because their God had neither name nor image. They were often asked, "Where is your God?" Down the centuries Christian theologians have tried to define the word 'God'. St. Anselm of Canterbury defined God as "that than which no greater can be conceived". Thomas Aquinas suggested that God was 'the first cause', 'the prime mover'. In the 20th century, Rudolph Otto used the term 'Wholly Other', while Paul Tillich favoured 'Ground of Being.' These Christian thinkers were all trying to speak helpfully of Exodus's "He is who He is" and to make its meaning accessible to contemporary believers. We can be sure that they helped some people and deepened their faith, but left others baffled. There has always been a strand of thought in both Jewish and Christian theology which admits that it is impossible to speak decisively about God. Several examples of this are given in the comments on Psalm 13.

In the Septuagint, the Greek version of the Old Testament, the divine name is 'Kyrios', which in English is rendered 'Lord'. It is significant that in the New Testament 'Kyrios' or 'Lord' is often applied to Jesus. For Christians his resurrection revealed that he was not only the Christ, the Jewish Messiah, but also the second person of the divine Trinity, the Son of God. Peter, in his speech on the day of Pentecost told the crowd, "Let all the house of Israel therefore know assuredly that God has made him both Lord and Christ, this Jesus whom you crucified." (Acts 2.36).

Reverence for God's name was always regarded as of the utmost importance, and the third of the Ten Commandments is, "Thou shalt not take the name of the Lord thy God in vain…" This kind of reverence seems to have died in our society. The name of God, protected in the Old Testament and in the Jewish faith, is, as it should be, a mystery to most people. Nevertheless, exclamations like, 'Oh, my God!' are commonplace and used without thought by people who, if questioned, would say that they do not believe in God. People use the name 'Jesus' and his title, 'Christ', not expecting anyone to be offended. The same would not be the case if the names 'Allah' or 'Mohammad' were used so lightly. Perhaps we should read the Ten Commandments more often in Christian worship (as we used to do), and remind ourselves of the way we have allowed our standards to fall.

Psalm 55

The text of this psalm is confused and it may be that we have a mixture of what were originally two separate poems. Or the confusion may be the result of the psalmist's distraught state of mind, causing his thoughts to jump about, returning to things he has already mentioned.

The psalm is an impassioned plea to God for relief from the attacks of enemies and, what he finds particularly hurtful, the disloyalty of a friend. The depth of his misery comes out in the words of verses 1 to 5. He is *distraught, in anguish* and *terrors; fear, trembling* and *horror* come upon him. He imagines getting free from it all, flying away with the freedom of a bird to a place of peace and safety (vv. 6-8).

In verse 9-11 we learn that it is institutional corruption that chiefly horrifies him. He speaks of *violence and strife in the city, oppression and fraud.* Like the prophets, he realises how oppression of the weak by the powerful, and the exploitation of the poor by the rich undermine the well-being of society. Amos speaks out against the traders and merchants who long for Sabbath to end so that they can get back to cheating the public; to "buy the poor for silver and the needy for a pair of sandals." (Amos 8.6).

In verse 12 the psalmist speaks of the personal distress he feels because a *familiar friend,* formerly a close companion, is among those who mock him. This has so hurt him that he returns to it in verses 20 and 21, describing the treachery in precise and penetrating word pictures of butter-smooth speech and oil-soft words.

In verses 16 to 19 and 22 and 23 he proclaims his trust in God's mercy and justice. He will badger God morning, noon and night, and is sure that God will hear his prayer and humble his aggressors (v.17).

He concludes the poem by imagining the terrible fate of his enemies. Of course, this imagining may be no more an expression of what he thinks will really happen, than his imagining of himself flying away like a bird. He writes as a poet. After the flight of fancy he ends with a firm declaration of faith: *But I will trust in thee.*

A recording of "O for the wings of a dove," (inspired by verse 6 of this psalm) sung by boy soprano Ernest Lough was made in 1927, and was extremely popular in the 1930s, 1940s and 1950s, through the very bleak war and post-war years. It is a beautiful performance and the peace which breathed through the words and music spoke to many people's longing for peace and serenity after living through the years of conflict, death, uncertainty and destruction. In a world which continues to be war- and conflict-torn, some of our generation find help in parts of Tennyson's *In Memoriam* written to mark the death of his close friend, Arthur Hallam. Different poetry has been set to different music for a different generation. Like verses 6-8 of this psalm, a slightly edited version of stanza cv (105) of *In Memoriam* has been set to music by Karl Jenkins in his *The Armed Man; a Mass for Peace*, composed in 2001. The words used in the Mass are:

> "Ring out the thousand wars of old.
> Ring in the thousand years of peace.
> Ring out the old, ring in the new.
> Ring happy bells across the snow:
> The year is going, let him go:
> Ring out the false, ring in the true.
> Ring out old shapes and foul disease:
> Ring out the narrowing lust of gold:
> Ring out the thousand wars of old,
> Ring in the thousand years of peace.
> Ring in the valiant man and free,
> The larger heart, the kindlier hand;
> Ring out the darkness of the land:
> Ring in the Christ that is to be."

Listening either to Ernest Lough or Karl Jenkins brings a fresh dimension to the words of this psalm.

Psalm 56

The text of this psalm is very 'corrupt'. Nevertheless, a pattern emerges with a repeated plea or lament, each followed by a refrain (verses 4 and 10) which expresses trust in God. The poet asks God to be *gracious* to him by protecting him from his enemies. As is often the case in the psalms, we do not know who the enemies are nor how they *fight against* him *proudly.* Their opposition seems to be both personal – *they have waited for my life* – and institutional – *they seek to injure my cause.* Their opposition does not seem to be open and legitimate because *they lurk* and *watch my steps.*

Whatever the cause and whatever the injury or distress they are inflicting, the psalmist is deeply affected. He speaks of sleepless nights and weeping (v.8). He asks God to take careful note of his sufferings.

Having made his complaint, he declares in faith, or perhaps it is only in hope, that his enemies will be *turned back* because God is on his side (v.9). In verse 10 as in verse 4 he says that he *praises God's* word. This could mean that he has been scrupulous in his observance of God's word in the Law. He believes that he has kept his side of Israel's covenant with God, and he therefore expects God to respond and protect him.

He has cleared his mind of the worries that oppressed and confused him; his opening prayer has been answered; God has been gracious. He will now offer sacrifices in gratitude because his life is on a firm footing. The dark days of his struggles are behind him. He can go confidently forward guided by the light of life (vv.12, 13).

Put thou my tears into thy bottle. What a wonderful expression of faith that God is concerned with our slightest joys and sorrows. Nothing is too small or insignificant to bring before God in prayer. Each person is like a beloved only child in God's eyes. It is as if he had no one else to worry about. In his first letter St. Peter encourages his fellow Christians to trust in the loving and trustworthy God. "Cast all your anxieties on him, for he cares about you." (I Peter 5.7). It seems that the writer of this psalm had experienced that care.

We might note again that Carl Jenkins uses the Authorised Version of the opening verse of this psalm in his Mass 'The Armed Man'.

Psalm 57

Confidence in God and the joy it brings spill out of this psalm despite the problems which beset the author.

It begins, like many psalms, with a cry to God for mercy, for shelter from the storms of conflict that surround him. To shelter *in the shadow of thy wings* may be a pleasing poetical way of speaking of God's loving protection, or it might indicate that the psalmist is worshipping in the temple and the overshadowing wings are those of the cherubim spread above the ark. This interpretation is given strength by the mention, in verses 7 and 8, of melody and musical instruments which, as we know from many references in the Old Testament, played an important part in temple worship.

As is so often the case, the precise details of the psalmist's woes and who is causing them are not given. The generalised terms would make it possible for the psalm to be used by different people on different occasions. This is not so dissimilar to the way Christians use hymns and prayers in public worship, each worshipper filling out the words with their own thoughts and needs. In Lent we all might sing, *Lord Jesus, think on me, and purge away my sin...* but we each have our own sins in mind, and they will differ widely from those of the people around us who are using the same words.

The refrain in verse 5, and again in verse 11, is a prayer that God be recognised as the only God, ruler of heaven and earth. These verses sound very much like a formal congregational response to words spoken by an individual.

The psalmist feels as if his difficulties are *storms of destruction* and those who cause them *trample upon* him – as though they hardly notice he exists. We sometimes use the expression 'walking all over' someone to describe an arrogant disregard for another person, their rights or their opinions. But the psalmist's enemies are also like wild animals, predators, man-eaters, and they scar and wound him with their words (v.4).

After the first congregational response in verse 5 he continues to list his woes. He is the victim of plots and traps. Again, he uses terms from the hunter's skills; they set a net and dig a pit. These schemes did not work and their plots rebounded on themselves (v. 6).

He clearly attributes the failure of his enemies and the very satisfactory punishment which they brought upon themselves as the working out of God's justice, and in verse 7 he begins a hymn of praise. He prepares to sing, accompanied by lute and harp, and perhaps by the whole congregation. He proclaims the firmness of his trust in God; *my heart is steadfast* (v.7). He wants his public thanksgiving to be shared, not just by the congregation but by *peoples* and *nations.* He will be singing of the immeasurable love and faithfulness of God (v.10).

The psalm ends with a congregational refrain proclaiming God's universal rule, over both heaven and earth (v.11).

Many Christian hymns are written in the first person. We can briefly mention a few : "Just as I am, without one plea"; "My God, I love thee, not because I hope for heaven thereby"; "Jesus, lover of my soul"; "Jesus, these eyes have never seen that radiant form of thine"; "My song in love unknown"; "I bind unto myself today..."; "I heard the voice of Jesus say." There are many others, and like this psalm, they offer each worshipper the opportunity to make the prayer and praise their own.

Psalm 58

Like the beginning of the Book of Job, the opening verses of this psalm are set in the court of heaven. Yahweh, the God of Israel, is the supreme God and he criticises the lesser members of the court, the baals or foreign gods of whom we hear much in the historical books of the Old Testament – Dagon, baal of the Philistines, Chemosh, baal of the Moabites, Milcom, baal of the Ammonites, and others. In this mythology of the heavens their responsibility was to maintain justice among men. But they have shirked or ignored the task. In verse 1 God asks them if they *decree what is right.* In verse 2 he answers his own question; of course they do not, and the injustice which originates with them in heaven results in injustice and violence on earth.

Verse 4 and 5 begin to recount the earthly results of that heavenly dereliction of duty. It means that people grow up and live in an atmosphere of wickedness and dishonesty. They become as dangerous as poisonous snakes, and are deaf to any attempt to bring them to reform themselves (vv. 4, 5). A number of violent metaphors follow, asking God to render harmless the wickedness of the ungodly. It is as if they were wild animals. With their teeth and fangs they tear apart both individuals and society (v.6). He asks that they might lose all influence, becoming mild and harmless like water, grass, a snail or even an aborted birth – a potential life which achieves nothing and passes unnoticed by all but those personally involved (vv.6, 7, 8). He asks that the wrong-doers and their evil influences be quickly swept away (v.9).

In verse 10 he looks forward to the day when justice will be established on the earth, and in another extravagant metaphor he pictures the righteous, like a victorious army, marching forward through the blood of the conquered enemy.

The psalm began with God's condemnation of the useless gods who did not ensure that there was justice on earth. At this point, the psalmist has reached a vision of justice established, and wickedness removed and forgotten. The God of Israel will overrule the lesser gods and his justice will be observed on earth (v. 11).

This striving for social justice is a vital part of the Christian faith. In his book *True God*, Kenneth Leech stresses this and its link with the faith of the Psalms and the Prophets. He writes, "The neglect of the Old Testament and of the essential 'Jewishness' of Christian theology and spirituality has led to the most appalling distortions of the gospel. The contempt for the material world and relapse into pagan approaches to matter, nature and history; the 'privatising' of God and the false interiority which reduces spiritual life to an inner experience of the individual; the loss of the link which joins social justice to spiritual insight: these and many other evils are connected with the neglect of the Old Testament roots of the Christian faith."

Returning to the psalm, it would be surprising if we did not shudder at the words of verse 10 which picture the righteous man bathing his feet in the blood of the wicked, and some modern lectionaries allow the verse to be omitted. We should remember that we are reading a poem. Vigorous word images wake us up and make us think carefully about the meaning. An author or speaker, in order to ensure that his readers or hearers pay attention, might well use exaggerated pictures which will bring them up short and make them think. We might take as modern examples of this the opening of Hilary Mantel's *Wolf Hall* or Ken Follett's *The Pillars of the Earth*. We don't easily put the book down. Like any brilliant and effective public speaker, Our Lord was not averse to using startling imagery. Consider *Depart from me, you cursed, into the eternal fire prepared for the devil and his angels.* (Matthew 25.41). He didn't say it to a particular group of people, it was in a story. But he could be sure they listened and perhaps took in the moral of his story.

Psalm 59

This is a lament by someone who is being persecuted. As is often the case we cannot be certain who the persecutors are. In the first four verses it sounds like an individual lament as the psalmist claims his innocence and describes his enemies as *bloodthirsty* and *fierce.* The psalm's heading ascribes it to David when the jealous Saul was seeking to be rid of David and the threat he posed to Saul's kingship.

However in verse 5 the enemies seem to be foreigners. Perhaps the psalm comes from a date much later than David when foreign kings had conquered Jerusalem. Their soldiers could swagger arrogantly about the city, confident in their strength and terrifying the people of the city. They are likened to wild dogs, hunting in packs, roaming wherever they like in the city (vv. 6, 7).

The psalmist believes that despite their fearsome appearance and their ability to hurt and to frighten, in God's eyes they are nothing. He laughs at their antics (v.8). So, in a refrain to be repeated at the end of the psalm, he addresses God as *my Strength* and *my strong tower* (vv. 9 and 17).

Verse 11 has probably been copied incorrectly at some time. Scholars suggest that it should probably read *Show them no mercy.* That would fit much more comfortably with the pleas that they should be *brought down,* made to *totter,* and finally be consumed so that *they are no more.*

The wild dog refrain is repeated in verses 14 and 15. This suggests that this may be a liturgical hymn with one person voicing the lament, another voice or a small group singing the feral dog refrain and perhaps the whole congregation singing the *O my Strength* refrain.

The voice of lament is turned into praise in verse 16. The pleas he made in verses 1-4 have been answered, and he knows that God is utterly dependable.

Once again we might note that Carl Jenkins, in his work, *The Armed Man : a Mass for Peace* uses the first two verses of this psalm, along with verses from Psalm 56, using the Authorised Version of the Bible, to create very effectively a sense of fear and foreboding.

In this as in many other psalms we can wonder at and admire the strength of the faith of the psalmist. Of course times were very different and there was no real option of atheism. Belief in God or gods was universal and atheism generally amounted to disregarding the laws of a god you believed existed. Now, when it is no longer fashionable to believe in God, it is harder to cling to faith when life becomes difficult. We can be grateful for the notable examples of some of the Christian saints; we might, for example, consider the life and suffering of 'The Little Flower', St. Theresa of Lisieux, or the life and work of Mother Teresa, and the example of the martyr Dietrich Bonhoeffer. Or we might be able to think of a Christian man or woman whom we know personally, who quietly and faithfully has maintained their faith while dealing with their own or a loved one's suffering. They are people who can join the psalmist and say *thou, O God, art my fortress, the God who shows me steadfast love.*

Psalm 60

Like many others, this psalm is best understood as a dramatic act of worship using different voices. The choral drama is used to lift the worshippers' hearts and minds from the misery of defeat to the acknowledgement of Yahweh's universal rule and the hope that he will again give Israel victory.

Verses 1-2 seem to speak of an overwhelming defeat for Israel's armies. This can only be explained by their assuming that God was no longer leading them and ensuring their victory. His withdrawal has left the nation scarcely able to stand. Instead of being upright and strong, they reel about like drunken men (v.3).

Verse 4 and 5 soften the claim that it is God's doing, his fault that they have been defeated. He still offers leadership to those who look for it. His steadfast care for Israel is likened to God's setting up his banner as a rallying point.

We then come, in verses 6-8, to words spoken by God. Perhaps a priest or other temple official would say or sing the words. God's sovereignty over all the peoples of Canaan is proclaimed. Canaan is God's land, and it is therefore in his power to apportion it as he will, as he did when he gave much of it to the invading tribes of Israel. All people are his people and are therefore subject to his care and judgement which extend far beyond Israel (Ephraim) and Judah. Moab, Edom and Philistia are spoken of slightingly and we are perhaps hearing the politically correct words of a priestly author charged with arranging the act of worship at which the king and other important citizens would be present.

Verses 9-12 could well be words spoken by the king. It was he who had suffered the defeat referred to at the beginning of the psalm, and now, after the assurance of God's sovereignty, he utters confident and morale-boosting words: *Who will bring me into the fortified city?* He is longing to exact revenge, and Edom is the local enemy he selects for his vengeance (v.9). But he is still not sure of success because he is not certain that God is on his side (v. 10). So the final two verses are a plea for God's help.

We notice that the person changes from *me* in verse 9 to *us* in verses 10, 11 and 12. So perhaps these final verses are a congregational response, adding their plea to the prayer of the king and bringing the dramatic act of worship to a close.

When British Christians say or sing the National Anthem, if it is not just before a football match or to mark the presentation of medals at a sporting event, the first verse becomes for Christian believers, a prayer for a well-known person with heavy responsibilities whose own Christian faith is real and profound. The little-known and rarely used second verse is: "O Lord, our God arise, Scatter our enemies, And make them fall; Confound their politics, Frustrate their knavish tricks; On thee our hope we fix; God save us all." Such words strongly suggest that the nation considers itself to be God's chosen people, and like the psalmist, its members call on God to act in their favour. Patriotism seems natural and admirable, but just beneath the surface of patriotism lurks nationalism, with its suspicion and even hatred of other countries.

Peace is as elusive now as it was in the psalmist's day – or any other day. We must pray for peace – for the politicians who alone can create it, and for those who suffer because of the absence of peace – combatants, refugees, the injured, the bereaved, the dead, the oppressed. Our task is to pray for peace and to work for it. Jesus said, "Blessed are the peacemakers." He said nothing of peace-lovers. The psalmist knew how hard it is for humans to live at peace among themselves. We need God's help because, as the psalmist said in verse 11, *vain is the help of man.*

Psalm 61

Though the speaker is 'I', asking God to hear 'my cry' and 'my prayer' this might still be a psalm for congregational use. If so, as we have noted before, it is like many Christian hymns such as "All my hope on God is founded", "Firmly I believe and truly", "Just as I am without one plea." Such hymns, and there are many of them, are sung congregationally but each worshipper fills the words with her or his own thoughts.

The psalm begins with a cry for the assurance of the closeness of God. It feels to the psalmist as if he calls to God *from the end of the earth.* God's seeming remoteness is a recurring problem for all who pray. We think God doesn't hear or, if he does hear, he doesn't answer. It is hard to accept that because the answer is not what we want, we do not recognise it. Or perhaps the answer is, 'Wait'. All who pray can readily sympathise with the psalmist's feeling of God being distant.

By verse 3, however, he is ready to acknowledge that God is his protector, his *rock,* his *refuge,* his *tower.* Again those who pray will recognise the feelings expressed in verse 4, *Let me dwell in thy tent forever.* When the nearness and reality of God is experienced, we want to cling to it rather like Peter on the Mount of Transfiguration, trying to cling on to a moment of revelation, saying, "Master it is well that we are here; let us make three booths, one for you, one for Moses and one for Elijah" (Mark 9.5).

The psalmist believes that he can have the constant assurance of God's presence by being in the temple, God's earthly *tent* or dwelling, worshipping under the canopy of the wings of the cherubim. He believes that by being there he is sure of his place in the community of the faithful (v.5).

The psalm then becomes a prayer for the king. The king is the embodiment of the nation and his health and prosperity is that of the nation. Verses 6 and 7 sound like a congregational prayer. They ask that the king may live and reign a long time, thereby ensuring national stability. Verse 7 acknowledges that the king reigns as God's viceroy. He must rule with justice and mercy on God's behalf. He needs, therefore, to be endowed with God's *steadfast love and faithfulness.*

The psalm ends with a vow that he will sing God's praises *day after day.* This *paying of vows* may well mean the intention to join in the daily worship of the temple.

Those moments which are sometimes called 'mountain-top' experiences, after the events on the Mount of Transfiguration, come infrequently, and some of the most faithful and devout Christians never have such an experience. Nevertheless, most believers can look back to moments of special blessing, perhaps on pilgrimage, in retreat, especially at a moving service, in the quiet of meditation, looking at the night sky or some other wonder of nature, or being challenged and inspired by a preacher. The lesson from the Gospel narrative is that no matter how exalted we may feel on a particular occasion, we have to learn to treasure it, then come down from the mountain and move on. When Peter, James and John returned from the mountain top with Jesus, they were immediately approached by a man who complained that he had brought his sick son to the other disciples and they were unable to cure him. Jesus wasn't pleased with his disciples. (Mark 9. 14-29). We cannot live for ever on the mountain top. We must come down and live with our own and other peoples' limitations and failures, realising that Our Lord is with us as much in our moments of failure as he is in the precious moments of exaltation.

Psalm 62

It seems as if the psalmist might have spent the night in silence, praying and keeping vigil, in the hope that somehow, perhaps in a vision (Daniel 2.19), or in a dream (Matthew 1.20), or by a voice (I Samuel 3.2,3), God might make himself known. In both verse 1 and verse 5, which are so similar that they seem to be a refrain, he speaks of waiting for God in silence. He receives the message that God is to be trusted; human help is of no use, *he only is my rock and my salvation.*

His confidence in God shines out throughout the psalm despite the deceitful opposition he faces. The attacks on his honour (v. 7) have weakened him so that he is like a tottering wall, ready to collapse. His opponents are set on pushing him over, saying kind things to his face but secretly cursing him (v.4).

In the midst of his distress he clings to his belief that God will deliver him from trouble, and for the third time says that God is his rock, the foundation on which his life can stand firm against all assaults. In verse 8 he encourages others to share his faith. Like him they must *pour out their hearts* before God. He will be their rock and refuge too.

Verses 9 and 10 speak of the transience of all earthly things. High and lowly alike are *but a breath* seen against the eternity of God. Ill-gotten gains are no guarantee of safety or happiness. Indeed, riches of any kind cannot be depended upon to bring happiness or security. In speaking to the rich young man Jesus could see that despite all his virtues he did not really own his wealth; it owned him, he could not live without it. Jesus went on to say to his disciples that it would be very difficult for rich people to become members of God's kingdom. They found that very difficult to understand. (Mark 10.17-26).

In direct contrast to earthly success and wealth, God has real power. That is the recurring message in God's revelations of himself in nature, in history and in the words of the prophets. But God's power is not power that will overwhelm and crush. It is the power of love – *to thee, O Lord, belongs steadfast love* (v.12).

The contrast between power as understood and exercised by humans and by God is spelt out quite shatteringly in God's answer to Job in chapters 38-41 of that book. The gap between the human and the divine is infinite and unbridgeable from the human side. Christians believe that God bridged the gap in the person of Jesus.

Twice the psalmist says *Truly my heart waits silently for God* (vv.1 and 5). The great teachers of prayer stress the importance of silence. Too often we think that when we pray we have to mention all sorts of matters to God—as if he didn't know all about them. This is sometimes the case in public worship when Intercessions can sound like a summary of the day's news. Generally speaking, there ought to be more opportunity for silence in public worship. But it is in times of private prayer that we can create space and time to listen to God instead of making him listen to us. It is not a simple matter. We quickly fill an empty silence with our own thoughts and worries. But a significant period of time spent silently saying a prayer like the 'Jesus Prayer' can still our minds and allow us to do what the psalmist did, and *wait silently for God.* (There is no single authoritative version of the Jesus Prayer. A simple form is "Lord Jesus Christ, Son of God, have mercy on me, a sinner").

Psalm 63

There are several indications in this psalm that the speaker is in the temple in Jerusalem. It is possible that the speaker is the king.

He begins by describing his longing for God. His whole being, body and soul, is thirsty for God as a man in a desert place thirsts for water. We who live in a temperate climate need to be reminded of how powerful an image this would be to someone in the scorching heat of a Middle Eastern midday. If this is the prayer of a pilgrim it is possible that he had experienced the torment of thirst on his journey to Jerusalem, like the pilgrim in Psalm 84.6.

But he has reached Jerusalem and has *looked upon* God in the temple. This may refer to a specific moment in the temple liturgy when the presence of God was publicly acknowledged, or it may be that his being in the sacred place assured him that he was indeed in the presence of God. He promises life-long thanksgiving for the assurance of God's steadfast love, which to him is the most precious thing in life (v.3). The lifting of his hands in prayer and the calling on the name of God sound like formal liturgical actions, and he therefore sees himself as a constant, or at least regular, worshipper in the temple.

In contrast to the thirst he describes in the first verse, he now feels sated with God's love. It is as if he has been the honoured guest at a banquet. His lips, as they praise God, seem to taste God's goodness (v.5). He lies awake at night, not worrying, but considering the wonder of God's love. Again, in verse 7, it sounds as if he is in the temple because his songs of joy are uttered *in the shadow of thy wings,* perhaps under the canopy shaped by the outstretched wings of the cherubim.

Verse 8 contains a picture of a parent and child or perhaps of someone who cares for an elderly, injured or disabled person. The feeling of insecurity and danger make the child or the invalid cling to the one who cares for them. They do this confidently, knowing that they are loved and that that love will be demonstrated in the gentle care that is given. We can understand this verse as a picture of God's love for each individual. In Hosea 11.1-4 there is a beautiful, lyrical picture of God, as a loving parent leading by the hand his beloved child, Israel.

In verse 9 the psalm takes on a more public aspect. Because he is sure that God cares, that he nourishes and upholds him, he believes that those who seek his downfall must themselves fall. He pictures them as vanquished on a battlefield, slain by the sword and their bodies the prey of scavengers (vv.9, 10). There is no reason why we should imagine the poet who wrote these words meant them to be taken literally.

The closing verse contrasts the dignity and success of the king, as the representative of the nation, with the fate of those who seek to undermine him with lies.

The psalmist's joy at being in the temple and the feeling of assurance it brings him is not an uncommon experience. It is something pilgrims often feel. After a long and sometimes arduous walk, to Santiago de Compostella for example, to be finally in the sacred place, brings joy, relief and wonder. Any pilgrim to the Holy Land will have felt it as they stand on the shore of the Sea of Galilee or walk the Way of the Cross, or stand at dawn at the Garden Tomb. In Celtic Christianity. there is the concept of the 'thin place', where whatever divides time and eternity, earth and heaven, human and divine, is very thin and glimpses of the other side can sometimes be seen. In his lovely book *Sun Dancing*, Geoffrey Moorhouse describes his first visit to Skellig Michael off the west coast of Ireland. "As I climbed the path winding up to the ancient constructions near the top of that cliff, I sensed that I was on the threshold of something utterly unique... nothing in my experience had prepared me for this huddle of domes, crouching halfway to heaven in this all but inaccessible place, with an intimidating immensity of space all round, where it was easy to feel that you had reached a limit of this world. A holy place to be sure, which would have still been so, even if it had never known the consecrated life of prayer."

Psalm 64

The text of this psalm is disordered and the meaning of some words and phrases is uncertain. Nevertheless the overall meaning is clear enough.

The psalmist asks God to listen to his *complaint.* He is the victim of slanderous enemies who plot against him. Their attack is vicious and it hurts him. Their tongues are like swords, their words like arrows, as they attack the psalmist and other *blameless* members of the faithful community (vv.3, 4). This is not just the wild imagining of the psalmist. There is much in the prophets about the problems caused by those who have deserted their national and ancestral faith in Yahweh and "gone after other gods." Here we are told that they are proud of their deceit and complacently imagine that their wrong-doing can be concealed (vv.5, 6).

How wrong they are! Of course God knows what they are doing, and God's *arrows* will be more effective than theirs! Like them, God will act *suddenly* and they will be publicly humiliated (vv. 8, 9).

The final verse, in a few words, stresses the joy of believers. They will *rejoice in the Lord and take refuge in him,* and they will *glory.*

As is often the case in the psalms, we do not know who the enemies are. They could be business rivals or political opponents. They could be religious opponents such as Jeremiah faced, men of faith who believed Jeremiah was undermining the nation's morale with his prophecies. (Jer. 20.1, 2; 26.7-9; 38.4-6).

The longing for justice which comes out clearly in this as in many other psalms is deep-rooted in humanity. At its simplest it comes out in the child's 'It's not fair'. It is a feeling that does not go away with age. The faith of the Old Testament held that at death one went to Sheol and was cut off from God. You could neither receive mercy nor give praise. (see Ps. 88. 4, 5 and many others). The desperate need for justice was one of the main reasons for the development of a belief in life after death. It was felt that the Maccabean martyrs deserved some reward and we find such hopes developing in Daniel 12. 2-3 and II Maccabees 7. 9 and 12.44.

Christians believe and, in the *Apostles' Creed*, state that Christ will come again to 'judge the living and the dead'. In the Book of Revelation there is a visionary attempt to describe the end of all things, when justice will be done. It is difficult to accept that the wicked will be horribly punished when the judge is to be Jesus. It is rather easier to believe that wrongs will be put right, and pains and sorrows abolished when God "will wipe away every tear from their eyes, and death shall be no more." (Rev. 21.4).

Psalm 65

If a Christian harvest festival service contains a psalm, this is likely to be the one chosen. Celebration of a good harvest may well have been the original purpose of this psalm, though the thanksgiving for God's generosity in a fertile earth takes up only a third of the poem.

The opening verse with its mention of Zion and the performing of vows suggests strongly that the psalm was used in temple worship either as a regular thanksgiving or perhaps on a particular occasion such as giving thanks for a remarkably bountiful harvest.

People come to God because of their feelings of guilt and the knowledge that God is merciful and forgiving (vv.2, 3). They feel great joy sharing in the temple worship and being close to God in his earthly dwelling, *thy holy temple* (v.4).

Verse 5 begins a celebration of God's power, his *dread deeds* in creation. Yahweh is no local god, no baal, but is *the hope of all the ends of the earth.* Even the sea, that dangerous and unpredictable element, was tamed by God in his creative acts (vv.6, 7). The whole world is witness to the majesty of God. Each dawn and dusk proclaim his wonderful plan and the order he has imposed on chaos (v.8).

Verse 9 begins the beautiful thanksgiving for the fertile land. Everywhere God's provision of water is vital – in river and in rainfall, enabling the grain, which is also God-given, to grow. We are reminded how important and uncertain water is in arid areas of the earth. Harvest time is the crown of the year. The poet pictures nature dressing up to celebrate. The hills are clothed in joy. The fields decorate themselves with sheep. The valleys cover themselves with grain and sing for sheer joy. The poet quite wonderfully transfers human emotions to the land itself.

In the western world harvest time has lost much of its ancient power. Here most people live in towns and cities and are divorced from the land. Our unthinking expectation is that we should be able to eat any fruit or vegetable from any part of the world at any time of year. We, who are so comfortable, ought to think more seriously and act more generously to help those for whom harvest is still a matter of life and death and for those in our own society who do not share the general prosperity.

Psalm 66

The psalm begins with a call to *all the earth* (vv.1, 4) to join in the singing of God's praises. In practice, it is a call to the congregation in the temple to represent the response of all people to the might and majesty of God.

Though he is God of all nations (v.7) he has chosen Israel as his covenant partner. In verse 6 his wonderful deeds at the Red Sea as they escaped from Egypt, and at the River Jordan entering the Promised Land, are recalled. They serve as reminders of the whole of Israel's salvation history.

God's care always continued in difficult times and he ensured their safety when their lives were at risk (v.9). It is acknowledged that obeying God is not easy, and at times they have been severely tried. The trying times are not described in detail but *affliction on our loins* sounds like some kind of epidemic. They were made subject to other nations, and only after passing through various dangers, *fire* and *water,* did they come into a place of safety (vv. 11, 12).

After this congregational hymn of praise for God's universal rule and his special care for Israel, in verse 13 the psalm becomes an individual prayer of thanksgiving. The speaker promises that he will fulfil the vows he has made and will offer the appropriate sacrifices. He had promised these when he was in trouble and God had saved him. He then invites his fellow-worshippers to listen to his story. It was because his heart was pure than God heard and saved him (vv.16-19).

Once again, as in Psalm 15, we learn of the crucial importance of purity of heart. This is much more important than the vows and sacrifices mentioned earlier in the psalm. It is our inner attitudes, not our external observances, that matter. There can be no purity of action without purity of heart. Besides saying that the pure in heart are blessed and they will see God, (Matthew 5.8), Jesus also taught that impurity of heart leads to impurity of life. (Mark 7.21, 22). It seems as if the psalmist instinctively knew this.

Psalm 67

Like Psalm 65, this is a hymn thanking God for a good harvest. We only become fully aware of that in the last two verses.

It is beautifully balanced poem beginning with a prayer for God's continued blessing on his people. The phrases used are very similar to those of the Aaronic blessing in Numbers 6.24-26. The worshippers are gathered to thank God for his blessing at harvest time, and they pray that *all nations* will come to acknowledge that it is Yahweh, God of Israel, who controls nature. The baals of Canaan, who were believed by their worshippers to control the fertility of land, animals and humans, have no power whatsoever. It is more usual in the psalms for Yahweh to be extolled as the Lord of history than Lord of nature, but the belief is always there that he not only created the world but continues to sustain it.

The psalmist declares that Yahweh is the only God, and in verse after verse, he prays that *the nations, the peoples,* and *the ends of the earth* will come to acknowledge that truth.

Verses 3 and 5 are a refrain, perhaps sung by the congregation, praying that all people will praise the God of Israel. The nations are not asked to worship Yahweh without reason. Verse 2 speaks of his *saving power,* verse 4 of his justice and guidance. The immediate example of God's goodness is to be seen in the harvest. The bounty of God in the harvest has fulfilled the longing expressed in verse 1; God has blessed them and there is good reason for all to be in awe of his grace and power.

This psalm used to be very familiar to regular Anglican worshippers. It was set as the alternative canticle to the Nunc Dimittis at Evening Prayer in the Book of Common Prayer. Very fittingly, those canticles followed the reading of the New Testament lesson. Having heard the good news of the Christian message in the reading, it was appropriate that the congregation should say or sing, "*Let the people praise thee, O God, let all the people praise thee.*"

Psalm 68

As we read this psalm and find it difficult to discern a common thread or purpose, it comes as no surprise to be told by scholars that the text is very corrupt, that is, disordered. Some suggest that the psalm consists of parts of several poems put together at random. Others have said that it is a collection of the first lines of poems or songs. That, of course, would mean that we are reading what in our hymn books would be called the Index of First Lines. Whether it is a whole poem or consists of parts, there is a great deal in it that speaks to us of God.

The opening words, *Let God arise* could refer to a moment in the temple liturgy when, somehow, the presence of God was conveyed to the worshippers, perhaps by a procession and 'enthronement' of the ark beneath the cherubim, or by some other means. The awareness of God's presence is so strong that his enemies, those who do not acknowledge his Lordship, melt away like wax before a fire, while his worshippers are *jubilant with joy* (vv. 1-3).

Verse 4 sounds like a congregational refrain, and the uttering of God's name, here translated as *the Lord* may also be a jubilant part of the temple liturgy.

In verses 5 and 6 the nature of God is proclaimed. He is merciful and cares for the unprotected, the homeless and prisoners. We might speculate that Jesus had this psalm, and probably other psalms, in mind when he told the parable of the sheep and the goats. (Matthew 25.31ff.).

In verses 7-13 the poet looks back over Israel's salvation history, God's care for them throughout their years in the wilderness and the spectacular and terrifying phenomena that accompanied the giving of the Law at Mount Sinai. (Exodus 19.16-19). The presence of God accompanying Israel and leading its army caused opposing kings and their armies to flee, leaving spoil on the battlefield which the women sort out and plunder. It seems as if the discovery of one little treasure is remembered (v.13).

Verse 14 records another folk memory, not recorded elsewhere in the Old Testament, when a military victory seemed to be marked by unusual weather. Great mountains are imagined looking with envy at Mount Zion because, small though it is, God has made it his earthly dwelling (vv.15, 16).

Verses 17 and 18 seem to describe a procession through Jerusalem to the temple, re-enacting in idealised form the conquest of Canaan, with captives in chains and the tribute of conquered kings borne in triumph.

We then come to what sounds (as in verse 4) like a congregational refrain, celebrating the *salvation* which God gives to his people (vv.19, 20).

Verses 21-23 sound vindictive, balancing God's goodness to Israel with his punishment of the ungodly. It may be the hyperbole of poetry or it might be a real wish grown out of much fear, oppression and suffering.

In verse 24 we are clearly in the temple, witnessing the procession as the ark is solemnly carried and set in its accustomed place. The liturgy is made resplendent with music and probably dance by the young women with timbrels. The representatives of the various tribes of Israel can be seen in their proper places – a very distinguished gathering.

A prayer begins in verse 28 asking God to use his power. Some foreign nations already acknowledged Yahweh's greatness and bring gifts, but there are many others, no better in their understanding than cattle; they need to be trained to accept the truth and offer proper worship to Yahweh.

The psalm ends with a call to the congregation to join in singing the praises of Yahweh because he is Lord of the heavens and the earth, and he has chosen Israel as his covenant people.

It is significant that in the midst of this rather jumbled or complex psalm, sounding out clearly, is the oft-repeated message that it is God's nature to care for the needy. Some words of Leonard Cheshire, the much decorated Second World War pilot-hero and subsequently the founder of the Cheshire Homes for people with incurable illnesses, are appropriate. He wrote, "Christ goes about this world as a beggar, in disguise, stretching out His hand for alms. He comes in the guise of a bereaved child, a widow, one who is lonely or homeless or sick, or unpopular; he is there in the consummate bore, the convicted thief or liar, the sensual and worldly, the frivolous modern pagan… ever asking for our love and gentleness and *reverence,* our courtesy and sympathy."

Psalm 69

This moving psalm contains, for Christians, several reminders of the Passion of Jesus. After Psalm 22 it is the psalm most often quoted in the New Testament.

It is the anguished prayer of a devout man who knows he is not perfect and who hopes that his sins will not bring shame and dishonour on other believers. He is suffering physically, mentally and spiritually and believes that it is God who is punishing him. He accepts that such punishment is just, but what he finds unbearable is the way his detractors seize on his weakness and pain, and try to humiliate him further. He has many detractors and is slandered and accused of theft and, though innocent, has been required to make restitution (v.4).

He acknowledges that he has sinned and that God has made him feel ashamed. That shame has also alienated him from his family (v.8).

One of the reasons for his being victimised seems to be his open devotion to God and his zeal for worship in the temple. In verse 35 the rebuilding of the cities of Judah is mentioned. This seems to date the psalm at a time after the return from the Babylonian exile, when the temple had been rebuilt and its patterns of worship restored, but other towns and cities in Judah were still lying in ruins. He has been sneered at for his devotion, for his open display of penitence in fasting and the wearing of sackcloth. Gossips and drunkards make up songs about him, which suggests that he was a person of some importance (vv 9-12). St. John (2.17) tells us that Jesus' disciples remembered verse 9 of this psalm when Jesus drove the money changers and dealers in sacrificial animals out of the temple.

The psalmist repeats his plea for God's help. Again he feels as if he is being overwhelmed by what is happening to him—he is sinking in the mud and without God's help he will die (vv. 13-15).

Varying the words but not the plea, he appeals passionately to God: *Answer me, Hide not thy face, draw near, redeem me, set me free.* He feels broken and utterly alone. There is no one to pity or comfort him. Both in this feeling of isolation and in the words of verse 21 we are led to the Passion of Jesus; *they gave me vinegar to drink.* (Matthew 27.34).

In verses 22 to 28 his anger finally bursts out. From the depths of distress his hatred of his enemies wells up and he calls for vengeance. As is usually the case, it is difficult to know who the enemies might be. Speaking of their *camp* and their tents may simply mean their dwellings, or he may be referring to the camps of opposing armies or a marauding desert tribe. Whoever they are, he wants them to suffer as he has suffered. In the Acts of the Apostles (1.20) we find verse 25 applied to the fate of Judas. In contrast we are reminded of Jesus' refusal to ask for vengeance. His words were, "Father, forgive them; for they know not what they do." (Luke 23.34).

The psalm closes with verses in which the poet assumes that God will answer his prayer and will help him. Then he will be able to join in a liturgy of thanksgiving in the newly rebuilt temple. It will be a song of thanksgiving which he believes will be more pleasing to God than the re-established rituals of sacrifice. He reminds his fellow-worshippers that what has happened in his own case is what all people can expect from Yahweh who *hears the needy, and does not despise his own that are in bonds.*

The final verses praise God who is proving his faithfulness to his chosen people by the rebuilding of the nation on its return from exile.

Those who openly admit their faith in God, and perform actions which make their devotion obvious, are often the butt of remarks both good-humoured and malicious. Going to work or to school with an ash-marked forehead on Ash Wednesday is not always easy. A young man or woman at school or college who is known to be a believer can be deeply hurt by the nickname 'God-botherer'. There have recently been several high profile cases in which the public profession and practice of one's faith is deemed unnecessary, offensive or unlawful. We should remind ourselves that what Christians might have to put up with in the western world fades almost into insignificance when compared with the sometimes barbaric physical suffering which Christians are having to face in the Middle East and in some parts of Africa and Asia.

The psalmist had borne this 'cross' and his thoughts and words take us on to the cross of Christ, his thirst, his solitude, his pain, his being mocked and, what is hard for his followers to imitate, his forgiveness of those who did such things.

Psalm 70 (See Psalm 40, verses 13-17 for almost identical words).

Psalm 71

In several verses the psalmist reveals that he is an old or at least a mature man. It seems that he is being maliciously persecuted and he asks God for help. Even as he asks, he declares that God is for him a place of safety, a *rock of refuge, a strong fortress* (v.3). He has, in the past, experienced the help for which he is now praying.

He speaks more fully of his dependence on God, then of the attacks of his persecutors. God has been his *hope* and *trust* not just from his youth, but from birth (vv. 5, 6).

In verses 7-10 it seems as if his self-confidence and perhaps his public reputation have weakened as he has aged. His enemies sense that he has lost God's support and they think they can therefore attack him at will (v.11). Again he prays that his revilers may be seen for what they are and put to shame, bringing an end to their ill-will (vv. 12, 13).

He promises to maintain his hope and confidence in God, and says that in public worship he will recount God's *righteous acts* and *deeds of salvation* (vv.14-16). He looks back over his life and can

128

see the guiding hand of God (v.17), and he therefore praises God now as he did when he was a young man. This probably means that he will make a public declaration, not only of his personal debt to God, but the debt owed by the nation. He will recount the salvation history of Israel to *all the generations to come* (v. 18).

Again in verses 20 and 21 he speaks of his confidence that the help and mercy that God has shown him in the past can be depended upon in the future.

The psalm ends with another promise to join in worship in the temple and, in a formal and public way, accompanied by music, he will sing the praises of God. Those who attacked him and made his life a misery have been disgraced and therefore silenced. The praise of God is now the only sound.

The promises made in verse 18 that future generations will be taught about the faithfulness and mercy of God is a very important aspect of Judaism. The great declaration of faith, *the shema,* proclaiming the oneness of God is followed by the instruction, "These words which I command you this day shall be upon your heart, and you shall teach them diligently to your children." (Deuteronomy 6.6, 7). In obedience to the words of Deuteronomy 6.20ff, it is the continuing tradition that in the table liturgy of the Passover meal the youngest present should ask the question, "Why is this night distinguished from all other nights?" This opens the way for the answer, "We were slaves unto Pharaoh in Egypt, and the Eternal, our God, brought us forth…" There is then a recital of the beginning of the salvation history of Israel from God's choosing of Abraham and the patriarchs to the deliverance from Egypt. Year by year the instruction about teaching the children is formally obeyed at this meal as well as more informally as children are taught about their ancestral faith.

It is a great strength to a religion when it is rooted in the home and family. No doubt, even in Judaism, this is being eroded by the demands and stresses of modern life. We might wonder if Christianity has lost its family roots. Do any Christian parents today kneel at the bedside and teach their children to pray? Are there many family meals which begin or end with a grace? It is on Christian parents and families that the responsibility for the future of the faith depends. It is not the responsibility of schools and teachers in a secular state. The teaching of Religious Education is vital to a properly rounded education, but it is not, nor should it be, an opportunity for evangelism. A Christian school will commend the faith it professes by its Christian ethos, its loving care for its members and its dedication to seeking the truth more than by stressing particular aspects of the faith. In the Anglican Church, the Mothers' Union (often made fun of even by its supporters), lays stress on the importance of marriage and family life. Its teaching and example are needed more urgently today than when it was founded by Mary Sumner in 1876. We should pray for the Mothers' Union, for teachers of Religious Education, for all Christian teachers and all Christian parents and families.

Psalm 72

The title of this psalm is 'A Psalm of Solomon'. It is clearly a prayer for the king and the opening verse could mean that Solomon, the king's son, was praying for David his father. As the name of the king appears nowhere in the psalm, it is more likely to be a formal liturgical prayer written for use at the enthronement of any king.

Because of the mention of foreign kings falling down before the king of Judah or Israel, paying tribute and offering gifts (vv. 10,11), this psalm has traditionally been used by the Church in the season of Epiphany, celebrating the visit of the Wise Men or Kings to the infant Jesus, "falling down and worshipping him," and bringing gifts. (Matthew 2.11).

The king of Judah does not rule in his own right. He rules on behalf of God. It is therefore right that the first gifts that are asked for are justice and righteousness (v.2). Only after that is power requested, and it is the power to do good. In verse after verse the people who are God's primary concern are mentioned—the poor and the needy. The king is responsible for their welfare.

God is asked to grant the king a long life and therefore a long reign, increasing the likelihood of peace and stability for the nation. It is recounted that, at the beginning of his reign, Solomon asked God for "an understanding mind to govern thy people." God was pleased that he had not asked for long life or riches, and promised that they would be granted him along with the understanding mind he requested. (I Kings 3. 9-14).

Verses 6 and 7 ask that the land might be fruitful and that the king's reign might be characterised by righteousness and peace.

Verses 8-11 look forward to the king's rule being extended across the earth, again not for reasons of power and aggrandisement, but so that the righteous and peaceful reign under God may benefit all people.

Once more the king (and people) are reminded that he reigns on behalf of God and therefore the *needy* and *the poor, the weak and him who has no helper* become the king's responsibility. He must protect them against oppressors and their lives, *their blood,* must be precious to him (v.14). In the reign of the righteous king, the earth will be blessed, and people of all nations will count their lives blessed because of the king (v.17).

This psalm is the final one in the Second Book of the Psalter. It may be that the two concluding verses are a doxology which have been added to the psalm in order to bring this section of the Psalter to a fitting conclusion. It is also possible that the verses are an integral part of the psalm and for that reason the psalm was chosen to conclude Book II.

In the Targums (Aramaic translations or paraphrases of books of the Hebrew Bible) this psalm is treated as Messianic, and for Christians, using it in the season of Epiphany, it becomes a prayer for the coming of God's perfect kingdom, which, they believe, was announced and inaugurated by Jesus. The vision of a world ruled by Christ, in which the needy are cared for and peace and justice are maintained, is a vision of the kingdom of God for which Jews and Christians continue to pray.

Psalm 73

This is the opening psalm of Book III of the Psalter. It is the declaration of a very honest man who does not shy away from confessing his envy of those who ignore or despise God, but nevertheless, seem to prosper.

He begins with a very orthodox statement, that God cares for the upright because of their purity of heart. Many times in the psalms we learn that purity of heart, as opposed to formal religious acts, is what is important to God and opens the way to him. (Ps. 24.4).

In verse 2 he begins his personal confession. He admits that he had almost been carried away with envy of the rich and powerful. They seem immune to the troubles that ordinary people suffer (v. 5). He describes their sleek, self-satisfied appearance, eyes peering out of the fat folds of their faces. They are proud, arrogant, violent, condescending and malicious. They talk as if they can challenge heaven and rule the earth (v.9).

People have been taken in and do not see how self-regarding the wealthy are. Having successfully hoodwinked the people they assume that they are also cleverer than God. Scornfully they ask *is there knowledge in the Most High?* The psalmist thinks that his attempts at righteousness, at purity of heart, have probably been wasted effort. He has felt *chastened* rather than rewarded (v.14).

Nevertheless he remains faithful though he cannot understand the apparent injustice of life. He can make no sense of it (vv.15, 16). Then he tells us that it was while he was in the temple on some occasion, possibly a pilgrimage or a great national festival, that the answer came to him. Rather as Job was compelled to look at his problems from a wider than personal perspective, so the psalmist, realising that only God sees the whole picture, and experiencing the awe-inspiring presence of God in the liturgy, begins to look at things in a new way. Popularity and powerful positions in society are *slippery places,* and it is easy and not uncommon for the rich and famous to fall. Wealth and public prominence can be swept away as easily as a dream disappears when one awakes (vv. 19, 20).

He now admits that before he understood these things he had been stupid, hardly human, in his understanding of God's justice. Nevertheless, unlike the ungodly, he remained faithful, and God continued to guide him rather as a parent guides a small child through a crowd, gently holding his hand (vv.23, 24).

He has come to realise that knowing God is the most important thing in his life and, despite his vulnerability, he trusts that God will see him through his troubles (vv.25, 26).

The two closing verses are similar to those at the end of many psalms, contrasting the fate of the wicked with that of the righteous. The final verse reminds us that the psalmist is most probably in the temple. *It is good for me to be near God* could refer to a moment in the liturgy when the presence of God was declared or simply to the confidence he feels in being close to the ark, the symbol of the presence of God. It could also mean that he had reached a fullness of faith which assured him that wherever he was, he was always in the loving presence of God.

As we read this psalm we become aware of how little the world has changed, and how little people have changed. The successful often find it difficult to remain humble. It also seems that in every generation there are prominent, clever people who, like the scoffers in verses 8 and 9, scorn people of faith.

The timeless truth of verses 18 and 19 is also evident in society. Each generation seems to have its own equivalent of the Profumo Affair, when, a prominent and highly regarded figure falls because of human weakness. In using that notorious and perhaps dated example, we should always remember that John Profumo spent the rest of his life in works of charity, atoning for his failing. Ours would be a better society if all who abuse the power and privilege of office, and all in public life who disgrace themselves were honest and humble enough to do the same.

Psalm 74

This is communal lament. *We* suffer because God seems far off, and in verse 1 it appears that God has cast off *us* for ever. The lamentation is a grieving over the destruction of Jerusalem and the devastation and desecration of the temple. It is likely that the destroyers are the armies of Babylon which overran Jerusalem in 586 B.C., that destruction being the forerunner to the exile in Babylon. It is possible, however, that it refers to a later attack on the temple by the armies of Syria under Antiochus Epiphanes in 167 B.C. Antiochus desecrated the temple by entering the Holy of Holies. He also caused sacrifice to be offered to himself, as the God-King, on the altar

The terrible things that have happened lead to the tenor of the first three verses which constitute a bold rebuke to God. They say that he seems to have forgotten the very people whom he had chosen specially to bring his blessing on all mankind. He has also forgotten and deserted the temple on Mount Zion, the place he chose as his earthly dwelling. God is asked to return, to visit Jerusalem and see for himself what the enemy has done.

Verses 4 to 8 recall in painful detail how the invading soldiers ransacked the temple and hacked to pieces its beautiful carved woodwork. We can gain some idea of how shocking to the people of Jerusalem such a desecration of the temple would be, when we read in Jeremiah how some people regarded the temple as the guarantee of their safety. They believed that God would never let anything happen to his temple. Jeremiah assured them that they were quite mistaken. (Jeremiah 7.4).

The worshippers saying or singing this psalm are frustrated and despondent because God seems not to care. He no longer makes his will known through prophets, and the enemy gloat and mock at his seeming powerlessness. God is charged with inaction; *why dost thou keep thy right hand in thy bosom?* It is like saying that God has put his hands in his pockets and is doing nothing (v. 11).

The despair is then put aside as the overwhelming power of God is remembered. They realise that the chaos of the destruction of Jerusalem is as nothing compared with the chaos which God transformed into order in his act of creation. Verse 15 then recalls how he continued to reveal both his power and his special care for

Israel, providing water when they were thirsty (Exodus 17.3-7), and drying up the water of the Red Sea when they needed to cross. (Exodus 14.21, 22). Again in verses 16 and 17 God's power in creation, his ordering of the universe, is acclaimed.

At verse 18 the psalm becomes a plea to God to defend his own honour. Those who do not know nor worship him speak scornfully of him. The psalm demands that God should defend his name, his reputation (v.18); that he should care for his chosen people (v.19), remember the covenant he made with Israel (v.20) and, as always, care for the downtrodden, the poor and the needy (v.21). In the final two verses God is again asked to put an end to the continued soiling of his reputation.

We should remember that like the nation of Israel, each individual has their own 'salvation history'. This is the narrative of God's dealings with us, and our dealings with God. As Israel constantly did, and as this psalm does, it is important to be able to reach back into our personal salvation history and find strength and support. We can recall the moments in our lives when we were filled with the certainty that God cared for us. It might be connected with a particular event or a particular person or place. It is good to think back and create a reservoir of such occasions or moments so that we can draw on them when we most need to reassure ourselves of the steadfast love and help of God.

Psalm 75

This is a hymn designed to be used in the liturgy of the temple. It is permeated by a feeling of cheerful faithfulness.

It starts with a brief congregational song of praise. The people say that they are thanking God because they have been reminded of his care for them in the recounting of his *wondrous deeds* in the retelling of their salvation history.

In verse 2 the voice becomes that of God, probably spoken by a priest. He says that the people who count themselves faithful and righteous long for the day when he will judge all people and nations. He reminds them that he alone will choose the time for judgement. Meanwhile he sustains the earth, even though it totters because of the evil that men do. He advises the boastful to be humble. They seem to be behaving like bulls or stags in the mating season (vv.4, 5).

We noted in Psalm 48 that the mysterious and unknown north was regarded as being the abode of God. So advancement for nations and individuals cannot be found in the surrounding nations, in the east, south and west. They might be allies, but equally they might be enemies. God alone raises and abases.

Verse 8 seems to allude to some sort of trial by ordeal. All will have to drink the cup of wine which God presents to them. The wicked will be intoxicated and lose their senses. We are left to assume that the godly will find it wholesome and strengthening.

At the beginning of the psalm the people sang as a congregation, *we give thanks.* At the end, and following the warning of God's cup of judgement, each individual speaks for him or herself. Personal faith has been strengthened and so they sing, *I will rejoice; I will sing.*

Verse 10 is the familiar statement of faith in God's perfect judgement through which the wicked will be rendered harmless and the righteous will receive honour.

The picture of the wicked as aggressive rutting animals is a telling one. It is difficult for anyone to strike a proper balance between striving to do the best with the gifts God has given them in life, and allowing crude, selfish ambition to take over. When we feel aggrieved with our lot, that life is treating us unfairly, we do well to recall the words of Jesus about seats of honour at banquets, and leave it to others to draw attention to any strengths or virtues we may possess. (Luke 14.7-11).

Psalm 76

The opening verses celebrate Jerusalem's status as the holy city. It enjoys that status because David chose Mount Zion as the place where the ark, the symbol of the presence of God, would be kept. Verse 1 declares that both Israel and Judah, united briefly under David and his son Solomon, know God and acknowledge his *name,* Yahweh, which declares his nature; "He is who He is." (Exodus 3.14).

Verse 3 may refer to a particular victory or it may be looking back more generally over the nation's salvation history, or recalling the victories which had been necessary to effect the conquest of Canaan. Those victories, won, in human terms, by national heroes such as Moses, Joshua, Gideon, Saul, Jonathan, David and others, were in reality God's victories. Verse 6 seems to be looking back at the destruction of the Egyptian army at the Red Sea. No one can withstand God's power.

After looking back over their God-directed history, in verse 7 the psalm begins to look to the future. God's judgement is not something they must wait for; it is present and will ensure the safety of all who are oppressed (v.9).

Even anger, which seems to be a political, military or, more probably, simply a human characteristic, will eventually be displaced by the desire to praise God (v.10).

The psalm ends exhorting the congregation to make vows and bring gifts to offer in the temple's worship. Because of his stern justice and concern for the oppressed, kings who are oppressors need to regard God as *him who is to be feared.*

Judaism, Christianity and Islam all speak of God's judgement. In the *Apostles' Creed* Christians say that they believe that Christ "will come again to judge the living and the dead." However, in John's gospel (12.31) Jesus says, "Now is the judgement of this world." Whatever may be the nature of the final judgement, it is certainly true that we are judged now, judged constantly, by the life of Jesus. He is the standard against which Christians must measure themselves. We are judged now and, knowing our constant failures, we cast ourselves on God's loving-kindness and forgiveness.

Psalm 77

The psalmist laments the apparent withdrawal of God's favour. Verse 9 succinctly expresses his feelings: *Has God forgotten to be gracious? Has he in anger shut up his compassion?*

Perhaps these are the words of the king, speaking on behalf of the nation at the annual renewal of his enthronement vows. For much of the psalm the subject is 'I', and if the 'I' is the king, the wider concerns of some of the verses fall into place. Also, if the king is the speaker, then he must be recalling his enthronement at which he was commissioned to rule on behalf of Yahweh, the real and eternal king of Israel. He is being reminded of the responsibilities he took upon himself, of the expectations of the people and his own expectation of the constant help of God.

The words of verse 1 would be as appropriate in private prayer as well as in a public liturgy in the temple though it seems more likely to be the latter. The king *cries aloud* so that God cannot miss his complaints. He says that he has prayed tirelessly, day and night, but finds no reassurance from God, no comfort (v.2).

His fervent praying causes him great distress (v.3). He has sleepless nights and he is speechless with weariness (v.4). In his prayers at dead of night he looks back over his life to try to recall how he may have offended God and so caused him to withdraw his care and favour. He begins to think that God has forsaken him and the nation, so abandoning the covenant agreement (v.8).

In verse 10 he asks if God's power, his *right hand,* has become weak. Is that what has happened? He soon dismisses the thought that his own and the nation's woes are because God has somehow weakened, and he seeks reassurance by looking back at God's great acts on behalf of the nation, his *wonders of old* and *his mighty deeds* (vv. 11, 12). In a very generalised way he thinks of God's help in the past. The crossing of the Red Sea and the terrifying phenomena at Mount Sinai are alluded to in verses 16-18.

It was perhaps the thought of God's presence and control of the waters of the Red Sea and the Jordan that leads the psalmist to picture God striding through *great waters* and, of course, leaving no footprints. This helps him to understand his dilemma and answers his questions. He realises that God's ways are indeed real and effective, but men are often blind to them. They fail to see the signs of God's actions which are like footsteps in the sea.

The psalm has an almost pastoral ending. The footsteps of God may be invisible, but he guides his chosen people by the hands of great and holy men like Moses and Aaron. Perhaps the psalmist/king has now realised that in his generation the hands by which God leads and guides his people are his own.

The psalmist's cry that God should do something, and his question, *has his steadfast love for ever ceased?* is answered by the final verse of the psalm. God does indeed act, but he uses human means to accomplish what he intends to do. This is an important lesson. Jesus said that it was not those who make the correct religious noises who would enter the kingdom of heaven, but "he who does the will of my Father who is in heaven." (Matthew 7.21).

It is possible to make prayer, especially intercessory prayer, a substitute for action. We can pray, "Lord, I commend into your hands my friend who is sick, the starving children of the world, my neighbour who is disabled. Please help them." What answer is there? Quite often God seems to say, "Thank you. We will certainly do something for them. Yours are the hands we shall use to push your neighbour's wheelchair. Yours is the bank balance we shall reduce to help the starving children. You will be my presence when you write to or visit your sick friend." He did it *by the hand of Moses and Aaron.* He always uses human hearts and hands, including yours and mine, to effect his will.

Psalm 78

The opening verses tell us that the speaker is a teacher of Wisdom. The words *parable* and *dark sayings* are characteristic of Wisdom teaching. The aim of Wisdom is to instruct people how to live in the way God requires, that is, by keeping the Covenant law. Such a life will bring 'blessedness', the quality of life outlined in Psalm 1.

The command to each generation that they must teach their children and grandchildren the 'salvation history' of the nation is recalled in verses 3-7. But in verse 8 the teacher admits that time after time, despite the *glorious deeds of the Lord,* they have fallen from the faith. Because Israel (Ephraim) failed to keep the covenant, forgetting God's mighty acts which had been witnessed in Egypt, their armies have been defeated. The acts of God which persuaded Pharaoh to let them leave Egypt were forgotten. Even the wonder of the crossing of the Red Sea and the marvels which occurred when they were travelling through the wilderness have gone from their memory (vv.11-16). They doubted whether God could give them food in the wilderness. They were shown to be faithless when he gave them manna, *the bread of the angels,* and quails in great number (vv.17-31). Again and again, as soon as they were helped, as soon as they felt safe, they abandoned their faith in God and forgot that all their good fortune was God's doing (vv.32-37). Despite their disloyalty God did not totally withdraw his mercy. Like a loving parent he finds reasons to excuse them; they are only *flesh, a wind that passes and comes not again* (v.39).

The teacher returns to an earlier theme (as a good teacher will). Verses 42-52 recall in some detail the mighty acts of God in Egypt, culminating in the death of the first-born (v.51). These 'plagues' persuaded Pharaoh to allow the people of Israel, who were his supply of slave labour, to leave the country. Then God led his people through the wilderness and, driving out the Canaanites, settled them in their Promised Land.

Even that was not enough. Like the generations before them they abandoned the worship of Yahweh and attached themselves to the baals, the gods of the land. Verses 60 and 61 seem to refer to the capture of the ark by the Philistines recorded in I Samuel 4.11. The sanctuary at Shiloh was desecrated and so God abandoned it (v.60) and allowed the surrounding peoples to attack and harass the settlers. (The narratives recording these difficult years of settlement are recorded in the books of Judges and I Samuel).

Eventually God decided that he would do something drastic. It was as if he awoke from sleep (v.65). He rejected the powerful tribe of Ephraim (in the person of Saul), and chose the lesser tribe of Judah (in the person of David), and because Zion, Jerusalem, was God's chosen home on earth, David chose it as his capital city (v.68).

The choosing of David, related in I Samuel 16.1-13, is here described most tenderly. David is chosen because he is a good shepherd, and the qualities of a good shepherd who cares for his sheep and lambs, who leads them, protects them and feeds them is the model for all rulers of Israel. (See Ezekiel 34).

The clear teaching of the psalm is that despite God's readiness to forgive and to act on Israel's behalf, his care is quickly forgotten and people go their own way. In generation after generation the pattern was repeated throughout the nation's history. Hope comes in God's three-fold choice of Judah, Jerusalem and David. David is the ideal godly king; *with upright heart he tended them, and guided them with a skilful hand* (v.72); the desired pattern for all rulers.

There is a Messianic feel to the closing three verses. Despite David's all too obvious human failings he was remembered as the ideal king with an unswerving faith in God. For Christians, Jesus, "born of David's line," is the ultimate good shepherd who not only tends and guides his people, but laid down his life for them.

Psalm 79

The agony and shame caused by the sight of Jerusalem, and the temple in particular, being laid waste by foreign soldiers, is plain from the beginning. In the psalmist's mind even the deaths of soldiers and citizens seems to be of less importance than the desecration of the holy city. They have been attacked, defeated, massacred and mocked, not only by the conquerors, but by nations looking on and rejoicing in Judah's downfall. The conquest of Jerusalem by Babylonian forces in 586 B.C. seems to be the appropriate occasion for the psalm's composition, though, as noted in thinking about Psalm 74 it might be the ravaging of the city by the Syrian king Antiochus Epiphanes in 167 B.C.

After the cry of pain in verses 1-4 comes the desperate plea to God, *How long, O Lord?* It is assumed that what has happened is God's will. He is angry with his people and is punishing them. As his wrath is described as *jealous* (v.5) it seems as if apostasy, the worship of other gods, is seen as the reason for God's anger. But even in the midst of his despair the psalmist's faith shines through. Eventually God will spare them because they are his special people.

The question is how long will the agony go on; how long before God forgives Israel and turns his wrath on the peoples who worship other gods (vv.5-7).

In verse 8 he wonders if they are being punished for the sins of their ancestors. In the public worship of the temple the nation's 'salvation history' was recounted, and the mighty works of God and the failings of their forebears were constantly put before them. The idea of communal sin and corporate responsibility, even across generations, was strong. It is set out in the third of the Ten Commandments: "I the Lord your God am a jealous God, visiting the sins of the fathers upon the children to the third and fourth generation of those who hate me, but showing steadfast love to thousands of those who love me and keep my commandments." (Deuteronomy 5. 9, 10). This seeming injustice is challenged by Ezekiel who teaches that God counts every person responsible for their own good or bad actions. (Ezekiel 33.12-20).

In verse 9 a further plea is put to God. If he is not ready to forgive them because they have sinned, will he perhaps forgive them in order to protect his own honour and reputation, *the glory of his name*? If he does not act, other nations will assume that the vaunted God of Israel is powerless or absent. If, however, he avenges the conquest of Jerusalem his power will be demonstrated to the nations (v.10).

The psalmist's faith is again revealed in the claim that God can save even those whose fate seems sealed (v.11). When he does that, the taunts that have been directed at God will be silenced, and those who mock, will be punished. It is assumed that this will happen, and then generation after generation of Israelites, *the flock of thy pasture,* will thank and praise God for ever.

As we read the opening verses of this psalm we can feel the depth of passion and horror at what has happened in Jerusalem. Psalm 74 also lamented these events, and in even greater detail. How could these things happen when there, in the temple, stood the ark, sheltered by the outspread wings of the cherubim. There the worshipper came face to face with God. His presence was felt, and his loving care for Israel constantly celebrated. How could aliens enter and desecrate such a sacred place? It is significant that there is no attempt to evade responsibility. There is no suggestion that the opposing army might have superior weapons, greater numbers or be better trained. All those things might be true, but responsibility for their plight is accepted, and so they pray *forgive our sins for thy name's sake* (v.9).

Much in modern life encourages us to avoid responsibility and place the blame on others. We can too easily shift responsibility for our problems and their solving to other people or organisations, to the government, the local council, teachers, social workers or the health service. We understand how some people do suffer and are perhaps led into wrong-doing because of the failings of previous generations—a drunken father, a drug-addicted mother and a host of other reasons. This is not unlike the reasoning of verse 8. Ezekiel is not happy with this approach and teaches individual responsibility. He writes, "It is the soul that sins, and no other, that shall die; a son shall not share a father's guilt, nor a father his son's." (Ezek. 18.20). While understanding that external influences of all sorts affect the way we and all people act, it is important that we are ready to accept responsibility for our own lives in an adult and mature way.

Psalm 80

The mention of the cherubim in the opening verse suggests that this is a hymn used in the temple liturgy. The refrain, *Restore us, O God; let thy face shine that we may be saved,* which occurs in verses 3, 7, 14 and 19 sounds like a congregational response to the lament uttered by one voice. Also, the plea that God's face should shine may refer to a particular moment in the liturgy when the presence of God is declared and made known to the congregation.

God is addressed fully. He is the shepherd of Israel, leading the nation in all situations. He is also their king enthroned in the temple in Jerusalem. The single voice cries out, *Stir up thy might and come and save us.* And the congregation responds with the refrain.

As in Psalm 79 verse 5, the question put to God is *how long?* How long will God be angry with his people? His failure to respond has allowed the destruction of the holy city and brought upon the nation a communal sadness. The surrounding nations are gleeful and scornful of Israel's fate (vv.5, 6).

Again the refrain calls for God to show himself and restore the nation. Its salvation history is recalled and taught in the lovely parable in verses 8-16, in which Israel is pictured as a vine which God brought out of Egypt. He cleared the ground for it by driving out the peoples of Canaan. Once planted, it struck deep roots and grew to a towering height, overshadowing mountains and the great cedar forests of Lebanon. Its branches spread East to the River (Euphrates) and west to the shore of the Mediterranean (vv.9-11). This idealised picture of the growth of Israel in its Promised Land then changes to one of damage and destruction. The walls of the vineyard have been broken down and all who wish may enter and plunder the fruit (v.12). Wild boar root up the vines and other animals can eat the young shoots. Men too have attacked the vineyard, felling and burning the vine (v. 13).

The reason for these disasters is that God seems to have stopped caring about his vineyard. The plea is that he should start to care again and restore the vineyard (vv.14, 15). The restoration will be effected by God's right-hand man, the king. Such salvation will assure the nation that God never ceases to care, though he may punish them. They will then be strengthened in faith and their worship will be sustained.

The psalm ends with a final congregational plea.

The parable of the vine is beautifully written and conveys many truths. To have a vineyard and to drink wine is the sign of a settled, peaceful and prosperous life. After the initial conquest of Canaan it would be some years before the Israelites could plant vineyards and drink their own wine. They doubtless took over the vineyards of the conquered peoples.

Isaiah too uses the image of a vineyard to represent Israel. He also says that God took immense pains over his vineyard and did everything possible to make it prosper. But it produced sour grapes. In anger God destroyed the vineyard because it did not fulfil its purpose. Isaiah's song of the vineyard says, "the vineyard of the Lord of Hosts is the house of Israel… he looked for justice, but behold, bloodshed; for righteousness, but behold, a cry." (Isaiah 5, verses 1-7).

Jesus took up the theme and described himself as the 'true vine' and his disciples as the branches. (John 5.1-11). As in Isaiah, good fruit is required and if branches are not fruitful they will be pruned and the cuttings burned. Only by remaining attached to the vine can the branches continue to live and yield fruit. The faithful practice of prayer, of reading the Scriptures, of receiving the sacrament, of being aware of our membership of the Body of Christ are vital for Christians. Through them we remain connected to the source of our spiritual life, to Jesus who is the root and stock of the faith. For, as he said, "apart from me you can do nothing." (John 15.5).

Psalm 81

There is an intense feeling of joy and celebration in the opening verses. The singing and musical instruments, timbrel, lyre and harp, suggest a festival occasion in the temple. In Leviticus (23.24) and Numbers (29.1) the shofar (ram's horn trumpet) is directed to be blown to signal the New Year. Reading this psalm therefore might place us at the New Year festival service which is observed on the first day of the Hebrew month Tishri, in our September. The psalm is used in Jewish worship at Succoth, the Feast of Tabernacles, kept between 15th and 22nd Tishri (in September or October). It is a harvest festival, and the concluding verse of the psalm suggests that it might be that festival which is being celebrated.

The first verse of the psalm invites the congregation to join in the shouts and songs of joy. It almost seems as if, at the end of verse 5, a rubric or part of a rubric, or perhaps a note that someone made in a margin, has strayed into the text. In verse 6 the words are to be understood as the words of God, probably spoken or sung by a priest or prophet. God reminds the people how he saved them from their slave labour as brick makers in Egypt, and gave them water to ease their thirst in the wilderness. He then reminds them that he alone is their God and they must worship no other. All the evidence of God's care is there if they will heed it: *O Israel, if you would but listen to me.* If they obeyed, their lives would be fulfilled (v.8). The picture of God feeding Israel seems to be that of a newly hatched young bird opening its mouth and its parent dutifully feeding it (v.10).

However, as was expressed agonisingly in Psalm 78, their forebears did not listen and did not learn. In punishment, God left them to their own inadequate devices. All this is instruction for the present generation. They are called to *listen* and to *walk in my ways* (v.13). In these verses, we receive the feeling that, like a loving parent, God is longing for his erring child to return. If only they will hear and return to him, he will quickly reveal his continuing love.

The psalm ends in a familiar way, expecting the working out of God's justice, under which the wicked will *cringe,* presumably when they realise how blind and stupid they have been. The godly will live, sustained by the very best of food, with *honey* and *the finest wheat.*

Making the experiences of past generations one's own is a strong feature of traditional Judaism. It is also a feature of Christian worship. At every Eucharist we hear the words of Christ, "Do this in remembrance of me." It is said that those words might be translated, "Do this to make me present." This making present is seen most clearly in the Three Great Days. On Maundy Thursday worshippers will be present at the Last Supper. In many churches, the feet of twelve of the congregation will be washed. After the Eucharist some people will then 'watch', keeping vigil as Jesus asked his disciples to do in the Garden of Gethsemane. On Good

Friday we will, in a variety of ways, be with Jesus on his way to Calvary, perhaps worshipping through *The Stations of the Cross*, or attending a service from noon till three o'clock, watching with Christ in the final hours of his life. On Holy Saturday we wait for the moment when, in a darkened church, fire is kindled and the new light, symbolising the resurrection of Jesus, is held aloft with the cry, "The light of Christ," to which we respond, "Thanks be to God." We make each stage of the Passion of Jesus contemporary with ourselves, and then on Easter Day we celebrate, not only that he rose from the dead just over two thousand years ago, but that "Jesus Christ is risen today."

Psalm 82

The opening verse seems to be a single voice announcing that the heavenly court is assembled and that Yahweh, the supreme and only real God, takes his place presiding over the lesser gods, the baals of Canaan and other national gods. Perhaps another single voice then speaks the words of God. In verse 2 he charges the lesser gods that they do not fulfil their responsibilities. Unlike Yahweh, who looks for righteousness and justice among men, they have dealt unjustly and showed partiality to the wicked. Verses 3 and 4 spell out precisely what they should have been teaching the human race.

The result of the dereliction of duty is that people do not know Yahweh. They live without the light of his covenant. They *walk about in darkness,* and the inevitable result is moral chaos on earth. Those lesser gods might be unimportant, but their failures have allowed injustice to flourish among men (v.5). Their punishment will be the withdrawal of their immortality. They will die like men (vv. 6, 7).

It is tempting to see this psalm as having single voices balanced by a final congregational response. A priest or prophet may have sung verses 2-4, speaking the words of God. Verse 5 could be the congregation's response, confirming that the shortcomings of the gods have indeed undermined the moral foundations of society.

God's judgement on the gods (vv.6,7) could well be the single voice again, and the final verse a great congregational cry to God asking him to *arise* and *judge the earth,* for he is the only God and all nations, including those who still worship the weak and useless godlings, belong to him.

The psalm forces us to ask the question, "Why is human life, both personal and communal, often so unsatisfactory or downright painful?" We ask why are the weak, the fatherless, the afflicted and the destitute, whose plight so concerned the psalmist, still so much a part of human life, even in an affluent and supposedly civilised society? The godlings of the court of heaven cannot be blamed; they do not exist. God requires us to do the job they were supposed to do. We need not despair. For millions of people, as the years have passed, life has become less nasty, short and brutish. Much of that improvement has been inspired and initiated by Christians. We should remember with gratitude Wilberforce, Fry, Shaftsbury and Nightingale, people of faith and action in our own nation. We should remember too Dietrich Bonhoeffer, Martin Luther King, Chad Varah, Nelson Mandela, Leonard Cheshire, Sue Ryder and Mother Teresa among the many Christians who, more recently, have sought to do the will of God and bring justice and kindness to human society. We should take pride in their work and not underestimate the difference each individual Christian can make.

Psalm 83

This psalm is a plea that God would put an end to the posturings of Israel's enemies which are not only a threat to the safety of the nation, but an insult to the sovereignty of God himself; *against thee they make a covenant* (v.5). Many nations are mentioned as being part of the threat, from small neighbours of a similar size to Israel to the super-power of the time, Assyria (vv.6-8). The psalm expresses the fear that some or all of their enemies might join in an alliance in an attempt to *wipe them out as a nation; let the name of Israel be remembered no more* (v.4).

The psalmist looks back, and in verse 9 recalls an occasion in the past when God helped Israel to triumph over great odds. The story is told in the Book of Judges chapters 4 and 5. Jabin, who ruled in Hazor, and Sisera, the commander of his army, were unexpectedly routed in battle and Sisera escaped only to be slain dishonourably; he was the victim of a crafty woman. Moving on to chapter 7 of the Book of Judges, Oreb and Zeeb, Midianite princes who thought they could *take possession… of the pastures of God,* failed against the God-inspired leadership of Gideon.

These backward glances into the nation's salvation history should reassure people that God is always in control, and that no matter how powerful their opponents might be, it is not the strategies of kings nor the might of armies which have the final word. God controls the destinies of nations just as he controls the forces of nature (vv.13-15). Sometimes the two are closely interwoven as in the story of Absalom's rebellion (II Samuel 18.8) or Elijah's contest with the prophets of baal. (I Kings 18.38).

The final three verses of the psalm tone down the cries for vengeance and slaughter; they ask God to fill their enemies with shame and to bring disgrace upon them. The ultimate reason for wanting this is not that they might be destroyed, but that they might share Israel's knowledge that Yahweh is the only God who rules *over all the earth.*

Verse 4, *Come, let us wipe them out as a nation; let the name of Israel be remembered no more,* strikes a chill into the heart of anyone who lived through the 1930s and 1940s, or who has studied the history of Hitler's 'final solution', his plan to wipe out the Jewish people. The founding of the modern state of Israel was the world's response to that infamous attempt at genocide. Little has changed. When the modern state of Israel was founded on 14th May, 1948 the armies of the Arab League states, Egypt, Jordan, Iraq, Syria and Lebanon, invaded Israel. Azzam Pasha, the secretary of the Arab League said, "This will be a war of extermination and a momentous massacre." Of course, in keeping with the nation's history, Israel proved remarkably resilient and indestructible. Sadly, the threats and counter-threats, the suspicions and the hatreds continue and some organisations, such as Hamas, still deny Israel the right to exist. Antisemitism, in its Jew-hating manifestation still has a vigorous life. All Jews, Christians and Muslims should do what Psalm 122 asks them to do and "Pray for the peace of Jerusalem."

Psalm 84

As a pilgrim nears the end of his journey he finds himself overwhelmed by the delight he feels at being in the place which God has chosen as his earthly home. He has come in sight of Jerusalem and can see the temple which has been his objective ever since he left his home. He is perhaps attending one of the pilgrim feasts or one of the great annual festivals. Verse 2 however could suggest that he is not in Jerusalem at all. He may be at home, seeing the temple in his mind's eye as he still *longs, yea, faints for the courts of the Lord.* Perhaps he is recalling a previous pilgrimage and the joy it gave him (vv.1, 2). On balance it seems more likely that he is a pilgrim basking in the joy and wonder of being in Jerusalem, looking round and noting all sorts of delightful details.

So he feels jealous even of the sparrows and swallows who can make a permanent home in the temple buildings. He imagines how delightful it would be to be permanently in the temple, living and working there, bringing up his family in Jerusalem so that they would drink in the atmosphere and be enriched by it. Those who work in the temple are lucky—more than lucky, they are blessed (vv.3, 4).

Realising that such thoughts are little more than a dream, he acknowledges that he and all pilgrims are also blessed by their determination to journey to Jerusalem. The journey is not an easy one. The arid valley of Baca is clearly a danger to the travellers, but the hope which fills the pilgrims' hearts helps them to use the hardship of the journey to strengthen their faith. They will not fall by the wayside; they will reach their objective and enter and enjoy the presence of God in the temple (vv.5, 6). Verse 7 may mean (as in the New English Bible translation) that they move from outer to inner wall within the temple precincts as the procession moves on. Verse 8 begins a prayer for the king, the nation's shield and God's anointed. This may mean that the occasion is the annual renewal of Yahweh's kingship over Israel and the enthronement of his human representative.

In the final three verses the psalmist returns to his joy at being in the temple. It is as if his awareness of the presence of God allows him no doubt. He reverts to his earlier thoughts of the good fortune of those who work in the temple and who, day after day, can bask in the overwhelming feeling of the close presence of God. Perhaps the pilgrim is a man of substance and importance in his own community. Nevertheless, in the intensity of his fervour he declares that he would delight to have a menial task in the temple (v.10).

Verse 11 returns to a more realistic view of religious faith. Many times in the psalms we read that what matters in religion is not sacrifice nor any other outward ceremony (Psalm 15), but purity of heart or, as in this psalm, walking uprightly (v.11). It is moral quality and compassionate action that matter. Gerald Hughes expresses this powerfully in his book, *Walking to Jerusalem*: "God is a living reality, not a concept, and we meet him, not through uttering a creed, but in the way we live and relate to one another, to ourselves and to all creation."

This psalm reminds us of 'the beauty of holiness'. There is a strong feeling that the culmination of the pilgrimage, the liturgy in the temple, is beautiful and intensely moving, assuring worshippers that they are in the presence of God, and renewing and strengthening their faith.

Worship should always be beautiful, however simple or complex it might be. It is significant that at a time when numbers attending parish churches are generally declining, the numbers attending cathedral services are rising. A beautiful building, glorious music and well-conducted services attract people who find they want to worship the Lord in the beauty of holiness. They feel as the author of this psalm felt when he was in the temple in Jerusalem. Beautiful worship is as important in parish churches as in cathedrals. A clean and tidy building, well-produced service books, immaculate altar linen, readings and prayers that are audible and carefully prepared, dignified and unfussy leading of the service should always be found. Importantly, those who lead worship should have been taught the words of Thomas a Kempis in his 'Imitation of Christ'. He wrote, "Better mindful of other people's profit than your own devotion or spiritual taste." Beautiful worship not only gives glory to God, it also helps people to be aware of the presence of God. How important this is on occasions such as Easter and Christmas when many casual or irregular worshippers attend. Beautiful worship which creates a sense of the presence of God then becomes a means of evangelism. People might return for beautiful worship. They are unlikely to do so if what they experience is careless, unworthy and lacking any sense of the presence of God.

Psalm 85

This psalm is characterised by great beauty in both thought and in language. The first three verses may have been sung by a priest or prophet to declare to the congregation and, at the same time to remind God, that in the past he has often forgiven the nation's sins and restored it to peace and prosperity. The very human emotion of anger or wrath is attributed to God, but as is clear from the psalter as a whole, God's wrath is not personal vindictiveness but the inevitable outworking of the justice which has been built into his creation. We see that the psalmist readily admits that God's anger was always the result of the nation's iniquity and sin (v.2). *Iniquity/sin* and *wrath/anger* are a good example of the parallelism which is characteristic of Hebrew poetry.

In verses 4 to 7 it seems as if the congregation responds, voicing its prayer. The peoples' question is whether God will continue to be angry, or will he act as he always has in the past and forgive them. They make their petitions, *Restore us again* (v.4) and *show us thy steadfast love, O Lord* (v.7).

The congregation's question is answered by the priest or prophet who asks that God's words might be spoken through him. The answer given speaks of multiple blessings because God's glory, his presence, will dwell in the land (v.8). The blessings will be peace and other qualities of life which embody the way God intends that humans should live together. There will be *steadfast love, faithfulness, righteousness and peace.* We are inevitably reminded of St. Paul's list of the fruits of the Spirit in Galatians 5.22. His list is 'love, joy, peace, patience, kindness, goodness, faithfulness, gentleness, self-control'. Paul, a Pharisee, learned in the Scriptures, can hardly have been unaware of this psalm as he wrote those words.

When people live together as God intends, the creation itself will share in the well-being; *faithfulness will spring up from the ground and righteousness will look down from the sky* (v.11). If humans lived according to the list of blessings, whether from the psalmist or from St. Paul, the world would be changed: God's kingdom would come on earth as it is in heaven. Until such a state of affairs exists the best-intentioned relief schemes will only patch things up. We must do that, of course, but we should also be aware that it is never enough.

A final note. This psalm has proved itself a rich quarry for the makers of liturgies. Verse 7, with its very clear parallelism was incorporated into The Lesser Litany in both Morning and Evening Prayer in the Book of Common Prayer: "O Lord, show thy mercy upon us: and grant us thy salvation." Verse 6 is also used in the Night Office of Compline.

Psalm 86

The psalmist immediately throws himself on God's mercy. He is powerless to help himself; he is *poor and needy.* Only God can help him. The opening four verses sound very self-centred. The words *I* or *me* occur seven time in those verses, and even allowing for parallelism, there is no doubt that his own needs and feelings are what preoccupy the poet and, quite properly, he brings them to God.

By verse 5 he is able to look away from himself and towards God. He states that God forgives and lavishes his steadfast love on all who pray to him (v.5). With that as the general truth on which to build, he can confidently ask God to come to his aid in his particular *trouble.* At this point we do not know what the trouble is.

He turns to God again, proclaiming Yahweh's sovereignty over all other gods. No other god can do what Yahweh does. In time the sovereignty of Yahweh will be acknowledged by all nations because, after all, he has created them (vv. 8-10).

In verse 11 he asks for instruction in God's *way*. This means help in understanding and keeping the covenant. (Psalm 119 is devoted entirely to this quest, and several verses of that psalm come very close to this verse: *Teach me, O Lord, the way of thy statutes* (119.33), *teach me thy statutes* (119. 124,135 and others).

He believes that God has answered his prayer, and he gives thanks with all his heart and promises to praise God for ever, because God has somehow plucked him back from the brink of the grave, from Sheol, where he would be out of reach of God (v.13).

In the closing verses he spells out what his troubles are, and it is clear that, though he is now confident that God will help him, the troubles have not gone away. Some men are conspiring against him because they do not honour God as he does. He prays that God will pity him and give him strength to face his troubles.

His prayers have brought him to a very realistic and constructive way to face his problems. We should not expect God to remove all difficulties, but we should ask him to help us to face them and deal with them. The Christian faith is rooted in the belief that God entered the human condition in the incarnation of Jesus. He has shared our life and therefore understands our needs. The psalmist's need in this case is for reassurance in situations in which he is uncertain and afraid, fearing that his troubles might be too much for him. In several psalms and in the prophets we find God pictured as a loving parent, taking their fearful child by the hand and leading them to safety. In his Christmas broadcast on radio in 1939, just months after the start of the Second World War, King George VI quoted lines from the poem *God Knows* by Minnie Louise Haskins. His words gave comfort and hope to many in those dark days. "And I said to the man who stood at the gate of the year: Give me a light that I may tread safely into the unknown." And he replied: "Go out into the darkness and put your hand into the Hand of God. That shall be to you better than light and safer than a known way."

Psalm 87

This is a hymn of praise, celebrating Jerusalem as God's holy city. God chose Jerusalem because he loved it above all other cities (vv.1, 2). In verse 3 the psalmist listens to the words, probably the songs, of his fellow pilgrims. It is totally appropriate that 'Glorious things of thee are spoken, Zion, city of our God' has become a favourite Christian hymn of praise, though there is nothing specifically Christian in its wording. It celebrates the *solid joys and lasting pleasures* that membership of a faithful worshipping community confers. It is, of course, a fact that for Jews and Christians Jerusalem is the religious capital of the world. For Muslims it ranks third after Mecca and Medina.

In verse 4 we hear of the nations from which the pilgrims have travelled; Egypt (Rahab), Babylon, Tyre and Ethiopia. We should remind ourselves of the vast distances pilgrims from those places travelled. It would always be an arduous journey – no tour guide, airline and coach travel for them. The pilgrims may be dispersed Jews or converts to Judaism. They can all say that they were *born in her* because Jerusalem is their spiritual home, the place where their real life, the life of faith began, and from which they receive continuing spiritual nourishment.

Here is no exclusive 'sacred nation' theology. Rather, the promise made to Abraham that through his descendants all the nations of the world would find blessing, is being fulfilled. Here we see the hope of a universal faith in the one true God. Christianity, growing out of Judaism has inherited this hope, inspired by the inclusive example of Jesus and the belief that he sent out his followers to bear witness to him from Jerusalem, into Judaea and Samaria and to the end of the earth. (Acts 1.8 and Matthew 28.19, 20).

Verse 7 reads like a rubric, an instruction telling worshippers what to do next. Here the singers and dancers are instructed to perform "All my springs are in you." That is almost certainly the first line of a hymn. It is rather like saying, "The choir will now sing 'Glorious things of thee are spoken'." Of course, it means they will sing the whole hymn. It reminds us that the Evangelists tell us that when on the cross Jesus said, "My God, my God, why hast thou forsaken me?" It seems very likely that Our Lord was reciting the whole of that psalm as a dying, devout Jew might well do.

Psalm 88

As we read this psalm we can feel the pain and sadness that fills the poet's life. He is troubled in body and soul. He feels close to death and is regarded as a man whose life is as good as over (vv.4, 5). He attributes his sufferings to God. *Thou has put me in the depths of the Pit… Thy wrath lies heavy upon me… Thou hast caused my companions to shun me…*

Punished by God, forsaken by his friends, he nevertheless, clings to faith in God as his only hope. In verses 1, 9 and 13 he recalls how he prays constantly, pleading that God should answer him. This is no sudden onset of illness or distress; it is not the inevitable weakening of the body in old age. His hold on life has been precarious throughout his life; he feels as if he has been *afflicted and close to death from my youth up* (v.15). There is a poignant sadness in verses 16 to 18. When he most needs the support and encouragement of human love and companionship, the only things that are close to him are God's *dread assaults.* The psalm ends with no sign of hope.

The pains and sorrows of this life are not the poet's main worry. Repeatedly he speaks of his dread of death, of going down into Sheol (v.3), the Pit (v.6), Abaddon (v.11): three names for one place of horror. It is not the horror of physical punishment as in some Christian and Muslim visions of Hell. It is the greater horror of being totally separated from God. Of course we realise that the vivid descriptions of physical suffering are an attempt to communicate, by picture language, how terrible separation from God must be. For the psalmist God's wrath is preferable to God's absence, because his wrath is just and will be accompanied by mercy and loving-kindness.

Many psalms express this fear and sorrow at the prospect of being beyond the reach of God. *Are thy wonders known in the darkness, or thy saving health in the land of forgetfulness?* (v.12). We find the belief stated in Ecclesiastes 9.10 as the author teaches Wisdom to his readers: "In Sheol, for which you are bound, there is neither doing nor thinking, neither understanding nor wisdom." We might also recall that in Jesus' parable of the Rich Man and Lazarus both die and go to different places, Lazarus to 'Abraham's bosom' and the Rich Man to a place of torment. The Rich Man, however, thinks that nothing has changed and that Lazarus will still be at his beck and call. He asks Abraham to send Lazarus to bring him some relief. Abraham says that they are both receiving their just reward... "And besides all this, between us and you a great chasm has been fixed, in order that those who would pass from here to you may not be able, and none may cross from there to us." (Luke 16.26).

There was no belief in personal resurrection within Judaism until the time of the Maccabees, when the number of Jewish martyrs forced people to reflect that surely God would not let people die for their faith in him without some sort of reward. The beginnings of this belief in a resurrection of the righteous dead appear also in Daniel 12. 2, 3, written in the time when the Maccabees were fighting Syrian oppression. This hope developed, and in the gospels we read that in the time of Jesus the Pharisees believed in the resurrection of the dead while the Sadducees did not. (Mark 12. 18-27). St. Paul, on trial in Caesarea before the Jewish king Agrippa and the Roman governor Festus, knew that he could divide the court, which was made up of Pharisees and Sadducees, by saying that he was being accused of believing in the resurrection of a dead man. (Acts 26.6-8).

In the creeds Christians affirm their belief that after his death Jesus 'descended to the dead'. Traditionally known as the 'harrowing of Hell', this was the opportunity given to all who had not been able to hear the message of Jesus, including the patriarchs and prophets of the Old Testament. The only reference to this in the New Testament is in I Peter 4.6 which says, "This is why the gospel was preached even to the dead, that though judged in the flesh like men, they might live in the spirit like God."

There is a strange but striking story about the harrowing of Hell in the apocryphal Gospel of Peter. It records that on the Sunday morning after the crucifixion, emerging from the tomb were two gigantic figures whose heads reached the heavens. They were escorting an even greater figure whose head overtopped the heavens. Behind them came a cross. We are not told whether the cross was a conventional wooden one or whether we are intended to imagine people being lead out in a crowd in the shape of a cross, or again whether we are to understand it to represent the crucified Christ. The text reads "And they heard a voice out of heaven crying, 'Hast thou preached to them that sleep?' and from the cross there was heard the answer, 'Yea'." That ancient Christian story would have reassured the psalmist of the hope of resurrection, just as it was intended to encourage the Christians of its own time.

Psalm 89

This is the final psalm of Book III of the Psalter. The closing verse seems to be a doxology added to bring the book to an appropriate conclusion.

The psalm moves from being a hymn praising God's power, revealed in nature and in the history of the nation, to one of lamentation over the current political situation. Emerging throughout is the importance of the Davidic royal house.

We can imagine the first four verses being spoken or sung by a priest, introducing the twin themes of God's power and his representative on earth, the Davidic king, or we can read the whole psalm as the words of the king himself. In verses 5-18 Yahweh is celebrated as the supreme God, incomparably superior to any other so-called gods or heavenly beings (vv.5-8). It was he who created order by overcoming and taming chaos (Rahab). He is no local god but the creator of everything – heaven, earth, north, south. He is not only a God of power however, *Righteousness and justice are the foundation of thy throne; steadfast love and faithfulness go before thee* (v.14).

Israel's place as God's chosen people makes the nation specially blessed, and those who are taking part in this festival liturgy are the fortunate representatives of the whole nation (vv.15, 16). Possibly the priest's voice takes over again for verses 19-37 in which the covenant made with David and his descendants is celebrated. This would suggest that the psalm is part of the annual enthronement festival at which the king's status as God's anointed was celebrated, along with the renewal of the Covenant in which the nation acknowledged that their real king was God himself.

God promises to be with the king, giving him wisdom (v.22) and military success (vv.23-27). The king will honour God, acknowledging that his success is due to no virtue, strength or wisdom of his own, but entirely to the help of God. As the king honours God, God will continue to support the royal house (vv.27-29).

Then comes a word of warning. Tactfully it is not aimed at the present king, but at his successors. If they fail to keep the covenant God will punish them, but whatever happens, God himself will be steadfast and faithful. *I will not violate my covenant, or alter the word that went forth from my lips* (v.34).

Verses 39-45 look to the current situation. Gone are the grand dreams, the wishful thinking. The present situation is so desperate that it looks as if God has actually broken his part of the covenant and rejected Israel. Jerusalem and outlying cities are in ruins. The treasuries have been looted (v.41), and the nation is regarded with contempt by neighbouring peoples. The king, as commander-in-chief, has been defeated, and he no longer has any authority to rule (v.44).

The psalmist asks, *How long* will it be before God changes his mind and uses his power to restore the nation and its king? That question, used so often in the psalms, reveals the deep faith of the psalmist. No matter how desperate the situation, God is still there, his covenant still stands. God's righteousness, justice, steadfast love and faithfulness (v.14) are unchanged and will, in God's good time, be lavished once more on his people.

We might reflect that throughout the history of Israel and Judah the hopes placed on the Davidic kings were unrealistic. Too much was expected of any fallible human being. Eventually, the hope for a second David was pushed into the future. Such prophetic hopes are set out, for example, in Isaiah (9.2-7) which speaks of a child being born who will be the Prince of Peace, whose reign would be endless 'upon the throne of David'. The same prophet (11.1-10) speaks of the hopes resting on the 'shoot from the stump of Jesse'. Jesse was the father of David.

When the followers of Jesus became convinced that he was God's representative, his anointed Son, for whom the nation had been waiting, they were keen to establish that Jesus was 'of David's line', and assurances appear in the pre-nativity stories in Luke's gospel. Zechariah, the father of John the Baptist, praises God for raising "up a horn of salvation for us in the house of his servant David" (1.69). It is also noted that Joseph is of the "house and lineage of David" (2.4). The genealogies in Matthew 1.6 and Luke 3.31 also make a point of Jesus' Davidic lineage.

The title 'Christ' is commonly used as if it were a name. It is the Greek for the Hebrew word 'Messiah'. Both words mean 'the Anointed One'. Pilate's question to Jesus at his trial, "Are you the king of the Jews?" (Mark 15.2) is ironically apposite. For Christians Jesus was, despite appearances, the 'king of the Jews' just as his ancestor David had been. He became incarnate in order to establish the Kingdom of God, and he will, in the end, rule over all people— just as the psalmist hoped. The early Christian hymn, composed or quoted by St. Paul in his letter to the Christians in Philippi, looks forward to the time when the exercise of God's power will be universal and all people will acknowledge the kingship of Christ: "God has highly exalted him and bestowed on him the name which is above every name, that at the name of Jesus every knee should bow, in heaven and on earth and under the earth, and every tongue confess that Jesus Christ is Lord, to the glory of God the Father." (Phil. 2.9-11).

Psalm 90

When Thomas Ken wrote his hymn, "Awake, my soul, and with the sun, Thy daily stage of duty run..." he may well have had this psalm in mind. The psalm is a meditation on the contrast between God's eternity and the brevity of human life. It begins with the acknowledgement that God has been the nation's *refuge* down the ages. But the history of the nation is as nothing compared with the timelessness of God. God was God before he created the earth. Man may be the crown of creation, but just as he was formed from dust (Genesis 2.7), so his body must dissolve again into dust. What for man is a long time is a mere instant to God (vv.3, 4).

Death is one thing that humans can be certain about. They are like grass which springs up but dies quickly, scorched by the Middle Eastern sun. But perhaps death is not the only certainty for humans. Sin is as universal as death, and it inevitably calls down on itself the wrath of God. Such punishment is not vindictiveness but the natural outworking of God's justice; sin creates its own punishment.

The psalmist suggests that it is man's sinfulness which limits his life to a mere 70 or 80 years. As in the second creation story in Genesis, it is sin which brings mortality to the human race. (Genesis 2.17 and 3.19). Perhaps the psalmist has in mind some of the remarkable ages recorded in the nation's history and mythology. In the early universal myths in Genesis men are close to God and live very long lives; Adam 930, Enoch 905 and, famously, Methuselah 969 years. When we come to more historical figures we find Abraham reaching 175, Isaac 180 and Jacob 147. It is as if generations of sinful human life have brought life expectancy down to its present paltry figure of 70 or 80. In our generation we are more likely to attribute the greater life expectancy of recent years to advances in medical science rather than a lessening of human sinfulness.

It is probably true that in today's mainly secular society, most people simply do not think about their sins and God's judgement. Reading the psalms, we realise it was always so. The psalmist believes that people need God's help to make them aware of their predicament (vv.11, 12). Having considered the fragility of human life and man's moral weakness, the poet cries out asking God to pity his servants. He knows that God will respond in mercy, but asks the commonly heard prayer of the psalmists, *How long?* When times are bad God's response always seems to be delayed.

He asks that the days and years of affliction might be balanced by an equal time of gladness (v.15). This seems to be the prayer of a wise and thoughtful man, who realises that most people have their ups and downs in more or less equal proportions.

The psalm ends with a prayer that God will make his doings apparent to his people. They cannot be expected to thrive on faith alone; they need some tangible sign of God's acts. If his people can see some sign of God's care for them, those alive now, and future generations, will have a real basis for faith. Finally, he prays that

God will bless their efforts to live as God would wish them to. *The work of our hands* will be the observing of the Covenant, their efforts to live personally and as a society in accordance with God's will (vv.16, 17).

Only in our generation and mainly in our part of the world has the general expectancy of life risen beyond 70 and 80. A cause for rejoicing for many, it is also a cause of worry and a painful problem for some individuals and families. The caring role of spouses, children, friends, and medical and social services is as important as scientific advances. On this matter Christians have much thinking and praying and caring to do. Some remarkable things have been done. Leonard Cheshire, a much decorated hero of the Second World War, was the British representative on the American plane which dropped the atom bomb on Nagasaki. Horrified by its destructive power and sated by the violence and destruction he had witnessed and contributed to throughout the war, he founded a chain of Leonard Cheshire Homes to care for people with incurable conditions. With his wife, Sue Ryder, he inspired many to bring hope and comfort to those nearing the end of their lives. The hospice movement, pioneered by Dame Cicely Saunders, is another wonderful example of faith in action, bringing God's loving-kindness and mercy to the dying.

Amid all the uncertainties of life one thing is certain, and that is that death will come to each of us. As that is the case, we should indeed do what Bishop Ken suggested in his hymn, and "Live this day as 'twere thy last."

Psalm 91

This psalm has parts for at least two voices and the references to the temple suggest that it was written for use in a temple liturgy. The closing verse mentions *long life,* a gift especially desired for kings because of the stability which a long reign would bring to the nation.

The first 13 verses are perhaps a congregational hymn, proclaiming confidence in God's protection. In some ways, the words would be most applicable to a liturgy in which the king and his soldiers dedicate themselves to God on the eve of battle. Assurances of safety, some quite unreal or at least exaggerated, strengthen this suggestion.

Abiding in the *shelter* and *shadow of the Almighty* may mean being present in the temple, where people could see the covering of the outstretched wings of the cherubim above the ark. For such worshippers God is a refuge and a stronghold.

The protection given by God is described in some detail in verses 3-13. The worshipper will be safe from those who hunt him, and he will be protected from the ravages of disease (v.3). God's protection is then expressed as being like that of a mother bird watching protectively over her young. Because of God's protection they will be safe night and day, from perils unseen in the darkness and those all too clear in the light of day (vv.5, 6).

Safety in battle is assured. This might be a pious hope that the king will be specially protected or, if it refers to any worshipping soldier, it offers unrealistic odds in battle. Generally speaking, a soldier enters a battle expecting to survive; it is almost impossible to imagine the reality one's own death. After battle, those who survive often feel privileged when they consider the fate of their comrades and think "there, but for the grace of God, go I." The encouragement to the worshipper comes to an end with the assurance that because he has made God his refuge, God will fulfil that function. Specifically, he will set his angels to care, preventing a slip or stumble (vv.11, 12). Dangers as lethal as those posed by animal predators will be walked over, unnoticed (v13).

The voice changes in verse 14 to that of God, responding to the vows of faith and loyalty which have just been made. These words may well have been spoken by a priest or prophet. God promises to deliver those who love him, those who know his name, that is, his nature. Those who are faithful will pray, and God will answer the prayer, giving safety and honour. What more could a soldier wish for? The final promise of long life may be intended particularly for the king, but again it is the hope of every person whose profession constantly puts their life at risk.

Verses 11 and 12 are familiar to Christians because they are quoted by the devil in the stories of Jesus' temptations. (Matthew 4.6 and Luke 4.9-11). Jesus, with rabbinic learning, used Scripture to dismiss the temptation. He quoted Deuteronomy 6.16, "You shall not tempt the Lord your God." It is salutary to be reminded that the devil can quote Scripture, and we should remember that verses plucked out of the Scriptures without regard to their context usually prove very little. Religious controversies and disputes, ancient and modern, show how the devil can use Scripture to promote his ends – suspicion, discrimination and hatred. The words of Scripture need to be read carefully and prayerfully and we must seek to understand them in their proper context.

Psalm 92

This is a hymn of praise, to be accompanied by music at a festival service in the temple in Jerusalem. The heading of the psalm says *A Song for the Sabbath,* which fits well with the three-fold mention of God's *work* in verses 4 and 5. The pre-eminent work of God is the act of creation, and the Sabbath was established to remember and celebrate God's resting from "his work which he had done." (Genesis 2.2). The continued keeping of the Sabbath is a reminder that God continues to work, keeping his creation in being and maintaining his covenant with his chosen people. The people *sing for joy* as they recall God's steadfast love and faithfulness (v. 2).

The ungodly who do not acknowledge God's majesty are simply too dull to understand (v.6). They may think that God has no power because they see the wicked flourish. The psalmist cannot and does not dispute this seeming injustice in human life, but he is not worried by it; he believes that God's justice will prevail in the end.

In verses 10 and 11 the focus changes to the first person, and we hear of *my horn, my eyes and my ears,* while it is *over me* that the fresh oil of anointing has been poured. Members of the congregation might each sing the words thinking of the conflicts and anxieties from which they have been delivered, but it seems more fitting that these verses might be a short statement spoken by or on behalf of the king. This suggestion is strengthened by the reference to his anointing, his pre-eminence and the downfall of his enemies.

In verse 12 we return to the congregational hymn celebrating how God makes the righteous flourish. As in Psalm 1 they are compared to a living, growing tree. Their roots reach down into the rich soil of temple worship, (v.13), and they live long and productive lives. Thus is God's righteousness and justice, which is invisible to the ungodly, clear to the righteous.

The psalmist's own peace of mind shines through this hymn. Despite the worldly successes of the ungodly he is able to rest steadfastly in his belief that in the end God's justice will prevail. We should note that his assurance is underpinned by his life of devotion. He joins in the temple worship. He praises God day and night (v.2), and his faith is like that of the righteous in verses 12-14, deep-rooted and sustained by the spiritual sustenance found in regular, dedicated worship and the fellowship of other believers. Faith, worship and fellowship are similarly vital ingredients of the Christian life.

Psalm 93

This is a hymn celebrating the kingship of Yahweh: *Yahweh reigns* or *Yahweh is king.* It was perhaps used in the festival liturgy marking the renewal of the Covenant, with the recognition that Yahweh is the nation's king and the earthly monarch his viceroy. The psalm might have been used at the enthronement ceremony of a king of Judah, clearly reminding him that, however powerful he might feel himself to be, he rules on behalf of Yahweh.

As in Isaiah's vision (Isaiah 6.1-8), there is no attempt to describe God upon whom no one may look and live. (Exodus 33.20). The poet simply clothes God in majesty and strength (v.1).

Verses 3 and 4 recall God's ordering of chaos in the act of creation. The *formless void* of Genesis 1.2 is usually linked by scholars with the slaying of the great sea monster, Tiamat, by Marduk, the hero-god of Babylonian mythology. The idea of God overcoming the destructive power of the ocean is a recurring feature in the psalms as a prime example of his control over nature. Sometimes the power is simply referred to as the ocean or the waters but sometimes, as in the Babylonian story, a named malignant monster is imagined. Thus we find Leviathan mentioned in Psalm 74.14, and God's triumph over the monster wonderfully described in Isaiah 27.1. In Psalm 89 verses 9 and 10 the name of the creature becomes Rahab. What is important to the author of this psalm is that God's rule over the forces of nature is as effortless as was his creation by his word of command: *And God said, "Let there be light." And there was light.* (Genesis 1.3).

It is this wonderful, powerful God who has chosen Israel as his special people through whom he will bring blessing on all humankind. (Genesis 12.3). The nation will accomplish this task by keeping the Covenant, the requirements of which are permanent, *very sure* (v.5). The keeping of the covenant makes the nation holy, set apart, and that holiness is concentrated and felt by the worshipper in the temple liturgy (v.5).

The picture of God overcoming and taming the forces of nature which, without his guidance, become alien and destructive, is brought home to us when we watch the destructive power of a tsunami or the pounding sea destroying the most modern of sea defences. It is a wonderful metaphor for the merciful power of a God who cares and is able to protect and save even in the most threatening situations. But what are we to think when thousands die as a result of the ravages of nature? What are we to say to those whose homes are flooded year after year, or to farmers whose crops are decimated by lack of rain or unseasonable cold or heat? Simply to say that God is actually in control is likely to persuade them that God does not exist, or that if he does, he is malignant and certainly not to be worshipped. It will be our actions rather than our words which might make sense. Strangely, it is easier in many ways to help those in need at the other end of the world than to help those nearest to us. It is always possible to donate to charities which provide aid and the means of rebuilding lives and homes when there is an internationally known disaster. Christian charities have a very good record in targeting the needs of disaster victims. It is more difficult to do something for farmers in our own country who suffer losses because of weather conditions or disease. It becomes yet another situation in which Christians have to take politics seriously, and try to ensure that governments, local and national, work to prevent or at least to minimise damage, and to pay adequate compensation to those whose livelihood has been destroyed.

The comments above regarding verse 4 and the allusion to God's creative power and the way in which, in Genesis, it seems to be an effortless act: "God said, 'Let there be light', and there was light." (Genesis 1), need balancing by the thoughts of W.H. Vanstone. In his book *Love's Endeavour: Love's Expense* he argued that authentic love is always limitless, precarious and vulnerable. He paints a picture of what God's love in the act of creation must have cost by telling, as a parable, a true story which is worth quoting in full. "A doctor tells of an operation which, as a young student, he observed in a London hospital. "It was the first time this particular brain operation had been carried out in this country. It was performed by one of our leading surgeons upon a young man of great promise for whom, after an accident, there seemed to be no other remedy. It was an operation of the greatest delicacy, in which a small error would have had fatal consequences. In the outcome, the operation was a triumph: but it involved seven hours of intense and uninterrupted concentration on the part of the surgeon. When it was over, a nurse had to take him by the hand, and lead him from the operating theatre like a blind man or little child." This, one might say, is what self-giving is like: such is the likeness of God, wholly given, spent and drained in the sublime self-giving, which is the ground and source and origin of the universe." Vanstone goes on to say, "It was no light or idle word but the Word of love, in which, for the sake of an other, all is expended, all jeopardised and all surrendered."

Psalm 94

The psalm begins with an unrestrained call for vengeance on the proud and *the wicked*. There is no doubt in the psalmist's mind that their punishment will come because, as the whole Psalter insists, Yahweh is a God of justice. So the question is not whether the wicked will be punished, but when, and we hear the common plea of many psalms, *how long?* (v.3).

The sins of the wicked are listed. They are arrogant and they use their strength to hurt the weak, the defenceless, widows, orphans, strangers and those who honour God. They think they will go unpunished because they believe that God knows nothing of their doings (vv.4-7). How foolish they are! Of course God knows. He created hearing and sight. The wicked think they are clever, but before God their cleverness is but a puff of wind (vv. 8-11).

In verse 12 the tone changes and, as we move through the rest of the psalm we see that the words might have been spoken by the king on behalf of the nation. The poet now celebrates the *blessedness* of those who have received God's punishment and who have learned from it and changed their way of life. They are now in a situation in which they can benefit from the teaching of God's law. There is no reason to worry about the seeming immunity of the wicked because, eventually, God's justice will be done (vv.12-15).

In verse 16 he calls on his fellow-worshippers to join him in his stand against the wicked. He recounts how he personally experienced the help of God without which he would have perished (vv. 17-19).

He declares that an evil and corrupt regime cannot claim to rule on behalf of God. Some *wicked rulers,* presumably in neighbouring nations, frame unjust laws and condemn innocent people. Their rule can never claim to be exercised under God (v.20).

The person who prays this psalm, perhaps the king of Judah, claims that unlike corrupt rulers, he has Yahweh as his *stronghold* and *rock of refuge.* His rule will be grounded securely on God and God's laws (v.22).

The psalm ends, as do so many, repeating that ultimately God's justice will prevail, and therefore the wicked will receive their punishment.

Yet again a psalm brings us face to face with the importance of integrity in people of power and influence. Such people are faced with enormous temptations to use their position to benefit themselves or their family and friends. The murder of widows, strangers and orphans (v.6) might be understood, in our day, as a

162

lack of real appreciation of the situation of the many who, by no fault of their own, are vulnerable and hurt. It might be a forlorn hope, but we should insist that moral concerns should be of more importance to rulers than their own re-election.

Psalm 95

The words of this psalm place before us a scene of enthusiastic, joyful worship. In the Mishnah, it is counted as a psalm for the New Year Festival and, as we read, we can hear the pilgrims encouraging each other to sing God's praises as they are about to enter the sanctuary (v.2). They are going to *make a joyful noise* praising Yahweh, the God of Israel. He is the supreme God; the gods of other nations are mere attendants at his court (v.3). His act of creation, bringing order out of chaos, proclaims his greatness (vv. 4, 5).

Having declared God's greatness, the worshippers urge each other to add actions to their words of worship; *let us worship and bow down, let us kneel before the Lord, our Maker.* He is the maker, not only of each individual but, more importantly, of the nation. God has chosen them, guided and protected them. He is their shepherd and they are his flock. They have much cause for praise and rejoicing.

In the final sentence of verse 7 we leave the congregational hymn and hear a command to listen to the voice of God, and from verse 8 onwards the words are God's, probably spoken by a priest or a prophet. The words are a warning lest those so enthusiastically singing God's praises should be like their ancestors and turn from praise to the doubting of God's care and power.

The event referred to took place during the years in the wilderness. After being led out of Egypt by Moses, time and again the people found fault with Moses, their criticisms of the human leader being in reality a cloak for their lack of faith and their criticism of God. They said that they would have preferred to have remained as slaves in Egypt than die of starvation in the wilderness. In response, God provided them with of the meat of quails and with manna. That did not stop the complaints: "Why did you bring us up out of Egypt, to kill us and our children and our cattle with thirst." At God's command Moses struck a rock with his staff and water flowed out. The place was called *Massa* (proof) and *Meribah* (contention) because there they put the Lord to the proof. (Exodus 17.1-7). So grievous was their sin of doubting God and in effect challenging him to act to fulfil their desires, that God denied that generation entry to the Promised Land.

The psalm ends on that solemn note of warning. We almost feel as if there should be a third part to the psalm, in which the worshippers promise trust in God, thus ending the hymn as it had started, with praise and rejoicing.

Because it starts with an invitation to worship, this psalm was placed in the Book of Common Prayer as the opening Canticle at Morning Prayer. It became known to generations of church-goers as 'The Venite' after the opening word in the Latin version. In newer versions of the Morning Office it remains as the opening canticle, though alternatives are offered, and verses 8-13 are often omitted.

Psalm 96

It was suggested above that perhaps a song of praise was missing at the end of Psalm 95. It is interesting that there is no heading separating Psalms 95 and 96 and they share a remarkably similar refrain – *For the Lord is a great God and a great King above all gods* (95.3) and *For great is the Lord, and greatly to be praised; he is to be feared above all gods.* (96.4). Perhaps the two psalms, like Psalms 42 and 43, were originally one hymn of praise.

We are commanded to sing *a new song* to Yahweh. The words *new song* appear also in five other psalms, and it may be that new songs were commissioned for specific festivals, perhaps to celebrate the New Year or the anniversary of the enthronement of the king.

The power and incomparability of Yahweh is celebrated. Other nations regard him as Israel's tribal deity, rather like their own baal, so the truth must be proclaimed to *all the earth* (v.12), *among the* nations… *among all the peoples* (v.3). The truth is that Yahweh is the only God, the creator, a God of *honour, majesty, strength* and *beauty* (v.6).

People are called to recognise the glory and strength of Yahweh and to worship him as is fitting. They are called to make a pilgrimage to the temple in Jerusalem, bringing the appropriate offerings. Then they will join in worship of the holy God in a spirit of holiness (vv. 7-9).

Once again, in verse 10, the duty of proclaiming the kingship of Yahweh is laid upon the worshippers. Their experience of knowing and worshipping the one true God is not something to be grasped and kept greedily to themselves. It is to be shared. They must say among the nations, *The Lord reigns.* He reigns as king and therefore as judge, and he will judge justly.

The insistence on the need for teaching the world that Yahweh is the one true God is in keeping with the covenant God made with Abraham through which God's blessing will be extended to all people. (Gen. 12.3).

The psalm ends with a wonderful explosion of praise and joy. Not just people, but the whole of creation, heaven, earth and sea reveal his glory and join in the praise (v.11). Nature itself will share the joy, fields and forests joining in (v.12). A similar, fuller and again wonderful poetic extravagance appears also in Psalm 65.11-16. It challenges us to recall times when we have felt that creation itself smiles and shares its God-given beauty and contentment with humans.

Like nature, man should rejoice because God will come to judge the world. His judgement will be utterly just.

Psalm 97

The Lord reigns or *Yahweh is king* is a proclamation probably made at the annual festival in which Yahweh was enthroned as the nation's king. Christians today, whose faith has been nurtured on centuries of monotheism are quite accustomed to referring to God as King. Hymns such as 'The king of love my shepherd is' (based, of course, on Psalm 23) or 'Rejoice, the Lord is king' (based on this and probably other psalms), have been widely used for generations. We sing with equal comfort a modern hymn such as 'The Servant King'. There is no problem for us to ascribe kingship to any of the Persons of the Holy Trinity, though in practice it is rare to find the word used of the Holy Spirit.

We are so accustomed to referring to God as king that we can miss what a challenging and revolutionary statement it was for the people of Israel to declare that their God, Yahweh, was the only God and therefore the universal king. It was a challenge to the neighbouring peoples, each of whom had their own god or gods, which the writers of the Old Testament call the 'baals'. Israel, in this psalm and in many others, as well as in the teaching of the prophets, insisted that there is no God but Yahweh. It should be remembered, however, that all too often their practice did not live up to their profession, and the prophets often rail against those of their people who found the cults of the baals all too attractive.

The opening verses of the psalm, speaking of *clouds and thick darkness* may be describing some spectacular piece of liturgical drama in the temple celebrating the enthronement of Yahweh as the ark was placed beneath the covering wings of the cherubim. Clouds of incense may have risen (v.2). Lights may have flashed like lightning, drums may have created 'thunder' and the trembling of the earth (vv.3-5). On the other hand the words of verses 2-5 may simply be recalling the terrifying natural phenomena which are said to have accompanied the making of the Covenant and the giving of the Ten Commandments on Mount Sinai. (Exodus 19.16-20).

The universality of Yahweh's reign is assumed in verse 1 with places far from Jerusalem being invited to join in the celebration. Again verse 6 claims that all people are witnesses to Yahweh's glory. The other so-called gods can lay no claim to such glory. Unlike Yahweh they are mere images, the creation of man. If those gods have any reality at all, they too must be worshippers of Yahweh (v.7).

The people of Judah are privileged. Those who dwell in Jerusalem (*Zion*) and the other towns and cities of Judah (*daughters of Judah*) are aware of their good fortune in being chosen by Yahweh as his special people (v.8).

The hymn ends, like Psalm 95, with a warning. God expects all people to live justly and to reject evil ways. Those who live in this way will be cared for by God. Verse 11 expresses beautifully their reward: *Light dawns for the righteous and joy for the upright in heart.* The final verse then returns to the note on which the psalm began: *Rejoice in the Lord.*

Light, promised to the righteous, was the first thing to be created by God's word after he had created the heavens and the earth. It was to illuminate his creation (Genesis 1.3). Simeon prophesied that the infant Jesus would become *a light to lighten the Gentiles.* (Luke 2.32). Jesus spoke of himself as the light of the world: "I am the light of the world; he who follows me will not walk in darkness, but will have the light of life." (John 8.12). In the Sermon on the Mount he said that his disciples would share the responsibility of being channels of God's light: "You are the light of the world." (Matthew 5.14). So Christians believe that Jesus is the light of the world, and has entrusted to his followers the task of lighting up the world with his truth and love.

Psalm 98

Starting exactly like Psalm 96, this is probably another song of praise for use at the annual enthronement ceremony at which Yahweh was acknowledged as the nation's king. The *new song* may be precisely that, something composed specially for the festival in a particular year.

Yahweh's kingship had been revealed in his leading Israel in its battles with other nations. What has happened throughout the nation's history, particularly in the God-inspired conquest of Canaan, should make it clear to *the ends of the earth* that Yahweh has chosen and loves and protects his people Israel (vv. 2, 3).

In verse 4 *all the earth* is commanded to break into songs of joy and praise. The next two verses reveal that it is the congregation present in the temple who will sing with enthusiasm, offering to God the praise which should be offered by all peoples. What they sing will be accompanied by the music of many instruments and the words might well be the *new song* of this psalm.

So verses 7-9 may be the song of joy or a part of it. Nature itself bears witness to the power of Yahweh; sea and land revel in the joy of it. All creation can rejoice that Yahweh is king, not only of Israel, but of the whole world. They can be glad because he will exercise his kingship, not with the fallible judgements of earthly rulers, but with perfect judgement exercised in righteousness and fairness.

We rush to judgement very readily. If times are hard it is somebody's fault—the greedy rich, the lazy poor, the untrustworthy politicians—certainly not us. We should be slow to judge, as Jesus advised in his Sermon on the Mount. (Matthew 7.1). But we cannot airbrush judgement out of the Christian faith. In the creed we say that we believe that Christ will return "to judge the living and the dead." We should expect judgement to be painful or, at the very least, uncomfortable for we all have things we are ashamed of and would prefer to keep to ourselves. God knows about all those things. However we also believe that the death of Jesus on the cross changed the way our sentences will be set. In his letter to the Romans St. Paul gave a picture of the last judgement. He said, "We shall all stand before the judgement seat of God." (Romans 14.10). The remarkable thing is that we shall all be found guilty, and then all declared innocent. That is the difference made by the life, death and resurrection of Jesus. We need not fear judgement, not because we are virtuous, or because sin doesn't matter, but because God is merciful and loving.

Psalm 99

This is another hymn celebrating the kingship of Yahweh. It begins, like Psalm 97, with the cry of triumph and faith, *Yahweh reigns* or *Yahweh is king.*

Verse 1 celebrates the actual moment of enthronement in the temple liturgy as the ark is placed beneath the cherubim. The earth quakes at the significance of the moment. This may simply be a reminder of the terrifying natural phenomena which accompanied the giving of the Law at Mount Sinai. (Exodus 19.16-19), or it may have been simulated in the temple ritual, perhaps with the sound of drums.

Yahweh's eminence as king is not merely over Israel, where it is acknowledged. It is over *all peoples* even if they do not know it (v.2). In verse 3 we have a refrain proclaiming the holiness of God. In almost identical words it occurs again in verses 5 and 9, where it is the climax of the psalm. The refrain celebrates the holiness of God and we might imagine it being sung by a priest or a choir.

God is to be worshipped because he is the *lover of justice,* he has *established equity* and he has *executed justice and righteousness* (v.4). As is taught in many psalms, those are the characteristics of Yahweh's holiness.

Verses 6 and 7 look back on some of the great leaders of the nation in the past. Moses is the towering figure of the Jewish Scriptures. Aaron, his brother, was the priest chosen by God to lead and direct the nation's worship (Leviticus 8.12, 13). Samuel, rather like Moses, was a leader in war and in peace, in religion and in politics. There is no mention of David, the ideal king, nor of any of his successors. The liturgy concentrates worshippers' minds entirely on the kingship of Yahweh. These three great men are held up as examples to be followed. They prayed to God and he answered them. They also kept the Covenant, though not perfectly, because God had to forgive them (vv.7, 8).

The psalm ends with its final refrain, which is a formal and, in reality, unnecessary command or entreaty that the people should worship God on his holy hill. That is, in fact, precisely what they are doing in the temple on Mount Zion. But it is a perfectly understandable way to encourage the worshippers and increase their devotion. In just the same way Christians sing the hymn "O worship the Lord in the beauty of holiness" to encourage themselves and each other in devotion.

In the letter to the Ephesians we read, "He chose us before the foundation of the world that we should be blameless before him." (Eph. 1.4). This psalm reminds us that, on the one hand, the holiness of God, and the holiness he wants his worshippers to exhibit, is a very practical matter which affects our life as a Christian community and in society in general, as much as it affects our private, devotional lives. God's holiness is revealed in his justice, equity and righteousness. On the other hand, God's holiness is to do with our being aware of the overwhelming gap between the human and the divine. Our knowing God as opposed to knowing about God, drives us to our knees as we come to realise that God not simply greater or more powerful but qualitatively different (Vanstone op. cit. p.73). Rudolf Otto in his "The Idea of the Holy" famously described God as the *mysterium tremendum et fascinans,* and recalled his own experience: "I have heard the *Sanctus Sanctus Sanctus* of the cardinals in St. Peter's, the *Swiat Swiat Swiat* in the Kreml cathedral, and the *Hagios Hagios Hagios* of the patriarch in Jerusalem. In whatever language they resound, these most sublime words that have ever come from human lips always grip one in the depths of the soul, with a mighty shudder, exciting and calling into play the mystery of the otherworldly latent therein." Otto echoes the psalmist's *The Lord reigns; let the peoples tremble… for the Lord our God is holy.*

Psalm 100

Verse 1 invites people of *all the lands* to join in this joyful hymn of praise. As soon as we reach verse 2 we know that this is a processional psalm sung as the pilgrims enter the sanctuary where they, representing the people of all lands, will be in the *presence* of God.

As we pass to verse 3 the people of other lands are gently moved aside as the praise turns to the means by which God's blessing will come upon all, through the unique relationship between Yahweh and Israel. Israel's God, Yahweh, is the only God. The worshippers are reminded that amongst all his wonders, his choosing of Israel and his leading of the nation like a good shepherd are chiefly to be praised.

The pilgrims encourage each other in their hymn as they pass through the gates and enter the sanctuary, moving ever closer to the presence of God. They are to give thanks for the privilege granted them, and to bless the sacred name, Yahweh (v.4).

The psalm ends with the oft-used declaration that Yahweh is good. He is not a tyrant god, like many of those of the surrounding nations, demanding child sacrifice or other abominations. Yahweh's nature, his *name,* is steadfast love and faithfulness. He has demonstrated it throughout the nation's history, and so trustworthy is he that they know his love will continue *to all generations.* As we shall see, Psalm 136 celebrates Yahweh's *steadfast love* in every verse, showing how it is the reason behind all God's actions.

The portrayal of Yahweh as the good shepherd is found, of course, most famously in Psalm 23. It is also in Psalm 80. But it is a recurring theme in the prophets too. In Isaiah's prophecy of the coming of God to his people, he wrote, "He will feed his flock like a shepherd, and will gather the lambs in his arms." (Isaiah 40.11). Jeremiah, speaking of the hope of return from the Babylonian exile, wrote, "He who scattered Israel will gather him, and will keep him as a shepherd keeps his flock." (Jeremiah 31.10). It is a prominent theme in Ezekiel's consideration of the nation and its unsatisfactory earthly rulers, who are worthless shepherds. God will do away with them and become their shepherd himself. (Ezekiel 34). Zechariah 10.2 and 11.16 also has much to say about bad shepherds.

It must have been with these references to shepherds, good and bad, in his mind and long meditated upon, that led Jesus to tell the parable of the Lost Sheep (Luke 15.3-7) and to call himself the Good Shepherd and the door of the sheepfold as recorded in the 10th chapter of John's gospel.

Psalm 101

The title of this psalm is *A Psalm of David for the thank offering.* It certainly sounds very much like vows made by a king, possibly on the occasion of his enthronement. It could be a form of royal dedication used in the liturgy at the enthronement of every king.

It is significant that the king considers himself and his duties and responsibilities before saying what he will demand of his subjects. He puts loyalty and justice first, and acknowledges that without the help of God he will not be able to maintain the standards at which he aims: *Oh, when wilt thou come to me?* He promises integrity and the avoidance of all that is *base* (vv.3, 4).

In verse 5 he moves on to consider the people around him, his court or his cabinet. He will require the highest standards from them, and will weed out those who prove themselves unable or unwilling to maintain the standards expected. These are not vague promises; they are not things to be aspired to. They are things to be done. A commitment is made to a daily examination of his advisers: *Morning by morning* he will examine those around him and dismiss the unworthy. They shall not be permitted to pollute Jerusalem, *the city of the Lord,* with their wickedness.

As we read these commitments we might wonder if this king was replacing a particularly corrupt regime. On many occasions in the historical books of the Old Testament, we read of kings who did not rule in the way that God required. Their reigns are usually summed up with a formula statement repeated on many occasions. Very often a father and the son who succeeded him are linked in condemnation. To take one example: "Nadab, son of Jeroboam, began to reign over Israel… and he reigned over Israel two years. He did what was evil in the sight of the Lord, and walked in the way of his father, and in his sin which he made Israel to sin." (I Kings 15.25, 26). The need for kings to select their advisers very carefully and to rid themselves of corrupt ones is expressed in the teaching of the Proverbs (25.4, 5): "Take away the dross from the silver, and the smith has material for a vessel; take away the wicked from the presence of the king, and his throne will be established in righteousness."

This psalm bears out Lord Acton's well-known saying that power corrupts and absolute power corrupts absolutely. At least at the beginning of his reign the king, speaking this psalm, knew of the dangers of power and the compelling need to watch carefully his own behaviour, and that of the people he chose as his companions and advisers. There is a good example of the malign influence of the wrong advisers in I Kings 12.1-17, when Rehoboam took the advice of his contemporaries, ignoring the wisdom of older counsellors. That mistake resulted in the kingdom, united under David and Solomon, being divided into Israel in the north and Judah in the south.

The standards for godly monarchs set out in this and other psalms form part of the Coronation Oath taken by the British king or queen. When Queen Elizabeth succeeded her father, George VI, she made the following informal commitment. "I want to ask you all, whatever your religion may be, to pray for me… to pray that Christ may give me wisdom and strength to carry out the solemn promises I shall be making, and that I may faithfully serve him, and you, all the days of my life." In those words, we hear unmistakable echoes of Solomon's request to God for wisdom when he succeeded his father David. In the Coronation service held on 2nd June, 1953 in Westminster Abbey, Elizabeth II was asked by the Archbishop of Canterbury, "Will you to the utmost of your power cause Law and Justice, in Mercy, to be executed in all your judgements?" She answered, "I will." Then he asked, "Will you to the utmost of your power maintain the Laws of God and the true profession of the Gospel?" Again she answered, "I will." The commitment required of a king in ancient Judah still deeply influences the way the British monarchy sees itself and its duties.

The Church of England, as the established Church of the land, has the privilege of appointing a priest to act as chaplain to the Houses of Parliament. We may hope that the chaplain sets this psalm, pointing out particularly the words of verse 6, before a Prime Minister when, having been elected, he or she chooses their cabinet members and advisers.

Psalm 102

This is counted as the fifth Penitential Psalm and its heading begins *A prayer of one afflicted.* It certainly describes much suffering in the first eleven verses, but underneath all the misery is the belief that God can change things. He can bring comfort and relief. Verse 12 is the turning point in the psalm. Up to that point the psalmist's sufferings have been his first concern, then verse 12 starts with a resounding *But* as the eternity, power and pity of God are called to mind.

The words of verse 1 have become familiar to many Christian worshippers as a versicle and response used in prayers of intercession; "O Lord, hear our prayer: and let our cry come unto thee." The psalmist asks God to listen to him, but fears that God is deliberately hiding his face, as if to turn his back on the supplicant who wants an immediate response (vv.1, 2).

In verse 3 he begins to set out his distress in detail. It seems he is sick with a high temperature and loss of appetite and weight. On top of his physical suffering he feels friendless, totally alone like a single bird of prey circling in an empty sky (vv. 6-8). Having said, in verse 5, that he has no appetite, he now says that he simply doesn't care what he eats or drinks (v.9). He believes his plight is because God has forsaken him. The wonderful expression *My days are like an evening shadow* may mean that time drags, and the hours are long like the shadows cast late in the day. Or perhaps he means that he fears that death approaches as the shadows of evening are followed quickly by the total darkness of night.

The tone of the psalm changes completely in verse 12. In contrast to his own misery and the brevity of his life stands the changeless eternity of God. The psalmist has only to think of God and his mind is filled with hope and confidence that God will, as always, *have pity on Zion* (v.13). The belief that God has chosen Jerusalem as his earthly dwelling gives confidence that he will act to protect the city. Jeremiah had to tell the people of Jerusalem in his day that there was no guarantee of safety in Jerusalem. They had broken the covenant and their superstitious repeating of the phrase, "the temple of the Lord", would do nothing to save them (Jeremiah 7.4).

Here the psalmist says how the people of Jerusalem venerate their holy city; *they hold her stones dear* (v. 14). This verse reminds us of the disciples of Jesus wondering with awe at the great stones of Herod's temple, some of which can still be seen today. The disciples said to Jesus, "Look, Teacher, what wonderful stones and what wonderful buildings." Rather like Jeremiah, Jesus had to temper their enthusiasm. "Do you see these great buildings? There will not be left here one stone upon another, that will not be thrown down." (Mark 13.2).

The psalmist expresses the hope that many nations will come to Jerusalem in awe of Yahweh. God will *build up* Zion and his presence will be known there (v.16). Any pilgrim who has visited Jerusalem will know that this prayer of the psalmist has been and is constantly being fulfilled. Though a troubled city, it is indeed the focus of pilgrimage and devotion for people of many faiths and nations.

Verses 15-22 tell us that future generations should be taught that Yahweh, the God who is revered in Jerusalem, cares for all the people of the earth. He is a merciful God, concerned particularly with those in desperate circumstances, including *prisoners* and those *doomed to die.*

In verse 23 the psalmist returns to his personal concerns. He continues to feel weak and believes he has not long to live. Perhaps he counts himself among those he spoke of in verse 20, who are doomed to die. Again he contrasts the brevity of his own, and perhaps of all human life, with the eternity of God. Even the heavens and the earth, which seem timeless and eternal to humans, are as nothing to God. He changes them as people change their clothes. God is unchanging, utterly steadfast, utterly trustworthy. Confident of this, his people can live without anxiety; all things are in God's hands.

It is inspiring to read of this man's problems and to see how his meditation on the mercy and unchanging nature of God leads him from despair to hope and confidence, not only for himself but for future generations. He would have agreed with Lady Julian of Norwich that "all shall be well, and all manner of things shall be well."

Psalm 103

This wonderful psalm celebrates the love of God which brings healing and forgiveness to body and soul. The poet begins by urging himself to praise God with his whole being; *all that is within me.* He speaks of his own experience when illness brought him close to death. Forgiveness and healing were God's gifts. His health was restored and he felt as strong and invulnerable as an eagle (v.5). Isaiah used the same imagery saying that "they who wait for the Lord... shall mount up with wings as eagles." (Isaiah 40.31). In both cases it is a wonderful image of effortless, soaring strength.

In verse 6 he moves from concentrating on his own experience of God's love to that of the nation. God's justice is enshrined in the Laws of the covenant made with Israel through Moses (vv. 6, 7). In the Law God revealed himself not only as just but as *merciful and gracious, slow to anger and abounding in steadfast love* (v. 8).

God has constantly revealed himself as forbearing and forgiving. It is as if the psalmist had in mind the account of God's mercy in permitting the making of a second set of stone tablets on which the Law was written to replace those thrown down and shattered by Moses in anger at the apostasy of the people. (Exodus 32.19). When the second pair of tablets were cut, we read, "The Lord passed before him, and proclaimed," in words surely echoed by this psalm, "The Lord, the Lord, a God merciful and gracious, slow to anger and abounding in steadfast love and faithfulness." (Exodus 34.6).

God's justice is tempered by his mercy (v.10). His steadfast love is measureless (v.11). He removes peoples' sins beyond reach (v.12). We find a picture of God behaving like a loving father, always ready to excuse his disobedient children. He is aware of human weakness. He created man out of dust (Genesis 2.7) and is fully aware how fragile and temporary he is (vv.15, 16). In contrast God is eternal and he constantly maintains his covenant love for Israel (vv. 17, 18).

The last four verses are a song of praise. God's total supremacy and universal rule are declared. All are called to bless God, beginning with those closest to him, angels and other heavenly beings, cherubim and seraphim. *All his hosts* may also refer to the angelic beings in a typical piece of parallelism. Or they may be the stars and planets, a different sort of heavenly body, as in Deuteronomy 4.19 and 17.3 and in Isaiah 34.4. After calling the whole creation, all God's *works,* to bless God, the poet ends as he began, urging himself to bless the wonderful God whom he knows; *Bless the Lord, O my soul.*

We find ourselves wanting to praise God when life brings us joy and fulfilment. It is a different and deeper feeling of gratitude when we know ourselves to be forgiven after having done things we should not have done or not done things which we should have done, as the old General Confession says. Such forgiveness creates within us a profound thankfulness and, like the psalmist, we thank God with our whole being.

Psalm 104

Like the previous psalm this one opens with the psalmist urging himself, *Bless the Lord, O my soul.* He closes the poem asking, in verse 34, that this psalm, his *meditation,* may be pleasing to God.

It is a meditation on the wonder, order and beauty of creation, and how it reveals God's careful conceiving and ordering of the universe. God himself may never be seen, but his presence is known because the majesty of creation, and the light which gives life to all creatures and by which nature is seen, are like garments concealing him (v.2).

From the mention of light, the first thing created by God's word of command, we are led through the acts of creation in a wonderful series of poetic images. The sky was stretched out by God, as a man stretches the covering over the framework of his tent. Clouds, wind, fire and flame are the means by which God controls nature.

As in Genesis chapter 1, and often in the psalms, water is regarded with awe, and feared as a dangerous element which threatens at all times to return and engulf the world, returning it to chaos. It is restrained only by God's mercy and power. Verse 8 paints an almost geological picture of the formation of hills and valleys, arranged by God to contain water in safe and useful places.

God has thought of everything. Properly controlled by God, springs sustain wild animals. Domesticated animals and humans are cared for by God's planning. Nor is it just the necessities of life that are provided. Along with the provision of the basic bread to sustain life, God has also provided wine to bring cheerfulness. Among the many uses of the vital olive oil is its ability to make a person's face shine with health and happiness (vv.14-16).

Birds are kept safe by being able to make their homes high in trees, far from the reach of their predators. Other creatures finds suitable habitat in what appear to be inhospitable places (vv.17, 18).

Nature is controlled, in God's plan, by the passage of night and day and the seasons. Nocturnal creatures can roam and hunt while man sleeps, and when they sleep, man goes to work. All is beautifully arranged by God.

Verse 25 returns to the great and mysterious sea, full of strange creatures. *Leviathan* (v.26) is sometimes the term used for the terrible and destructive force of the sea which God had to tame. The creature is the equivalent of Tiamat, the sea monster of the Babylonian creation story. Here, *sporting,* seems to owe something to the observation of whales surfacing or dolphins playing.

In verse 27 the poet reflects that God did not simply create things and abandon them to their own devices. He cares for his creation and maintains it. This reminds us of Jesus' words in John's gospel (5.17). He had healed a man on the Sabbath and was challenged because it was unlawful to 'work' on the Sabbath. His reply infers that even if God's work of creation was completed in six days, his work of maintaining his creation continues: "My father is working still, and I am working."

Humans are not immortal. Immortality was lost, according to the creation myth in Genesis, by Adam's disobedience. He had become a living being when God breathed his spirit into him. (Genesis 2.7). When God removes his spirit human life ends. But the life of humanity continues because God continually renews it.

The psalmist prays that God's glory, seen in his creation, will be everlasting. He admits that disasters do take place, earthquakes and volcanoes threatening human safety (v.32). Despite these he is determined to praise God as long as he lives, and asks that this poem, his *meditation,* may be pleasing to God.

The final verse is a prayer that the ungodly will not be allowed to spoil God's wonderful arranging of the universe, (what we might call the balance of nature), so that God's justice and mercy will flourish. Then the psalm is 'sealed' by the repetition of the opening cry, *Bless the Lord, O my soul.*

Psalm 105

The placing of the ark in the tabernacle, the tent which King David had prepared for it, was a very solemn occasion. It is recorded in I Chronicles chapter 16. Verse 7 of that chapter says that David "first appointed that thanksgiving be sung to the Lord by Asaph and his brethren." Asaph was the chief Levite. (I Chron. 16.4, 5). That song of thanksgiving has found its way into Psalm 96, verses 1-13, into verses 1-15 of this psalm, and into a few verses of Psalm 106.

If the first singing of the thanksgiving was at David's command, it appears that the tradition was continued at subsequent annual festivals at which the covenant was renewed.

Verses 1-6 call on the congregation to praise God as they enter the sanctuary of the temple which had been built as a more dignified, suitable and permanent place for the ark of Yahweh to rest. The ark was the symbol and guarantee of God's presence. The pilgrims are called to remember the mighty acts which God performed on behalf of their nation, which he had chosen as his covenant partner.

Verses 7-11 are the statement of their covenant belief, *He is the Lord our God.* They state that God is always faithful to the covenant promises which he made first to Abraham, and which he renewed to Abraham's son, Isaac and his grandson, Jacob. Then follows a reminder that the promised land, Canaan, was always a vital part of the salvation history of the nation. Verses 12 and 13 may at first sound like a description of the wilderness wanderings, but if so they are out of historical order. More likely they refer to the nomadic life of the patriarchs. Abraham, as the head of a semi-nomadic clan, was constantly on the move, as were many other similar groups at that time in history – about 1500 B.C. The psalmist here is perhaps making an allusion to the story of Joseph, when he was sent to look for his brothers who were caring for the family flocks. He was sent to Shechem, where they were supposed to be. But, seeking fresh pasture for their sheep they had moved away to Dothan. Genesis 37.15 says, "And a man found him (Joseph) wandering in the fields…" So these verses seem to record that God cared for them from the earliest days of their relationship with him.

The probable reference to Joseph leads on very naturally to an account of his rise to power in Egypt which is also seen as God's doing. Indeed, this is precisely what Joseph had told his guilt-laden brothers when they came face to face with him. (Genesis 45.5). Jacob/Israel and all his family went to Egypt at Joseph's invitation and at first they flourished there. The success of the immigrants was not to the liking of the Egyptians, and under a new Pharaoh they were oppressed and reduced to being slave labourers (vv. 23-25).

So God sent Moses and his brother Aaron, and through the 'plagues', culminating in the death of the first-born, Pharaoh was persuaded to let the people go (vv. 26-36).

They left Egypt laden with gifts from the Egyptians who were glad to see them go. With a pillar of cloud by day and a pillar of fire by night showing his presence, God led them through the wilderness. Food and water were miraculously provided, and they entered the

Promised Land, a people chosen and preserved by God to keep his covenant, through which justice and blessing would be brought upon all peoples.

By necessity the psalm gives a very brief summary of Israel's salvation history. It is a very selective and idealised summary. The continual grumbling of the people against Moses and God is not mentioned, nor the fact that none of those who left Egypt were allowed to enter the Promised Land, Moses among them. This idealised history of the nation is presented quite deliberately, to remind the pilgrim worshippers who hear it that it is now their responsibility to be perfect in their keeping of the covenant. They take that responsibility upon themselves as they share in this annual festival of worship and renewal.

Strong echoes of verses 8 and 9 are found in Luke's gospel chapter 1, verses 72 and 73. They form part of the Song of Zechariah, the father of John the Baptist. The song speaks of the covenant and the belief that God would save his people through a new Davidic saviour. Of this coming saviour, Zechariah's son, John, would be the forerunner, "for you will go before the Lord to prepare his way." (Luke 1.76).

For Christians Jesus is that longed-for Davidic saviour. When Israel failed to keep the covenant, Jesus, as the ideal Israelite took the place of the nation. He was not just the ideal Israelite, he was the ideal Israel or Jacob. He inaugurated the new chosen nation, with his twelve disciples, corresponding to Jacob's twelve sons, as the foundation. He renewed the covenant by his life, death and resurrection. At the Last Supper, he gave the cup of wine to his disciples and said, "This is my blood of the covenant, which is poured out for many." (Mark 14.24). No longer was the covenant a national matter. It was for all people as God's promise to Abraham had intended. Every time Christians receive the sacrament of the Body and Blood of Christ in the Eucharist they, like the pilgrim worshippers in the psalm, commit themselves to a renewed intention of keeping the covenant.

Psalm 106

We noticed that Psalm 105 pictured the nation in idealised form. This psalm looks at the reality, recounting many of the occasions throughout their history when they doubted God, forsook the Covenant and worshipped other gods. It is possible that this is largely a form of public confession for the nation's sins, used at the annual Covenant Renewal Festival.

The psalm begins with a familiar call to praise God *for he is good; for his steadfast love endures for ever.* Psalm 136 uses these words as a refrain in each of its 26 verses, and they appear in several other psalms as well. They must have been words familiar to all who worshipped regularly in the temple.

Verses 2 and 3 remind the worshippers that mere words do not constitute the praise of God. Actions, lives, characterised by justice and righteousness, are what matter. Each worshipper asks that they should be counted among God's *chosen ones,* part of the nation chosen by God as his Covenant partner (vv. 4, 5).

They seek to be honest in their confession. They admit that like each generation before them, they have failed to keep the Covenant. Their sins have been the result of their doubting God's power and steadfastness. So the historical recital of failure begins. Even before they left Egypt, the sight of Pharaoh's army pursuing them led them to criticise Moses. (Exodus 14.11, 12). Despite their doubts God saved them famously at the Red Sea and, as verse 12 records, they then sang God's praises. Their song of praise is recounted in Exodus 15 and tradition says that the angels joined in. We might be relieved to learn that a Talmud writer was troubled by this and taught that God interrupted the song of praise saying "My creatures are drowning in the sea – and you are singing? What if they are enemies of Israel and liberty – they are still human beings! How can you think of singing while human beings are drowning?" The Vigil in the Christian Easter Liturgy offers the use of both the narrative of the drowning of the Egyptian army in Exodus 14, and part of the song of triumph in Exodus 15. It should always make us feel uncomfortable. Perhaps our service sheets would be enhanced by a quotation from the Talmud.

The psalm then goes on to refer to other acts of disobedience. Jealousy and faithlessness are recalled as well as the fact that it was only the intercession of Moses that persuaded God not to destroy them (v.23). Similarly the drastic act of Phineas is remembered. He killed a Moabite cult prostitute and the Israelite man who was consorting with her in what would, by them, be understood as an act of worship of the baal of Peor (vv. 28-31).

Verse 32 reminds the worshippers of the price paid by Moses for his anger at Meribah, anger caused by the faithlessness of the people. He was not permitted to enter the Promised Land. He was only allowed to look at it. This startling and shocking event is thoroughly recorded. (Exodus 17.7, Numbers 27.13 and Deuteronomy 2.51, 52).

The nation's apostasy in worshipping the gods of the people of Canaan is recalled; cults which included child sacrifice. Deuteronomy 18. 9-12 gives a full account of the various practices which were an attraction to the people of Israel. It was this apostasy which angered God (v.40), and caused him to allow nations to defeat and oppress his people.

The extent of Israel's apostasy seems limitless, and then verse 44 begins, *Nevertheless...* Despite the nation's weakness and sin, God did not forget them nor did he forsake his side of the Covenant (v.45). Because of his steadfast love he brought them relief by causing even their enemies to pity them.

The overwhelming forbearance and love of Yahweh is the reason for the worshippers gathering on this occasion. They remind themselves of the failings of past generations in order to strengthen themselves to try to do better. They ask God to save them now, so that their praise and thanksgiving may be all the more heartfelt. The final verse blesses Yahweh, the God of Israel, and the congregation is bidden to respond *Amen.* This closing verse may be the reason that this psalm was selected as the final one in Book IV of the Psalter, or it may be an addition to the original psalm.

The psalm is about God's patience with his people, his readiness to forgive and to go on forgiving. Every Christian knows how important that is. The liturgical year has two penitential seasons, Advent and Lent. In practice, worshippers have to struggle to observe Advent, as the commercial and secular exploitation of Christmas commonly starts well before the beginning of Advent. Lent is much more generally observed, and particular services, such as those on Ash Wednesday at which worshippers are marked on their forehead with ash, are a public admission of our need for forgiveness. We can all look back, as this psalm does, and recall our habitual failure to live in imitation of Christ. Verses 2 and 3 of the psalm stress that actions speak louder than words and remind us that Jesus said, "Not everyone who says to me 'Lord, Lord' will enter the kingdom of heaven, but he who does the will of my Father who is in heaven." (Matthew 7.21). Words are easy and we can become skilful in using the right words at certain times to convince or impress people with our penitence and our commitment. But in the end only our deeds reveal our faith.

Psalm 107

This is the opening psalm of the 5th and final book of the Psalter.

The first and the last verses of the psalm celebrate *the steadfast love* of Yahweh. Between them, we have a hymn of thanksgiving, using the experiences of four separate groups of people who found themselves in serious difficulties. They appealed to God for help and were answered. Each narrative section ends with a refrain. It is possible that the psalm was for use at temple festivals with each narrative section recited or sung by a priest and the refrain and verses 33-43 sung by the congregation.

As in the previous psalm, the first verse is probably a versicle and response through which the congregation is called to thank God for his unfailing steadfast love.

The first narrative section in verses 2-7 could be recalling the wilderness wanderings from the Exodus to the settlement in Canaan, where they found *a city to dwell in.* However, more likely, it may speak of the pilgrims themselves gathered in Jerusalem. For some of them, the journey had been long (vv.3, 4) and hazardous (vv.4, 5) before they reached Jerusalem, which for a time would be their *city to dwell in.*

Verses 8 and 9 are the first refrain, calling the pilgrims to thank God for the way he preserved them when hungry and thirsty on their journey.

The next narrative (vv. 10-14) concerns prisoners who have no hope of release. Their plight is the result of their unfaithfulness and they do not deserve God's help (v.11). Nevertheless, God was their only hope and they cried out to him (v.13). God responded, not because of their merit, but because it is the nature of Yahweh to have mercy and so to free the imprisoned (v.16). This may refer to unfortunates in prison because of their lawless acts. It might also be a reference to the exiles planted in foreign countries after defeat by Assyria or Babylon. The Babylonian exile was looked upon as a national imprisonment and the return to Judah the result of God freeing them.

In verses 17-21 the sick are the focus of attention. Again, their plight is due to *their sinful ways* and *their iniquities* and again their plea to Yahweh, their only hope, was answered. Verse 22 suggests that the offering of sacrifice would be an appropriate thanksgiving for God's help, strengthening the assumption that we are reading a psalm used in the liturgy of the temple.

Verses 23-30 turn to the plight of seafarers. Today work at sea is a hazardous occupation. In the psalmist's day, it was even more so. The great and unpredictable power of the sea was the basis of the myths of sea monsters, such as Leviathan, and the characterisation of water and its power as having to be defeated and tamed by God in his acts of creation. The images in this section seem to reveal personal experience of the dramatic and terrifying rise and fall of a ship in high seas (vv. 26, 27). As in creation, only God can tame the sea, and in response to the sailors' prayer he imposes peace and quiet. The refrain in verses 31 and 32 suggests appropriate thanksgiving in public worship.

It is possible that verses 33-43 form a congregational hymn of thanksgiving with reminders of various episodes in the nation's salvation history. The drying up of the Red Sea, the provision of water in the wilderness, the settlement in Canaan and their flourishing life there are alluded to (vv.33-36). They sing of God's care in times of trouble (v.39), his help during foreign wars (v.40) and his care for the weak and needy (v.41).

What the psalm has demonstrated and celebrated is *the steadfast love of Yahweh* and while the wicked will be speechless, the *upright* and the *wise* will understand that the justice and mercy of Yahweh control both nature and human life.

There are clear echoes of verse 30 in the gospel stories of Jesus calming the storm on the Sea of Galilee. Mark (6.45-51) recounts the distress of the disciples, experienced seamen though some of them were. Jesus came to them walking on the water thus demonstrating God's supremacy over the sea, and his presence brought peace and calm. His words, "Peace, be still" take us back to verse 29 of the psalm. In John's account of the same incident (6.16-21), we find that "immediately the boat was at the land to which they were going" which seems to echo the psalm's *he brought them to their desired haven* (v.30).

Verses 23-32 of the psalm are regularly used at Lifeboat Services, annual events in many coastal towns, when the courageous work of those who man lifeboats is acknowledged, and the men and women of the crews are thanked. Along with the hymns, "Eternal Father, strong to save, whose arm doth bind the restless wave" and "Is your anchor sure?" this psalm brings home to the crowds, many of whom are holiday-makers come to enjoy the shallows of a benevolent sea, of the unchanging truth that the sea is dangerous, and that it is God who controls the sea and all nature, and that humans are puny and helpless without the help and mercy of God.

Psalm 108

Verses 1-6 of this psalm are almost identical with verses 7-11 of Psalm 57. Also verses 7-11 of this psalm are almost identical with verses 6-12 of Psalm 60. We need say little about them except that it is generally thought that copying and rewriting of some of the psalms took place during the exile in Babylon or after the return from exile, in order to make them suitable for use in the worship of the rebuilt temple in Jerusalem. What is important for us is that this psalm contains thoughts and words which were valued sufficiently to be repeated in the Psalter.

In verses 1 and 4 the word *steadfast* is used of the worshippers' devotion to God and of God's love for creation. The same English word translates different Hebrew words. God's *steadfast love,* his 'hesed' is his quality alone. Nevertheless for us, using the English version, it brings home the truth that we strive to imitate the goodness of God, and that is best achieved by steady, regular, unspectacular, 'steadfast' devotion. Faithful worship and righteous living are more important than intermittent bursts of emotional devotion. For priests, the daily saying of the Offices of Morning and Evening Prayer is a good example of such steadfastness. For many people, it will be daily Bible study, perhaps with the help of a study guide, or a quiet time in which we wait faithfully for God, listening to him in silent prayer rather than telling him things or asking for things. It is a reminder of Our Lord's teaching in the Parable of the Sower. People are compared to different types of soil and different locations for planting. It is not the ones who quickly believe, nor those who immediately receive the gospel with joy, nor those whose worldly interests are insurmountable who are fruitful. It is those who "hearing the word, hold it fast in an honest and good heart, and bring forth fruit with patience." (Luke 8.15).

Psalm 109

This psalm is often misunderstood. The shocking suggestions made in verses 6-19 are sometimes taken to be the words and hopes of the psalmist, spoken against his enemy. However, if verse 6 followed immediately after *they beset me with words of hate,* (v. 3), it would be clear that these vicious suggestions are in fact the accusers' charges against the psalmist.

This is the lament of a misunderstood and wrongly accused man. He claims, in verses 2-5, that not only are the charges against him false, but that they have been made maliciously and unfairly. He had always acted in his accusers' best interests. Commenting on verse 4 in which the psalmist says *In return for my love they accuse me, even as I make prayer for them,* Dietrich Bonhoeffer makes a challenging case for a Christian response. He writes, "In the New

Testament our enemies are those who harbour hostility against us, not those against whom we cherish hostility, for Jesus refuses to reckon with such a possibility. The Christian must treat his enemy as a brother, and requite his hostility with love. His behaviour must be determined not by the way others treat him, but by the treatment he himself receives from Jesus." He goes on to say "No sacrifice which a lover would make for his beloved is too great for us to make for our enemy." What very challenging words!

We know the psalmist's situation was extremely serious because in verse 16 we learn that he was being accused of causing the death of a poor man. The psalm begins with a plea to God to influence the court by speaking on his behalf, supporting his plea of innocence. Perhaps, his hope is that God will inspire him or those speaking in his defence so that the truth will be revealed and his innocence established.

After recounting in verses 6-19 the appalling charges being brought against him; in verse 20, he begins his counter-attack. He asks that the ill-will that has been directed at him should rebound upon his accusers. In verses 21-25 he tells us that the accusations have made him ill. He is physically weak and in his weakness he has become an object of ridicule. In his plight, he turns to God whose *steadfast love* is exactly the opposite of the malice he is suffering from men (v.21).

He repeats his prayer for God's steadfast love, and asks that his accusers may come to realise that he was not the cause of the poor man's death. It was God, or as might be said today, natural causes, that brought about the death (v.27).

He asks that God's blessing on him may nullify the curses of his accusers, and that they will come to feel the shame and dishonour they ought to feel when they realise how unjust and cruel they have been (vv. 28, 29).

The final two verses suggest that the psalmist's prayer has been answered and that he has been cleared of the charges against him. He will now make a public thanksgiving, praising God who helps the needy, especially people like himself who was almost unjustly condemned to death.

This psalm, particularly verses 22-25, was in the minds of the writers of the Passion narratives in the Gospels. Jesus as he hung dying on the cross was, like the psalmist, a man wrongly accused. The cruel treatment he had received after his arrest in the Garden of Gethsemane on the Thursday evening, culminating in the scourging, had seriously weakened him. The evangelists record the savage taunts of those who passed by. Like those who mocked the psalmist, they knew it all; they knew that he had asked for it. They wagged their heads in their imagined wisdom. (Mark 15.29). We are reminded, both by the psalmist and by the evangelists, that thoughtlessness can so easily turn into cruelty. We read and hear of many examples of cruel, malicious and quite thoughtless accusations being made these days by the instant publication of shallow thoughts on computer chat sites, so-called 'online bullying'. Some such attacks have driven young people to suicide.

Psalm 110

The psalm seems, at first, to consist of a number of separate statements about the role of the king. When we consider it as a piece of liturgy with different voices speaking different parts, and even containing rubrics instructing certain actions it all starts to fall into place and we see it as a part of the celebration of the enthronement of the king of Judah.

Verses 1 and 4 both quote the words of God. These parts would probably be spoken by a priest or prophet. In verse 1 God invites the human king to a place of honour at his right hand where he will receive the submission of his enemies. The king was God's representative and he ruled on behalf of God. With God's support and favour it is inevitable that he will be victorious over any rival kings and nations.

Verse 2 may well be describing a liturgical action, perhaps a procession. The sceptre is displayed as a symbol of the power which God gives to the king. The strange wording of verse 3 seems to suggest that like the freshness of morning dew, so the young king will have all the freshness of youth on his side.

Verse 4 declares that the king is also a priest after the pattern of Melchizedek, who was king of Salem, that is Jerusalem, in the time of Abraham. (Genesis 14.18). This verse about the mysterious priest/king, was used by the author of the Epistle to the Hebrews as a way of speaking about Jesus, the great and eternal High Priest, who offered himself as the final and perfect sacrifice. In practice, throughout the history of Israel the acknowledged priesthood of the Judaean king may well have been a way of balancing the power and influence of the Levitical priesthood.

Verses 5 and 6 look forward to the time when the king, on behalf of God, will bring all nations to judgement. If this is a part of a temple liturgy, it is understandable that it looks forward to the stern judgement of God putting the rulers and people of other nations in their place. A rather more circumspect view of the final judgement is found in Amos. He warns the people of Israel that the judgement will be as stern and painful a time for them as for their enemies. He tells them, "Woe to you who desire the day of the Lord! Why would you have the day of the Lord? It is darkness and not light." And he goes on to describe, amusingly, how inescapable God's judgement of them will be. (Amos 5. 18, 19).

The final verse sounds like a rubric telling the congregation that the king, newly seated on his throne, symbolically at God's right hand, and bearing the sceptre, the symbol of his authority, will now drink from a bowl or fountain as part of the liturgy. Whatever the king drank from developed over the years, in religious imagination, into a wonderful picture of a sacred stream. Ezekiel's vision of a new temple sees the stream, flowing from beneath the altar, feeding fruit-bearing trees in abundance and sweetening even the salt-laden Dead Sea (Ezek. 47). The image is found again, further developed, in the vision of the New Jerusalem in the Book of Revelation. (Revelation 22. 1, 2).

The deep desire for a godly and successful king, pictured as an ideal David, stayed in the mind of the people of Judah. But kings, all too human and fallible, came and went and, inevitably, all failed to live up to the nations hopes. So the hopes were pushed into the future, and the longing became a Messianic hope. In his own good time, God would send his representative who would fulfil all hopes and longings.

Jesus quoted the opening verse of this psalm in controversy in Jerusalem, saying that if David, who was assumed to be the author of the psalm, calls the Messiah-to-come *my Lord,* then he cannot possible be David's son or descendent, because no father would call his own son 'Lord'. It isn't an argument that takes us very far, but it does warn us not to use biblical quotations too literally and separated from their context.

For Christians Jesus is the longed-for ideal king. He showed himself to be both Messiah and 'Lord' by his death and resurrection. And it is as "King of kings and Lord of Lords" (Revelation 19.16) that he fulfils the hopes of this and other psalms. Recognised or not, Christ does reign, and will ultimately judge all people. Believing this, we should look again at what Amos warned about the Day of the Lord and those people who look forward to it, expecting praise and honour. It just might be rather different.

Psalm 111

This psalm, like the two that follow it, begins with the Hebrew word 'Halleluia', translated quite literally as Praise the Lord. The rest of that first verse tells us that the psalmist is part of the worshipping throng of pilgrims in the temple. He joins the company of the upright. The twofold theme of their prayer is the power and the merciful justice of God. God's power is seen in creation, his great and wonderful works, which bring pleasure to those who take the trouble to study them. But just as characteristic of God as his power are his righteousness (v.3), his grace and his mercy (v.4).

God's provision of food for those who worship him and are aware of his awe-inspiring nature possibly refers to the giving of manna during the wilderness wanderings. In those circumstances of need, God unhesitatingly provided for the well-being of his chosen people; he was *mindful of his covenant* (v. 5). It was also part of his covenant promise that he would give them the land he had promised to Abraham, *the heritage of the nations* (v.6).

Verses 7 and 8 bring out the reciprocal nature of the covenant. God is always faithful, and the terms of the covenant are eternal and just. Israel, for its part, must keep its side of the covenant, observing the Law with *faithfulness and uprightness.* Verse 9 again stresses the balance of the Covenant. It enacts *redemption* for his people. This 'buying back' may refer to their being freed from slavery in Egypt, or more generally to God's continuing care for them in many dangerous situations. That redemption requires the nation's obedience to be shown in their observance of the Covenant. God is not to be trifled with. His name, his nature, is holy and terrible, as was seen at the giving of the Covenant at Mount Sinai.

The final verse is a frequently used Wisdom saying. There is a further indication that this might be classed as a Wisdom psalm in the alphabetic order in the arrangement of each half of the verses. The pre-eminent example of this sort of arrangement in a Wisdom psalm is to be found in Psalm 119.

Wisdom is, to a large extent, a practical matter – the keeping of the Covenant. Understanding the Covenant is not a matter of learning and being able to quote: it is a matter of doing what the Law demands, *a good understanding have all those who practise it* (v.10). This final verse reminds Christians of Jesus' saying in the Sermon on the Mount, "Not everyone who says to me, 'Lord, Lord,' shall enter the kingdom of heaven, but he who does the will of my Father who is in heaven." (Matthew 7.21).

It has been suggested that besides verse 1 implying that the person praying is joining the worshippers in the temple, verse 5 might refer to a ritual meal that was part of the festival liturgy. For Christians the verse takes our thoughts to the Eucharist. In the Christian sacred meal, based on what Jesus did at the Last Supper, and on other occasions, we are reminded that Jesus said that the broken bread represented his body which would be broken on the cross, and the poured wine represented his blood which would be poured out for the sins of the world. God gives his people bread – bread in the wilderness of old, and bread in our personal, social, national and international wildernesses of today. As in the psalmist's time, it is our responsibility, as God's covenant partners, to live lives worthy of our calling; *a good understanding have all those who practise it.*

Psalm 112

This psalm is placed very appropriately next to Psalm 111. It takes up the theme of practical righteousness, the Wisdom which is God's gift to those who keep the Covenant. It also shares the feature of the alphabetical arrangement of the halves of the verses.

The theme of blessedness, wonderfully explored and explained in Psalm 1, is taken up. The person who lives according to God's Law is a blessing, not only to himself, but to all those with whom he has dealings. This whole psalm celebrates the joy, the satisfaction and the fruitfulness of a godly life.

The first verse makes the important point that the keeping of the Law is not a matter of steely determination; the good man *delights* in God's commandments. Then we are told that his righteous life will bring benefit to his family and their succeeding generations. There is no shying away from the fact that *wealth and riches* may well be the result of godly living. As in St. Paul's teaching, it is not money, but "the love of money which is the root of all evils." (I Timothy 6.10). Jesus could see that the rich young man who wanted to follow him was not the master of his wealth; the wealth was his master and he was unable to live without it. He could not make the sacrifice needed to become a disciple. (Mark 10. 17-22).

It is interesting that in many translations of this psalm the words 'the Lord' are inserted in the second part of verse 4. Certainly the qualities of graciousness, mercy and righteousness belong to God. But the Hebrew text does not have the word 'the Lord', and it makes perfect sense that the man who delights in God's Law, will come to share and exhibit those fundamentally divine attributes. As was stressed in Psalm 1, the blessed man will bring blessedness to others by the sheer quality of his life. It is as if he brings light into his own life and its rays illuminate the lives of others (v.4). We all know people whose gentle, kind and sunny disposition does exactly this.

Verse 5 then goes on to spell out some of the blessed man's virtues. He is generous and fair in all his doings. He is not immune to the difficulties of life, "the heart-ache and the thousand natural shocks that flesh is heir to." But his faith enables him to live with them and to deal with them. He can stand *firm, trusting in the Lord* (v.7). He need not fear the attacks of those who oppose him or who are jealous of him (v.8).

His use of worldly possessions is exemplary. As the psalms so often remind us, God's concern is always for the poor and the oppressed, the outcasts and the disadvantaged. The godly man of this psalm has cared for the poor, giving *freely* to those in need (v.9). In this he finds himself anticipating the teaching of Jesus, who told those comfortably off and able to invite people to dinner parties, that they should not invite their equally rich friends, but the poor – those who could not return the favour. (Luke 14.12-14).

The psalm ends drawing the contrast between the calm, outward-looking life of the righteous man, and those who do not attempt to live according God's Law. Their concerns are inward-looking, and they are jealous of the honour in which the good man is held, while being unable or unwilling to live as he lives.

Psalm 113

Despite the opening cry of Psalms 111 and 112, this psalm is regarded as the first of the Hallel Psalms. Together they comprise Psalms 113-118. 'Hallel' means 'praise'. The rubric in the Jewish Prayer Book says that these psalms are to be said "on New Moon, on Passover, on Pentecost and on Tabernacles, and on Chanukah."

Christians are accustomed to using the word 'Lord' as a title for God the Father and God the Son. It is not used of the Holy Spirit anything like as frequently. We are liable to forget that 'Lord' is the translation of the divine name, rendered in the Hebrew YHWH. This was the name revealed to Moses at the burning bush meaning "I am who I am," or "I will be who I will be." It is a personal name, revealing, or perhaps concealing, the mysterious, unfathomable nature of God.

Yahweh is no local or tribal god. As verse 4 reminds us he is *high above all nations,* the supreme and only God, and is to be praised through all time and in all places. Verse 3 may mean he is to be praised the world over, from east to west. Or it may mean that he is to be praised from dawn till dusk. Whatever is intended, it means that unending praise is the only proper response to Yahweh's majesty.

Verse 4 reveals that Yahweh is not to be thought of, as is often the case, as being 'in heaven'. He is as far above heaven as he is above the earth; he *looks far down* on them both (v.6). The spacial images are used to emphasise the qualitative difference between the divine and the human, between the creator and the creation. God is not a part of creation which is why we cannot see him. He is the cause, the reason behind everything.

Verse 7 reveals that this incomparable Creator-God is gentle and merciful. He is pictured, rather like the Good Samaritan, stooping down and helping up the poor from the gutter and the needy from the rubbish dump and enabling them to sit among the highest in society. Faith in Yahweh is the guarantee of social mobility. He also cares for the despised woman who cannot bear children, transforming her into the happy mother of a family. The psalmist might have had in mind the great heroines of the faith, Sarah, Rebecca and Hannah, all of whom were unable to bear children until God intervened. It was the case also with Elizabeth, the mother of John the Baptist. This revolutionary vision of God caring for those whom society neglects or despises, is expressed in Hannah's Song in I Samuel 2. 1-10, and is echoed in the New Testament by Mary's Song in Luke 1. 46-55. The message of this psalm, and of those Songs, is that worshippers of Yahweh, Christians as well as Jews, must be ready to be challenged by the God they say they worship, because he might well ask of them things which they may find difficult, upsetting and even distasteful.

Psalm 114

At the Passover meal the youngest present asks a series of questions which begin, "Wherefore is this night distinguished from all other nights?" The answers begin, "Because we were slaves unto Pharaoh in Egypt, and the Eternal, our God, brought us forth thence with a mighty hand and an outstretched arm…" The Passover festival has always been the annual reminder and celebration of liberty, the nation's release from slavery. It is a freedom festival. That is what made the timing of the arrest, trials and death of Jesus so significant. Pontius Pilate knew very well that if there was to be an uprising against Roman rule, it might well happen at Passover because at that time nationalistic fervour was at its height. That is probably why Pilate was in Jerusalem and not in his headquarters in Caesarea at that time. Jesus's opponents also knew full well that to have him accused of being a Messiah would ensure that the Roman authorities would have to take the case seriously. No wonder Pilate asked Jesus, "Are you the king of the Jews?"

It comes as no surprise to learn that this psalm is used as a Passover Hymn. It is made up of four well-balanced parts. The first section, verses 1 and 2 takes us back to the founding of the nation. Their ancestry, beginning with Abraham and the other patriarchs form the foundation for the nation's history which begins with the Exodus. In those days, before the conquest of Canaan and long before Jerusalem and its temple became the sanctuary of God, it was the people themselves who were God's holy dwelling, *his sanctuary* and *his dominion.* The mention of both Israel and Judah suggests that this was written before the destruction of the northern kingdom, Israel, by the Assyrians in 721 B.C.

Verses 3 and 4 record God's mighty acts in both nature and history. The crossing of the Red Sea, the central event of the Exodus (Exodus 14.21-22), and the crossing of the Jordan (Joshua 3.14-17) as the prelude to the conquest of Canaan, both by God's miraculous staying of the waters, are recalled.

In verses 5 and 6 the psalmist seems to mock the sea, the river and the mountains for their powerlessness before the might and will of God. Mountains skip like rams and hills like lambs. The poet knows his sheep, and is aware of the terror extreme weather conditions can cause in a flock. He seems to have in mind the remarkable events when the Law was delivered on Mount Sinai accompanied by quaking and thundering. He seems to enjoy a little ironical humour in these two verses.

But then in the final two verses seriousness returns. He speaks on behalf of God. Of course these things happen. Nature knows its place. What can it do but tremble in the presence of the Creator-God, who can not only stop a river and a sea, but can also bring water out of rock, when his people need sustenance. So the psalm ends on a high note. God is praised, not simply because of his power, but because of his graciousness. The water which he alone can rule and control, he provided for his people to sustain and preserve their life.

Psalm 115

This is a congregational hymn of praise to God. It seems to be part of a festival liturgy in which the nation gives thanks for its safety and its success. The psalm begins by stressing that what has been achieved is not due to the virtue or the cleverness or the hard work of the nation. It is all the result of Yahweh's s*teadfast love and faithfulness.*

While the liturgy celebrates the positive things in Israel's life, other nations notice its weaknesses and failures and perhaps the absence of any physical representation of Yahweh. They therefore question the power and existence of Israel's God and say, *Where is their God?* The traditional answer is that He is in heaven and is supreme over all things. The nations may not acknowledge his reality, but whether they know it or not, he is supreme over them as well.

Then in verses 4-8 there is a wonderfully mocking dismissal of the gods of the nations. They are not gods at all; they are mere puppets. While Yahweh is the creator God, maker of all things in heaven and earth, the gods of the nations are the creation of human craftsmen. They can have no likeness to the real God. They are like humans in shape, with human-seeming eyes, ears, noses, hands, feet and mouths. But they are lifeless and cannot see, hear, smell, walk or talk. Verse 8 comments that those who make such gods and worship them are like their gods; they are as wooden and useless as the gods themselves. Perhaps the psalmist intends those who sing this hymn to reflect that just as the nations are like their gods, so Israel should be like Yahweh, full of loving kindness and faithfulness. Isaiah of Babylon (Isaiah 44. 9-17) speaks with equal scorn of foreign gods, picturing a man cutting down a tree. With part of it he makes a fire and bakes bread or cooks meat, and with the rest of it he makes a god. Isaiah leaves his hearers and readers to acknowledge how ridiculous is such behaviour.

Verses 9-11 may have been said or sung by a priest, calling the nation, its priests and its people to trust in the continuing care Yahweh has for them; *he is their help and their shield.* It is possible that verse 11 refers to converted foreigners in the congregation. They were known as 'God-fearers'. (Acts 10.2). They too are called to trust in Yahweh.

In verses 12 and 13 the congregation responds that God has never neglected his care for them, nor he will in the future. He will continue to bless them all, unimportant and important alike, *both small and great.* (Rather oddly, the New English Bible reverses that order and has "High and low alike." It seems a strange translation and certainly reverses the priority given so often in the psalms to God's prime concern for the poor and needy).

The priest again, in verses 14 and 15, prays for God's blessing on all the congregation and their families, thus ensuring the future of the nation.

The psalm ends with a reminder of human responsibility. God rules in heaven over all things. But he has given responsibility for the earth to humans. This is precisely what the creation stories in Genesis teach. God's first words to the humans he has created are "be fruitful and multiply, and fill the earth and subdue it; and have dominion over the fish of the sea and over the birds of the air and over every living thing that moves upon the earth." (Genesis 1.28). Then in the second creation story we read, "The Lord God took the man and put him in the Garden of Eden to till it and keep it." (Genesis 2.15).

As the population of the world increases, human responsibility for the earth becomes an increasingly important matter. It is very difficult for the ordinary man or woman to decide about matters such as the causes of climate change, or the desirability of growing genetically modified crops. The experts on both sides claim to know the answers. We pray that vested interests are not allowed to warp judgement, and that the human race will fulfil its God-given task. In these matters very often God's work is being done by those who do not even acknowledge his existence.

In verse 17 we find the belief, so often mentioned in the psalms, that after death there could be no contact between God and man. For Christians, this is not the case. The need for this belief to be changed grew as Jewish martyrs in the days of the Maccabees were believed to deserve something more than annihilation. In the *Apostles' Creed* we say that Jesus 'descended into hell'. The usual understanding of this is that he used that opportunity to bring from there the righteous dead. This belief reflects the common human desire that justice should be done. How could we possibly believe in a resurrection life from which Abraham, Moses and all the other saints and prophets of the Old Testament were excluded? The Christian belief is not that immediately after death we 'go to heaven', but rather that we are in the keeping of the Lord until the final judgement when, like Jesus, we shall experience the 'resurrection of the body'.

The psalm ends with the rapturous worshippers promising that they will bless God now and forever.

Psalm 116

This is a passionate prayer of thanksgiving by someone who has been close, either to physical death or to the spiritual death of loss of faith. He is suffering from anxiety and depression (v.3). As we hear his prayer his problems are in the past, and he looks back to the wonderful moment when he realised that his prayers for help had been answered. Now he is overwhelmed by a feeling of undeserved salvation. In the elation he now feels he cannot imagine his gratitude ever lessening; *therefore I will call upon him as long as I live* (v.2).

Verses 5 and 6, like verses in many other psalms, reveal the believer's discovery of the nature of God: *Gracious is the Lord, and righteous; our God is merciful.* He cares for those who cannot care for themselves, here called *the simple.* He might just as easily have labelled himself 'poor' or 'needy'. Because of God's care his troubles are now over. He can put anxiety aside and his soul can return to being at rest. The writer of Psalm 37.7 similarly urged himself to *be still... wait patiently for him; fret not yourself.*

Verse 8 suggests that he had been very ill, at the point of death. In that state he realised that that he was beyond human help; *men are all a vain hope.* Only in God could he find true help (v. 11). This clinging to hope in God had been justified. God had brought him through his troubles.

In verses 12-19 he muses on how he can properly demonstrate his gratitude to God. He seems to be speaking this prayer during an act of public worship in the temple. His mind naturally turns to the traditional ways of worship offered by the temple liturgy. He will drink the ritual *cup of salvation* and make vows in the context of public worship. In both verses 13 and 17 he says he will *call on the name of the Lord.* The name of God, which we render 'the Lord' or 'Yahweh', was profoundly sacred because it revealed, as did all names, the character or the nature of the person who bore it. "Calling on the name of the Lord" in a temple liturgy must have been an act of the deepest significance, never to be undertaken lightly. Using the name of God would invest the vows and the drinking of the cup with the greatest possible seriousness. The psalmist's personal experience of God's grace, righteousness and mercy (v.5) has changed his life and he needs to tell others about his experience. As is often the case, profound experience of God compels a person to want to speak openly and urgently about it.

When Jesus' disciples asked him to teach them to pray, he could not have been more orthodox when he said their prayer should begin, "Our Father, who art in heaven, hallowed be thy name." That the holiness of God's name should be recognised is the first thing we ask.

In the Septuagint, the Greek version of the Hebrew Bible, the divine name, YHWH, is translated Kyrios, Lord. This is usage which English translations of the Old Testament have followed. There are exceptions, notably the Jerusalem Bible, which seeks to get nearer to the original, translating YHWH by 'Yahweh', which is probably as good a guess as can be made.

In the New Testament Jesus is often called 'Lord'. There is ambiguity because sometimes Kyrios means merely 'Sir,' a polite form of address. We see it in the words of the leper in Matthew 8.2; "Lord, if you will you can make me clean," and in the words of the Canaanite women in Matthew who addresses Jesus in this way three times. (Matthew 15.22, 25, 27).

After the resurrection, the early Christians came to use the word 'Lord' in a very different way. In his speech on the Day of Pentecost, Peter said, "Let all the house of Israel therefore know assuredly that God has made him both Lord and Christ, this Jesus whom you crucified." (Acts 2.36). The early Church was beginning to see that Jesus was much more than 'Sir'. He was both Jewish Messiah (Christ) and Lord and Ruler of all. We should remember that this was in a world in which the Roman emperor was regarded as supreme and divine. For Christians, Caesar's lordship was but a pale imitation of the true Lordship of Jesus.

The name *Jesus*, chosen under divine instruction (Luke 1.31), also became regarded as something more than a personal label. The early Christian hymn, composed or quoted by St. Paul, says that Jesus was of divine origin, but emptied himself of his divinity, to become human. He suffered an unjust and cruel death, from which God has raised him, or exalted him, "that at the name of Jesus every knee should bow, in heaven and on earth and under the earth, and every tongue confess that Jesus is Lord, to the glory of God the Father." (Philippians 2. 10, 11). Whoever wrote that hymn seems to have had in mind the words of God in Isaiah 46.23, that "to me every knee shall bow, every tongue shall swear."

The name of Jesus has come to hold much the same sacred significance for Christians as the divine name YHWH did, and does, for Jews. Many hymns have been inspired by this devotion: "At the name of Jesus every knee shall bow" is perhaps the best known. There is also Charles Wesley's "Jesus, the name high over all," and very many modern hymns.

Perhaps because of the hymn in Philippians 2, it is the practice of many Christians to bow their head or discreetly bend the knee, whenever in a hymn, prayer or reading the name of Jesus is used.

Such physical acts, just like the psalmist's drinking of the cup of salvation, reinforce the devotion of the worshipper. On the other hand, using the name of Jesus as an exclamation or profanity is meaningless to the user and hurtful to the believer.

Psalm 117

It is unlikely that the two verses which make up this psalm were intended to stand alone. They may originally have been the conclusion to Psalm 116 or the opening of Psalm 118. Perhaps they are simply part of a temple liturgy, a statement or invitation made by a priest at the beginning of an act of worship, calling the people to join in singing God's praises.

All nations are called to praise Yahweh, the God of Israel. The justification and reason for this universal invitation is that his people, Israel, have experienced God's steadfast love and faithfulness. They speak from experience. What they know and delight in, they want to share with everyone.

We might see a similarity to these two verses in Christian worship. The Eucharistic prayer is prefaced by what has been traditionally called the Sursum Corda (from its Latin original). The celebrant/priest says or sings, "Lift up your hearts." The congregation responds, "We lift them to the Lord. Priest, Let us give thanks to the Lord our God." People, "It is right to give thanks and praise."

This psalm also reminds us that we can too easily get a narrow and exclusive understanding of God's choice of Israel as his special people. This is to forget that they were chosen for responsibility, not privilege, and from the outset their task was to bring all peoples to the worship of the one true God whose characteristics were steadfast love, faithfulness, justice and mercy. As was so often the case, when their understanding and practice of their faith was becoming warped, they were called back by the prophets to living lives true to their status as the chosen nation. Amos says that all people are his chosen ones. Every nation, just like Israel, has its salvation history: "Are you not like the Ethiopians to me, O people of Israel? says the Lord. Did I not bring up Israel from the land of Egypt and the Philistines from Caphthor and the Syrians from Kir?" (Amos 9.7). This is a salutary warning to any person or any group of people who think that they alone have access to God and his truth and love.

Psalm 118

This is reputed to be Martin Luther's favourite psalm. It is a great hymn of thanksgiving with parts for priests, people and king. In the Targums (Aramaic translations or paraphrases of the Hebrew Bible) and in the Talmud it is set to be said or sung antiphonally, and it is certainly helpful if we imagine different voices playing their part. We are also helped by imagining the scene in the temple with procession, music, sacrifice, praise and prayer.

The opening verses, 1-4, and the closing verse 29 enfold the rest of the prayer, stating the theme which is the giving of thanks to God because *his steadfast love endures for ever.* This is the theme too of Psalm 117 and the two verses of that psalm may originally have been the beginning of this psalm.

Verses 1-4 were perhaps sung by a priest. The congregation consists of ordinary citizens (the House of Israel), priests, Levites and other temple functionaries (the House of Aaron) and converts, Gentiles who have come to the worship of Yahweh (God-fearers).

Verse 5 is the beginning of the prayer of the king. Political and military leaders never have untroubled lives, and perhaps that is certainly true in the Middle East. In this psalm the king, knowing that in reality Yahweh is the king of Israel, and that his own authority depends entirely on Yahweh's choice and commission, declares that in times of extreme difficulty he called for God's help and received it (v.5). He knows that God is a better ally than any human power (vv. 6-9). In arresting similes he describes how defeat stared him in the face. But then, through God's help, he was able to triumph (vv.10-13).

In verses 15 and 16 we hear the king quoting the battle-cries and victory shouts which have encouraged and emboldened his soldiers in battle. In the conflict he personally came near to death, but in the end God preserved his life. Therefore in public worship, he will recount how God had saved him (vv.17, 18). This public thanksgiving will be a formal act and he asks for the opening of the gates which bar the way to the sanctuary (v.19). He is answered by the gate-keepers. In this formal and rehearsed liturgy they state that the fact that it is the king demanding entrance is not enough. Only *the righteous* may enter. We are reminded of the stern conditions for entry laid down in Psalm 15. Ritual purity and public status are not even mentioned. The conditions are purely ethical. As he enters, the king offers his personal thanks to God for accepting him (v.21).

With the king and his procession in the sanctuary, the congregation offers thanks. In the recent conflicts, their king seemed to have been deserted or rejected by God, but in the end he was wonderfully vindicated. Perhaps there was a touch of eccentricity about the king. He had seemed like an irregularly shaped stone which the builders at first considered useless, but which turned out to be precisely what was required to complete and strengthen the arch they were building (vv.22, 23). In just that manner was the king the right man for the occasion. Verses 24 and 25 record the people's joy and their plea for God's continuing care.

In verses 26 and 27 we hear the priests' formal welcome of the king and his procession as they approach the altar to offer sacrifice. The king declares his personal thanksgiving and dedicates himself anew to the praise and service of God (v.28).

The psalm ends as it began, praising God because of *his steadfast love which endures for ever.*

This psalm with its image of the rejected stone being revealed as the vital one which completes and makes sense of all the others was quickly adopted by the early Church as an image which could be applied to the death and resurrection of Jesus. Death and apparent defeat were turned into life and victory by God's raising him from the dead. (Mark 12.10,11, I Peter 2.7). According to Matthew's gospel (21.42), Jesus himself used this image when in controversy with the chief priests and elders, who attempted to belittle him by asking by what authority he was acting. To them he looked like a useless stone, an oddity. Significantly, this exchange took place in the temple, the stones of which were legendary for their magnificence (Mark 13.1).

Again, when Peter and John were dragged before the same religious elite, accused of causing trouble by the healing of a crippled man and ascribing their power to do so to the risen Jesus, Peter turned to this psalm, well-known, of course, to his accusers: "be it known to you all, and to all the people of Israel, that by the name of Jesus Christ of Nazareth, whom you crucified, whom God raised from the dead, by him this man is standing before you well. This is the stone which was rejected by you builders, but has become the head of the corner." (Acts. 4.10, 11).

Psalm 119

If you have looked at this psalm you will know that it is very long. If you have read through it you will know that it is repetitious and feels rather artificial. You may also have noticed that at times it seems to use verses from other psalms. It is a psalm that stands out as being different from all others. So, before considering it more closely, let us read what Thomas Traherne said of this psalm in his *Centuries of Meditations,* (3.92). He wrote, "In the 119th psalm, like an enamoured person, and a man ravished in spirit with joy and pleasure, he treateth upon Divine laws, and over and over again maketh mention of their beauty and perfection. By all which we may see what inward life we ought to lead with God in the Temple. And that to be much in the meditation of God's works and laws, to see their excellency, to taste their sweetness, to behold their glory, to admire, rejoice and overflow with praises is to live in Heaven."

It is good to have such a positive and uplifting appreciation of the psalm because it is easy to think that the same thing is being said over and over again and, of course, in a sense it is.

It is an artificial construction, an alphabetical psalm with each of the eight verses of each of the twenty-two sections beginning with the same letter of the Hebrew alphabet. Thus all the verses 1-8 begin with the letter *Aleph,* the first letter of the alphabet, and verses 9-16 all begin with *Beth,* the second letter, and so on.

The psalm is a celebration of God's Law, the Torah. All but two of the verses (verses 121 and 122) use the word Law or a synonym such as *statutes, ordinances, precepts, testimonies, words, promise.* Even in this rather artificial composition, the author rejoices that when he faces life's problems, as in verses 61, 78 and 84-87, he finds reassurance and strength in the Law. The study of the Law is the perfect preparation for someone setting out on life's journey as an adult (v.9ff).

The Law is the revelation of the will of God and we might expect that obedience is required. What we find in this psalm, as in many others, is that obedience is merely the beginning. As in Psalm 1 verse 2, the man who is blessed *delights in the law.* We can almost regard Psalm 19 verses 7-14 as a summary of Psalm 119. Again the law is a *delight,* it makes the simple wise, it makes the heart rejoice, it enlightens the eyes, it is more valuable than gold and sweeter than honey. Psalm 119 is an embellishing and ornamenting of all those qualities of the law. The purpose of the Law is the moral and intellectual perfection of human beings. More than being mere rules of conduct for human life, it was seen also as a way of knowing God.

As Thomas Traherne said, to see God's demands for justice, mercy and compassion as a delight, and to be able to live joyfully complying with those requirements is to 'live in heaven'.

Sadly where there is law there is often legalism, and post-exilic Judaism developed a taste for legalistic disputation. Always it was with the best possible intentions. After all, how can laws which were framed for a pastoral or nomadic society be interpreted for city dwellers? The tradition of interpreting the Law to make it relevant seems to have begun with Ezra 'the scribe'. In Nehemiah 8.4 we read that Ezra read the Law to the people from a pulpit. But it seems not to have been a simple reading; interpretation and explanation were also given. "And they read from the book, from the law of God, clearly; and they gave the sense, so that the people understood the reading." (Neh. 8.8). Expounding the Scriptures and applying them to the daily lives of their hearers is what Christian preachers try to do in their sermons.

The tradition of debate and interpretation in Judaism developed, and sometimes it seems to have been less than helpful. When Jesus was asked what he believed about divorce (Mark 10.2-9), his questioners seem to have been trying to find out whether he agreed with Rabbi Hillel, a liberal, or with Rabbi Shammai whose interpretation was more conservative. Jesus went behind the interpretations to the words of Scripture themselves.

With the destruction of the temple by the Romans in 70 A.D. Judaism lost its altar. The sacrificial rituals could not be carried out and the priesthood became unnecessary. Judaism became a religion of the book or books. The Hebrew Bible never lost its centrality, but over the years much rabbinic discussion came to be written down in the Mishnah and in the two Talmuds, the Palestinian and the Babylonian. Most of the discussions were conducted to help devout Jews to live their lives according to God's Law under ever-changing conditions, though sometimes arguments seemed to be made almost for the sake of argument. In the Mishnah, there is a discussion about the requirement that the 'Shema', the prayer based on Deuteronomy 6.4 should be said at dawn. "When is dawn?" was the question. The answer arrived at was that dawn was when a blue thread could be distinguished from a green one. Perhaps it was that sort of rabbinic discussion that Jesus, who was himself referred to as 'Rabbi', was criticising when he said, "Woe to you, scribes and Pharisees, hypocrites! For you tithe mint and dill and cummin, and have neglected the weightier matters of the law, justice and mercy and faith; these you ought to have done, without neglecting the others." (Matthew 23.23).

It is very easy for people of faith to become legalistic. We can work out what we must do to be loyal to God and our tradition. We must receive Communion every week or every day, according to how we have been brought up. We must read the Bible every day. We must have a quiet time. We must go to confession regularly. We must have had a 'spiritual' experience. We must 'know Jesus personally', and so on. None of those things are bad. All of them are good. But more important, as Jesus said, are justice, mercy and faith. They are the weightier matters of God's Law.

Psalm 120

This is the first of the *Pilgrim Psalms*, (Psalms 120-134). In the Revised Standard Version of the Bible they are entitled 'Psalms of Ascent'. Such a title might suggest that particular psalms were sung at a certain points in the pilgrim procession into the temple, as they climbed the sacred Mount Zion, moving through the courts and into the building and coming closer and closer to the most sacred place, where the ark of God was kept.

It is a pilgrim's prayer of thanksgiving that the slanderous accusations made against him have been proved false. It was in his distress as the victim of lies and liars that he prayed for God's help (vv.1, 2).

Verses 3 and 4 suggest that the charges against him have now been dismissed and he wonders what punishment will be meted out to his accusers. The *sharp arrows* and *glowing coals* sound like vivid metaphors for severe punishment, rather like the medieval pictures of the torments of hell.

In verse 5 we hear the typical lament of a pilgrim. As he approaches the holy city, sees the temple and looks forward to sharing in its inspiring worship, he becomes very aware of how far away is his home, and therefore how unlikely it is that he will be able to make the pilgrimage again. Like the arrows and coals, the places he mentions are probably just examples. He could hardly live in Mesech and among the tents of Kedar. Mesech lies between the Black Sea and the Caspian Sea, whereas Kedar was a nomadic tribe of the Arabian deserts. He probably simply means that he lives a long way from Jerusalem, 'the back of beyond'. It is perhaps rather like the way people in the early 20th century used 'Timbuktoo' to mean any distant and unknown place. Wherever it is that the psalmist lives, it is, for him, a place of conflict. He wants a peaceful life and reconciliation with those who oppose him, but they prefer conflict. This is the situation which had caused the distress mentioned in verse 1, and from which he prays to be delivered. His pilgrimage may be an attempt to bring God's justice into the conflict and therefore resolve it once and for all.

It is one of the benefits of pilgrimage that the pilgrim is freed from the duties and responsibilities of everyday life. Journeying takes time, and time can be used for reflection and prayer. It provides an opportunity to think about one's life and to make plans to improve it. Whether the pilgrim travels alone or in a group these opportunities arise. Many people look back on a pilgrimage as a life-changing and faith-deepening experience.

Psalm 121

Jerusalem is a city of hills and valleys. Mount Moriah was the site of Abraham's attempted sacrifice of Isaac and it was the place chosen by David for the ark when he conquered Jerusalem. It became the Temple Mount or Mount Zion, and there Solomon built the first temple. Nehemiah rebuilt the temple on the same site after the return from the Babylonian exile, and Herod again used the site for his temple building. The Mount of Olives is the other 'mountain' in Jerusalem the name of which is familiar to Christians. It is mentioned as the starting point for Jesus' entry into Jerusalem, close to the villages of Bethany and Bethphage. (Mark 11.1).

In the psalm, after perhaps weeks of travel the weary pilgrim is nearing the end of his journey and in the distance he can see something of the hills and valleys and the great buildings of Jerusalem. As he raises his eyes to the sight, he asks himself if it can be really true that in that city he will find his questions answered and his problems solved (v.1).

He is answered with a resounding affirmative. It may be that from verse 3 the words were spoken by a priest, assuring the pilgrim of God's care. Or perhaps the psalmist answers himself and looks at his life as if from the outside. He is sure that Yahweh, the God of Israel, is indeed the source of all help. He is the creator of all things, so naturally, he has the power to help. Yahweh has not only the power but also the desire to help. God does not sleep; he misses nothing and knows a person's every need. Yahweh's care for the individual is as vigilant as his care for his Covenant people, Israel (vv.3, 4).

In a wonderful image, verse 5 pictures God as a slave, holding a shade over the exhausted traveller as he nears the end of his journey. God walks, unseen, at the pilgrim's right hand, so that he can attend to all his needs. As he walks on in the heat he can reach out his right hand and accept the proffered refreshment. God's care is as close and as thoughtful as that. The shade he carries protects the traveller from the blazing sun. The influence of the moon, believed to pose dangers, will also be kept at bay.

God's care will never cease. It is not limited to the special effort of a pilgrimage. He will watch over the believer's comings and goings, his daily round and common task, for ever.

The psalm breathes a quiet confidence in God. The question asked in verse 1 is answered with a lavish picture of God caring for people who know they do not deserve such care, and can hardly believe that it might be given. Jesus' disciples experienced similar shock and confusion at the Last Supper in the Upper Room when Jesus knelt down like a slave and washed their feet. (John 13.3-15). As we use this psalm we should remember what Jesus said about his act of humility and love. "If I then, your Lord and Teacher, have washed your feet, you also ought to wash one another's feet."

Psalm 122

The pilgrimage is over and the pilgrim looks back, counting the blessings it has brought. This may be the poem of an individual pilgrim or, possibly, a hymn provided in the Temple liturgy for the use of all worshippers as the pilgrimage draws to a close.

I was glad... He looks back to the joy of being invited, perhaps by a group of friends, to go on pilgrimage this year. Perhaps it was his first or his only pilgrimage, and every moment is stored up as a precious memory. He recalls the procession reaching the Temple gates, and no doubt going through the ritual questions and answers which are recorded in Psalm 24.7-10, as well as having questioned himself about his moral standing according to verses 3-6 of that psalm. The whole of Psalm 15 also deals with the ethical requirements for pilgrims.

Verse 3 speaks of Jerusalem as a strong city. This suggests that the psalm was composed either before the destruction of the temple and the city by the armies of Babylon in 586 B.C. or after Nehemiah had restored both temple and the city walls following the return from exile some seventy years later.

The psalmist notes, in verse 4, how pilgrims gather from all the tribes and areas of Israel. This is in accordance with the instructions recorded in Exodus 23.17, "Three times in the year shall all your males appear before the Lord God." Just how practical it was for this to be fulfilled is impossible to say. The festivals associated with harvest and vintage would be a natural period of rest in the working year after the frantic and worrying ingathering of crops.

Verse 5 recalls a scene in the Temple. Of all the glories to be seen there, it was the royal throne, the seat of the current representative of the house of David, which seems to have made the greatest impression on the pilgrim. Of course, if the psalm is a part of the formal Temple liturgy, it might be a way of confirming the Davidic line as God's choice, and boosting it in the minds and mouths of the pilgrims. It might have been a sort of *Jerusalem* or *I vow to thee, my country* for ancient Israel.

'Salem' or 'Shalom' means *peace*. The pilgrim is urged to pray for the city's peace. A reading of the *Books of Kings* quickly reveals that whatever peace the city enjoyed was fragile at best. David determined to capture the city because it was a formidable fortress. (II Samuel 5.6-10). Walls and other defences were built by him and by subsequent rulers. Down the centuries, in Biblical and post-Biblical times, due to its strength and its strategic position it has been a prize constantly sought by foreign powers.

Jesus would be fully aware of the city's fortunes recorded in the Hebrew Scriptures and of what had happened in the time of the Maccabees when the Seleucid king, Antiochus IV, Epiphanes, desecrated the city by building an altar to Zeus on the site of the altar of Yahweh. Jesus seemed to be aware also that another disaster would overtake the city in the life-time of some of his own disciples. "There will not be left here one stone upon another, that will not be thrown down." (Mark 13.2). The promised cataclysm came when Titus, son of the Emperor Vespasian, led the Roman army to destroy the city in 70 A.D.

Since then, and to the present day, the city has been fought over, damaged, desecrated and divided. As Jews try to secure the homeland they were given, almost as a reparation for the Holocaust, and as Palestinians of various faiths try to secure ancestral lands and a homeland of their own, the psalmist's prayer is as relevant as ever it was. "Pray for the peace of Jerusalem."

Psalm 123

Christians in many countries today might feel sympathy with the plight of the psalmist. His poem is the lament of a believer who is being treated with scorn and contempt by unbelievers – perhaps those who worship other gods or the unbelievers of his own nation.

He lifts his gaze beyond the torments and humiliations of his everyday life to Yahweh, *enthroned in the heavens.* His plea is not for revenge or for some exceptional favour, but the request of a trusted servant to his gracious and just master. Verse 2 contains the vivid simile of the servant and his master and the maid and her mistress. There are many examples in the Bible of mutual trust and friendly relations between masters and servants. In Genesis chapter

24 we read of Abraham's entrusting his servant with the crucial task of finding a suitable wife for Isaac. To appreciate the significance of such trust, we have only to remember how important was the very existence of Isaac, the child of promise (Galatians 4.28), whom his father almost sacrificed. God's promises to Abraham depended on the life of this child and his descendants. Or again, we might recall that the experience of Joseph in the service of a high-ranking Egyptian soldier was one of mutual trust and admiration, ruined only by Potiphar's scheming and unfaithful wife. We might assume also that the relationship between Elisha and his servant Gehazi was one of trusting friendship until it was destroyed by greed. (II Kings 5). In the New Testament the story of the centurion approaching Jesus to beg him to heal his boy servant shows a kindness and concern we do not readily expect from a soldier of an occupying army.

In verse 1 of the psalm the verb is in the singular; the psalmist speaks for himself. In verse 2 his thoughts and prayers have widened, embracing all the faithful. He pictures himself and his fellow-believers as the favoured servants and maids of the perfect master. There is no question of equality; Yahweh is the master. But he is known to be gracious and concerned for the well-being of his servants. Their service for him is not an arduous task or burden but a delight, and they know that in their need they can depend on his help.

It is only after the declaration of trust in God's readiness to help that the problems are mentioned. He and his friends have been ridiculed and scorned for their belief and presumably for living according to their beliefs.

For centuries, the Western world regarded itself as Christian. There have been religious wars, terrible persecutions and inhuman punishments. But in many ways those wars and atrocities were a measure of the respect, and certainly of the fear, with which the persecuted were regarded. Contempt was generally reserved for small, exclusive groups of believers. The Society of Friends was nicknamed 'The Quakers', a title which they now wear with pride. Mormons, Jehovah's Witnesses, Seventh Day Adventists and other small groups have come in for their share of mockery.

In recent decades in this country, the mocking of the Christian faith and practice has become widespread, the attitudes gaining some respectability from their association with high profile militant humanists and atheists. However, as Rupert Shortt points out in his book *Christianophobia*, these slights and criticisms are not of the same magnitude as the appalling persecutions of Christians in other parts of the world.

Let us return to the vivid picture of the worshipper as the servant of God. In the Scriptures servanthood is not demeaning. The Servant of Yahweh, spoken of by Isaiah of Babylon (Isaiah 42.1-4 and 44.1-5) is an honoured title which Jesus seems to have accepted as the pattern for his Messiahship. Certainly he taught his disciples that service was honourable and the readiness to serve a requirement for entry into the kingdom of God. (Mark 9.35). He said that he himself came to serve. (Mark 10.45). At the Last Supper he put his teaching into practice by washing his disciples' feet. (John 13.3-11). When the apostles found that their Christ-inspired practice of serving their fellow believers at table prevented their teaching the faith, it was decided to appoint seven assistants "to serve tables". (Acts 6.2). The qualities of these men soon led to their taking on more responsible tasks. Traditionally they have been called the Seven Deacons or Servants.

The Diaconate is the first order of the ordained ministry in the Anglican Church. Though there are some perpetual deacons, a person is usually a deacon for a year. It is a time of learning and, as its name suggests, service. The other two orders are the priesthood and the episcopate. Whatever jobs are done by the ordained ministry – parish work, chaplaincies in hospitals, schools and prisons, being a residential canon at a cathedral, being an archdeacon, a diocesan bishop or an archbishop – all are done by men and women in one of the three orders. A common and most valuable piece of advice which should be remembered by all who are ordained is, "Once a deacon, always a deacon." However seemingly exalted or important their rank or position might be, those ordained must always remember that they are servants of God and of all with whom they have dealings.

Today young people thinking about a career no longer think in terms of 'going into service', and the 'downstairs' of large houses is more likely to contain the children's table tennis table or dad's snooker table than a butler, housekeeper, cook and various kitchen maids. In spite of this, in our society most people are servants. Those who work in service, in hotels, restaurants, in the travel industry, retail sales and in many other ways – all are servants. It is important that their work should never be demeaning. In a very real sense anyone employed and paid by another is a servant, whether in a factory, on the land, in a firm of lawyers or accountants, in the media or in a city bank. Masters and mistresses are a much smaller group.

They bear great responsibilities. St. Paul wrote wise words about their approach to life: "Masters, treat your slaves justly and fairly, knowing that you also have a Master in heaven." (Colossians 4.1). The topic is dealt with in slightly more detail in Ephesians 6.5-9).

Christians should all be prepared to follow Our Lord's teaching and example. Whatever our position in society we must be ready to be servants to each other – in our families, with our friends, in church, at work and in all our relationships.

Psalm 124

Verse 1 sounds rather like the announcement of a hymn in a Christian act of worship: "We shall now sing *If it had not been the Lord who was on our side…*" Then, in verse 2, the congregation, *Israel,* joins in the singing of the psalm.

It recalls, mainly in general terms, God's constant support of the nation. The advantage of using general terms like *when men rose up against us,* gives each worshipper the opportunity to clothe the words with episodes from the nation's salvation history, or from their own experiences which mean a great deal to them, and speak to them of God's care.

Verses 2 and 3 look back to an unnamed but memorable act of salvation by God. The dominance which the escape from Egypt had in the nation's collective memory suggests that it is the flight from Egypt, pursued by Pharaoh's chariots, which might be the particular occasion the psalmist has in mind. Also the *flood, torrent* and *raging waters* of verses 4 and 5 seem to recall the crossing of the Red Sea, though the later crossing of the Jordan (Joshua 3 and 4) might also be a possibility. Later conflicts as they moved towards, and then into, the Promised Land, were against smaller and less powerful foes – *Sihon, king of the Amorites, and Og, king of Bashan,* as Psalm 135.11 recalls.

God is thanked for having saved the nation on the occasions when the people felt as if they were being hunted by a predator (v. 6). Their freedom is all the more miraculous because they were trapped, caught like a bird in a snare. This again sounds like the deliverance at the Red Sea when they were trapped between the sea and Pharaoh's army. (Exodus 14). By God's power the trap was broken and they escaped like a bird set free.

The final verse reminds the worshippers that as well as being the God of history, Yahweh is also the creator of all things.

Down the centuries the recalling and retelling of the nation's salvation history has been a characteristic of Judaism. There is an obligation to pass on the stories of God's saving acts to the next generation. Deuteronomy 4.9 says, "Take heed, and keep your soul diligently, lest you forget the things which your eyes have seen, and lest they depart from your heart all the days of your life; make them known to your children and your children's children." In obedience to this command the words of Deuteronomy 6. 20-25 are still repeated at every Passover Meal.

Christians recall their own salvation history in a similar way at festivals. The events of the life, death and resurrection of Jesus and the formative days of the early Church are recalled and celebrated at the great fasts and festivals from Advent to Pentecost. Like Israel, we look back to the foundation events of our faith, reassuring ourselves that by becoming one of us in the incarnation, God has shown himself to be unmistakably *on our side*. Like the Israelites of old and present day Jews, we know that because of what God has done in the past we can trust him in the present and in the future.

Psalm 125

Believers are compared to Mount Zion, the rock on which the temple was built. The significance of the Rock was commented on in the reflections on Psalm 27. We might say that the comparison should be the other way round. God's choice of Israel as his Covenant People pre-dated the choice of Jerusalem as the place of God's earthly dwelling. Both people and city have been chosen by Yahweh, and the choice stands for ever regardless of failures or triumphs, sins or faithfulness, defeats or victories.

David chose Jerusalem as his capital city, and it was through David's line that God determined the Covenant should be honoured. God spoke to Nathan, David's court prophet: "Go and tell my servant David, Thus says the Lord...When your days are fulfilled and you lie down with your fathers, I will raise up your offspring after you...and I will establish his kingdom. He shall build a house for my name, and I will establish the throne of his kingdom for ever. I will be his father and he shall be my son." (II Samuel 7. 5, 12-14). The special relationship with the house of David is proclaimed in Psalm 89: *I have made a covenant with my chosen one, I have sworn to David my servant: I will establish your descendants for ever, and build your throne for all generations.*

For Christians that promise is still being fulfilled through Jesus, 'born of David's line', and through the Church which he founded.

Verse 2 reminds us that this is a Pilgrim Psalm. It recalls the excitement felt by pilgrims as the first enthralling view of the hills and great buildings of the city comes into sight. We saw this also in the question with which Psalm 121 begins.

The first part of verse 3 states that because Jerusalem is God's chosen city, foreign, non-Davidic dynasties will never rule there. History proved this to be a false hope. Jeremiah saw that such hopes were futile if the people of Jerusalem did not live in accordance with the Covenant promises. Without righteous living, to depend for safety on God's presence in the temple was mere superstition. (Jeremiah 7.1-7).

The second part of verse 3 acknowledges that dangers exist. The lure of the agricultural gods of Canaan were a constant temptation to farming communities. The immoral cults of some foreign gods also had their attractions.

The final two verses ask God to act justly, blessing the righteous. As for the wicked, they will go to their just fate. No hope is expressed that they might change their ways. Unlike Jonah (4.1, 2), the psalmist has no shrewd suspicion that people will change and God will forgive. For Christians the life, death and resurrection of one 'born of David's line' gives hope even for those who do not acknowledge him. The closing verse reiterates and expands the vital prayer of Psalm 122 which we all share: "Peace be in Israel."

Psalm 126

The psalm consists of two parts, a beautiful song of thanksgiving, followed by a prayer that the nation's joy will continue.

Pilgrims to the Second Temple, restored by Nehemiah after the return from the Babylonian exile, ponder the wonder of the rebuilding of the temple and city, and the very fact that God has so ordered the events of history that the rulers of Persia had allowed and, indeed, encouraged the Return. Such events had been prophesied by Second Isaiah, who was living with the Jews in exile (Isaiah 45.1). The books of Ezra and Nehemiah record the events of the return and the restoration of buildings and religious and community life in the city.

The pilgrims stand in a city being transformed from ruin to something like its old beauty, and they can scarcely believe that it has happened: it seems almost like a dream (v.1). They look around and see a happy, noisy, bustling people. So remarkable is the change in the nation's fortunes that even other nations have to admit that Israel's God, Yahweh, has indeed *done great things*, and that is why they can celebrate (v.3).

In verse 4 the psalm becomes a prayer that the happiness they currently enjoy will be sustained. The elation and prosperity of the nation is like the apparently miraculous restoration of the seasonal wadis; dry and barren for much of the year, but in the rains turned into torrents of fresh water.

After the return from exile farmers had to sow in fields that had been ravaged by war and neglected by settlers. They sowed, but with little optimism. The prayer of the psalmist is that the harvest will be plentiful, a cause for rejoicing (vv.5, 6). Farming in a former battlefield is what many farmers in Belgium and France continue to do. Even today, after a hundred years, in the fields around Ypres shells and bombs are regularly turned up by the plough. They are placed in slots in the concrete masts carrying power cables and telephone wires where they lie safely until they are collected and properly disposed of.

The psalm reminds us how important are the giving of thanks and the cherishing of hope. It used to be commonplace for people to be told, "Count your blessings." In modern society a person is more likely to be told "Claim your rights." It is a very useful exercise to look back over a day, a week, a year, a life-time, and recall the many things for which we can be thankful. It may be the blessing of a happy marriage, a loving family, a fulfilling job, the gift of friendship, a special talent, the ability to listen to people, the gift of kindness, of caring for the sick – and many others. It is good to think how blessed we have been, and to thank God for it.

Hope is other thing the psalm teaches. Even when things do not look promising, with a loving God in control, we should not lose hope, we should not despair. The psalmist's *sowing in tears* and *reaping in joy* can be a metaphor for the fact that, as the crucifixion of Jesus demonstrated, God can bring transforming good out the worst of human suffering.

Psalm 127

Like the previous psalm, this also consists of two parts which link together very tightly. Along with the common title of psalms 120-134, *A Psalm of Ascents*, or *A Pilgrim Psalm*, this has the added words, *Of Solomon*.

Verse 1 begins to explain the added words. Solomon was legendary as a builder in the history of Israel. Famously, he built the temple. The process of building took seven years. It is interesting to note that he spent rather longer, thirteen years, building his own palace, which was larger than the temple. Perhaps the work on

God's house was considered more urgent! The psalm could also be referring to the restored temple, rebuilt after the return from the Babylonian exile. As this is a hymn for pilgrims to sing or hear, it seems that they are being asked to look around them. They see the magnificent buildings which look as if they will stand for ever. Jesus' disciples had identical feelings when they gazed on the colossal stones of Herod's temple. (Mark 13.2). They too looked immoveable, but Jesus told them that all would be thrown down— and much was thrown down by the Roman army in 70 A.D. Some of the vast stones of Herod's temple can still be seen; cut with wonderful precision and fitting perfectly together without mortar.

Whether he was thinking of the temple of Solomon or the rebuilt temple, the psalmist no doubt had in mind that though the word 'house' can certainly mean a physical structure, it can equally well mean a dynasty. The 'House of David' was doomed to failure if it did not stand firmly, with God as its foundation.

A further meaning the psalmist may have had in mind was the ephemeral nature of all human constructions. All human strivings and achievements, however wonderful, cannot prosper and last without the blessing of God.

Verse 2 drives home the message that we often think that everything depends on us, on our talent and our hard work. We 'burn the candle at both ends' because we think our contribution is so important. We give ourselves a role which is totally out of proportion. God does not want us to feel burdened. He gives rest as well as work. In the Sermon on the Mount Jesus told his disciples not to be anxious, losing sleep over tomorrow's challenges. "Do not be anxious about tomorrow, for tomorrow will be anxious for itself. Let the day's own troubles be sufficient for the day." (Matthew 6.34).

While making that point we might remind ourselves that the primacy of God in any endeavour does not relieve us of our responsibility. Often, answering our prayer, God will want to use our hands to do his healing or supporting work. This thought is built into the Mothers' Union Prayer, which ends, "empowered by your Spirit, may we be united in prayer and worship, and in love and service reach out as your hands across the world."

That prayer is a very appropriate point at which to turn to the second part of the psalm. Verses 3-5 are a celebration of family life. The psalmist speaks of *sons* when we would speak of 'children'. The social conditions of the time placed male offspring above female. Sadly that is still the case in some religious and social settings today. The alarming differences in numbers of requests for abortions for male and female foetuses in some communities show that such thinking has not been abandoned.

If children are a gift from God or *a reward* as verse 3 states, it is hard to justify any abortion. Many people who were born disabled lead happy and fulfilled lives, calling out love from their families and friends, and often returning it with interest. Of course, each case has to be considered individually, but the factors taken into consideration should be ethical as well as medical and social.

The psalmist refers to sons as *arrows* in their father's *quiver*. They would be his defence when he grew old and unable to look after himself. They are also his pride and he can boast of them when he is in public among his contemporaries. That is still a common fatherly activity, terribly embarrassing to the sons!

This psalm makes us ponder the value of family life. In our society, many children have to grow up without the stability of what Christians consider a normal family life, of support, discipline and learning the art of living helpfully and happily with others. Worrying statistics suggest that in Britain today more children are born out of wedlock than within it. Again studies show that those children have reduced chances in life. They are less likely to be successful at school and more likely to be involved in crime. For Christians the weakening of family life is a matter of serious concern. The Mothers' Union continues its quiet, but vastly important work, trying to promote and support marriage and family life across the world.

Psalm 128

There is an air of contentment about this psalm; life for the psalmist seems good. It continues the theme of Psalm 127 that the greatest blessing anyone can enjoy is a happy family life. In addition, this psalm teaches that work is a blessing rather than a burden; there is happiness in enjoying the fruits of one's labours.

Verse 1 recalls so many other psalms, Psalm 1 in particular, in seeking to define true blessedness. Being aware of the total otherness of God, the vast gulf between the divine and the human, fills one with awe, the fear of the Lord. Once that is understood and accepted everything else follows naturally.

Work, which in the second creation story seems to be a curse on humankind (Genesis 3.17-19), is seen here as a blessing with its own satisfaction and rewards. It is a way of ensuring the continuance of the family in the future.

As in Psalm 127 children are regarded as a blessing. The background to this stress on the importance of children is not only that they were an economic advantage or necessity, with each extra pair of hands valuable in the support of the family. Also in the national religious memory was the anxiety caused by childlessness for Abraham and Sarah, Isaac and Rebekah, Elkanah and Hannah. Only by God's will were children born to them. They were his gift and they proved themselves to be of crucial importance in the fulfilling of God's plans for Israel, and through Israel for the world.

Here the child-bearing wife is compared to a fruitful olive tree, the fruits vital and satisfying a whole variety of needs. A man with such a wife and family is truly blessed (vv.3, 4).

The final two verses sound like a formal priestly blessing. Perhaps the psalm was used towards the conclusion of a pilgrim liturgy. The mention of *Zion* and *Jerusalem* strongly suggest this. These closing words could be the pronouncing of God's blessing on the pilgrims as they prepare to leave the holy city and return to their homes, their families and their everyday working lives. The importance of children is stressed again in verse 6, a prayer that the pilgrims will live to see their grandchildren. The final prayer, as in Psalm 125, is *Peace be upon Israel.*

The psalm paints a picture of ideal family life and working life. Some people will remember the advertisements for food or furniture seen in the early days of television, the 1950s and 1960s. The family is in a cosy home, with father in pullover or cardigan, probably smoking a pipe. Mother, pretty and aproned, offering delectable food, and two neat and very clean children, one male and one female – the ideal family. Of course, as in the psalm, it was an idealised family. Though patterns of family life have changed in half a century, the truth that a stable, loving family is best for children in all sorts of ways, has not changed.

What about work? Patterns of work have also changed a great deal since the psalmist wrote. In our society, ever since the Industrial Revolution, which created vast numbers of repetitive jobs, many people have found their employment not a matter of fulfilment and enjoyment, but simply something they do to pay the bills. Office, factory or field can be wearisome labour. Charlie Chaplin, in his film 'Modern Times' showed with piercing wit and accuracy how dehumanising some forms of work can be. Christians must be aware of this and be troubled by it. We believe in a God whose main concern is always with the weak and down-trodden, with those who cannot always care for themselves. So Churches must ponder and work to make people's lives fruitful and fulfilling. It has always been a strength of the Churches that they produce people who are willing to give their time and talents by belonging to and often leading organisations in their local areas and communities. Uniformed organisations for children are a tradition in many churches. Locally Christians will generally have the talents to engage and encourage people in the arts, music, drama. Traditionally the men of Lancashire and Yorkshire whose days were spent in hard and often repetitive work down the pit or in cotton or woollen mills, found release and recreation in cricket and football clubs set up by local churches. It is important that Christians ask themselves what the Churches can do today to offer relaxation, stimulation and fellowship to those whose work is unfulfilling.

Psalm 129

Our general practice, in both public worship and private prayer, is to read a psalm as a whole, as if it were the utterance of an individual. Doing that we try to make the words relevant to our own life and faith. However, many psalms, and this is certainly one of them, yield a more fruitful meaning if we remember that they were composed for use in a liturgical setting, in an act of public worship for pilgrims in the temple.

Verse 1 was probably spoken by a priest or some other temple official. *Let Israel now say,* seems to be an announcement, "We shall now sing *Sorely have they afflicted me from my youth.*" In verses 2, 3 and 4 the pilgrims then take up the song.

As was customary at festivals, the nation's salvation history was recounted. (See Psalm 78.1-7). So packed was it with incident and meaning that it would necessarily be recalled in small portions. This hymn recalls times of oppression and suffering. The nation still bears the scars of its hard times (v.3), but despite all, they have survived (v.2). That survival is because God has kept his promises; he is *righteous.*

The psalm then becomes a denunciation, even a curse, on those who have opposed or hindered Israel in the fulfilment of its God-given task. They are described as *all who hate Zion.* Rather than foreign nations, this sounds more like the dissident kingdom of Israel, which split off from Judah after the death of Solomon. They claimed to be worshippers of Yahweh and their rulers created new sanctuaries, like the one at Bethel, so that their people would not feel that they had to return to Zion (Jerusalem) to keep the pilgrim festivals. If the people of the northern kingdom were not, their leaders certainly were, among those *who hate Zion*. The worshippers' prayer is that the apostates' influence would be short-lived and judged as worthless.

The first half of verse 8 may be the end of the curse on Judah's enemies, the withholding of the expected blessing. The second half of the verse sounds like a final, formal blessing on departing pilgrims. It would be spoken by a priest – perhaps the same person who announced the psalm in verse 1.

There is something refreshingly honest about plain speaking regarding one's enemies or opponents. The prayer is that they will be prevented from promoting their hatred of Jerusalem. There is no suggestion that the people of Judah should take matters into their own hands, meting out the punishment which they consider appropriate. The details are left to God.

In a world in which wars, somewhere, never cease, and in which many nations have weapons of cataclysmic power, the Church has understandably felt embarrassed by some of its more militant-sounding hymns and prayers. Those who, as children, regularly sang, "Onward, Christians soldiers…" rarely have the opportunity today. Hymns which use the metaphor of war to describe the Christian's unremitting fight against evil are now rarely used, despite the magnificent tunes to which many of them are set. In some modern hymn books words with a possibly militant meaning are edited out. It is a sad and rather arrogant assumption by editors that Christian worshippers do not know the difference between using military metaphors, as St. Paul did, and the promotion of violence and hatred. At Baptism we enlist in Christ's army, the army of the Prince of Peace. We are marked with our common badge, the sign of the cross, which we wear, invisibly, for ever. Any Christian who does not feel engaged in a battle, within and without, against "sin, the world and the devil" hasn't really started living the Christian life.

Psalm 130

His writings reveal that Martin Luther was deeply aware of his own and all peoples' vulnerability to temptation; how ready we are to sin. This psalm was one of his favourites. As well as being a Pilgrim Psalm it is also counted as the 6th of the Penitential Psalms. Doubtless Luther found in it the assurance that God's power and readiness to forgive was far greater than human sinfulness. St. Augustine was another man whose writings reveal his fierce battle against his own weaknesses. It is said that he wrote this psalm on the walls of his cell when he was dying.

The psalmist cries to God *out of the depths.* What are the depths? Depths of guilt at his own sinfulness? Depths of despair that he cannot be strong and resist temptation? They may be the depths of physical pain or spiritual conflict. His own resources having failed him, he turns to God, pleading for a hearing (vv.1, 2).

In verse 3 he admits that his guilt is such that he does not deserve forgiveness, but he holds to his belief that it is God's nature to forgive; "c'est son metier," as the Empress Catherine the Great is reported to have said. The psalmist is filled with awe, *fear,* when he considers the amazing grace of God's constant readiness to forgive. It demonstrates the qualitative difference between the human and the divine. When one is confronted with this difference – that God is 'wholly other'– humans can only react like Abraham on whom the knowledge of God's presence produced "a dread and a great darkness." (Genesis 15.12), or like Moses at the Burning Bush, when "Moses hid his face, for he was afraid to look upon God." (Exodus 3.6).

Feeling his unworthiness and having confessed his sinfulness, the psalmist waits for God's response. His impatient longing for a sign of forgiveness is compared to soldiers on guard duty through the night, longing for the dawn. He is impatient, but knows that forgiveness, like the light of a new day, never fails to come. Confident of his own state of having been forgiven the psalmist calls on his fellow-worshippers, *Israel,* to share his faith that God's steadfast love and forgiveness is *plenteous,* more than enough to cover all human sinfulness. The closing verse is a further statement that God's love for Israel will always outweigh the nation's sins.

This psalm is a reminder that Jesus did not found a new religion. As the longed-for Messiah, the incarnate Son of God, he fulfilled, continued and widened God's covenant with Israel. He did not reveal a different God, but showed that the awe-inspiring God of the Old Testament was also our loving Father. The God he addressed as 'Abba' is the God of Abraham, Isaac and Jacob, the God of Moses, Samuel and Elijah, of Isaiah, Amos and Nehemiah. As Kenneth Leech wrote, "The Christian God is first of all a Jewish God." This psalm reminds us that Yahweh certainly evokes awe; as Psalm 111.9 says, *Holy and terrible is his name.* But in the blaze of forgiveness revealed in the life and death of Jesus, we sometimes forget that the awesome Yahweh was always characterised by mercy and loving-kindness: "The Lord, the Lord, a God merciful and gracious, slow to anger and abounding in steadfast love and faithfulness…" (Exodus 4.6).

People who try to live good lives are apt to be very aware of their failures; they can be burdened by their sins. Jesus shifted the emphasis, teaching by word and deed that God in indeed just and awe-inspiring, but that above all he is forgiving. This was expressed succinctly by John Taylor: "We are citizens of a forgiven universe."

Psalm 131

This is the prayer of someone who has entered calm waters after a stormy and turbulent life of striving. We do not know if his striving was for power or wealth or position or popularity. Nor do we know if he achieved any of those things. Whether he did or not, he has now realised how empty such trophies are. He has come to realise the truth which Jesus expressed in his paradoxical sayings about the first and the last. The psalmist may also have experienced a foretaste of the kingdom which is open to the child-like (Mark 10.13), and in which the great must be ready to serve (Mark 10.44).

He is now content to think about lesser matters. Perhaps he has discovered the beauty of God's creation, the uncountable wealth that true friendship creates, the importance of little things and little people. He did not find security and peace through his own strivings, but finds them now in total dependence on God and his loving care. He feels like a child, blissfully happy, totally unaware of any danger because he rests securely on his mother's breast.

What he has experienced in his personal life he believes is possible for everyone, and he calls the congregation, *Israel,* to share his hope.

Is there then no place for striving? It seems to be natural, fitting and beneficial for young people to engage in athletic activity, in sporting competitions. It seems natural that children compete and compare their school marks with each other. We can assume that it is natural and indeed, enjoyable, because of the readiness of adults with all sorts of education, background and talents to engage in pub quizzes or television quiz shows as well as in sporting contests. It seems fitting, therefore, that God-given gifts of all kinds – physical, intellectual, artistic and moral – should be exercised and developed. Indeed, Jesus' parable of the talents seems to point to just that conclusion. (Luke 19. 11-17). Those with great gifts of any kind should develop them and use them for the good of all. Striving to do things well is admirable. But the readiness to cheat, to take unfair advantage and to glory in success is as wrong in life as it is in sport.

This psalm seems to be the relieved prayer of one who has left behind the competition and bustle of life. Such a peaceful period in later life is a great blessing, but it does not come to everyone. Those, like the psalmist, lucky enough to enjoy it are able to *be still before the Lord* (Psalm 37.7), but stillness and quietness in the presence of God are yet more important for those still engaged in the bustle and competition of life.

Psalm 132

This Pilgrim Psalm seems to be part of a liturgy used at the Festival of the Dedication of the Temple, in which the sacred ark was carried in procession and placed in its traditional resting place "beneath the cherubim." The major theme of the psalm is God's choosing of David and his descendants to exercise divine rule on earth. Very closely interwoven with the theme of the Davidic dynasty is that of God's choice of Jerusalem as his earthly dwelling place.

It is significant that verses 8-10 of the psalm appear, with very slight variations, in 2 Chronicles 6, verses 41 and 42, as the conclusion of Solomon's prayer at the dedication of the temple which had been built under his orders.

As they sing verses 1-5 the worshippers are reminded that though Solomon built the temple, his father David had striven hard and long to make it possible. *The hardships he endured* would include his years as a reluctant rebel against King Saul, his securing Jerusalem as his citadel (2 Samuel 5. 6-10), and his determination to protect the ark by finding a safe place for its keeping. (2 Sam. 5. 12-16). 2 Samuel chapter 7 tells the story of David's desire to build a 'house' for God, and his being told that not he, but his son, would be the one to accomplish it.

Verse 6, *the fields of Jaar* probably refers to the account in 1 Samuel 7.1 of the ark being 'lodged' at Kireath-jearim for twenty years.

The pilgrims encourage one another to enter the temple and to worship in God's presence, which was guaranteed by the sight of the ark (v.7). Many Christian hymns use this sort of mutual encouragement: "Come, let us join our cheerful songs with angels round the throne…", "Come ye faithful, raise the anthem," and many more.

Verse 8 would be spoken or sung as the ark moved in procession to its resting place. Verse 9 prays that the priests and other temple officials who are officiating may lead lives worthy of their calling.

The appropriateness of this verse has caused it to be included in the Lesser Litany in the Offices of Morning and Evening Prayer: in the Prayer Book version, "Endue thy ministers with righteousness; and make thy chosen people joyful." Verse 10 seems to be the climax of all the petitions, being a prayer for the king, David's successor, God's anointed.

God's promise to David that his desire to build a house for God was displaced by God's promise to build a 'house', a dynasty, for David. (2 Sam. 7.16). That house would last for ever if only his successors observe the Covenant (vv.11, 12).

The rest of the psalm, while never leaving the theme of the Davidic house, dwells on the choice of Zion/Jerusalem. David's choice of the city as his capital was guided and confirmed by God, who *desired it for his habitation* (v.13).

God's words in verses 11-18 were probably spoken by a priest. They promise that God will make Jerusalem (and that would be understood to include the surrounding towns and countryside) a prosperous and compassionate society in which the poor would not lack food (v.15). The citizens, priests and people, *her saints,* will be aware of God's care for them and will therefore be filled with joy. The royal house will be strong and its future secure, (*the horn* being a symbol of power), and the king will rule by the guiding light of God's law. (See Psalm 119, verse 105). The king's enemies will be put to shame, making the rule of the righteous king of Judah shine all the more brightly.

It is important to note that in this rather formal liturgical psalm God's care for ordinary people and the poor in particular, is mentioned before his concern for the priests and other 'religious' people, the *saints.* Christianity shares this view of spiritual priorities. Just as this psalm (and many others) talk of the setting up of God's rule on earth through the righteous reign of the house of David, so Jesus' first words in St. Mark's gospel are "The time is fulfilled and the kingdom of God is at hand; repent and believe in the gospel." (Mark 1.15). The kingdom or reign of God is the keynote of Jesus' preaching. So for Christians, spirituality is not simply a private matter between each individual believer and God. We are the Body of Christ, and Christianity is a corporate religion because it seeks to transform society. It is an incarnational religion and therefore people's bodies as well as their souls are important. We must always seek to care for the poor, whatever their poverty might be – economic, educational, cultural or spiritual – before we can be comfortable in our own feelings of devotion.

Psalm 133

The theme of the blessedness of family life, celebrated in Psalms 127 and 128, is continued here. Unity in a family was important in nomadic and farming communities for safety and for the management of flocks and herds. Cooperation and understanding were vital if the work was to be done properly. Also, for most of the period of the Old Testament, it was believed that life ceased completely at death. There was no individual future life or resurrection to be hoped for. Therefore the only way a person's life could be continued was in their children and grandchildren. We might note that Genesis chapter 13 records the consequences of disagreement between the herdsmen of Abraham and those of his kinsman Lot. It was decided that the survival of both parts of the clan could only be assured by the allocation of different grazing areas.

Verse 1 seems to be very aware of famous examples of bad relationships between brothers. The most famous, of course, was Cain and Abel, but there was also Jacob's fierce rivalry with his elder brother Esau. That personal antagonism was seen as the origin of the traditional and mutual hatred between Israel and Edom (Genesis 27). Joseph's differences with his brothers are the theme of one of the most accomplished narratives in the Old Testament (Genesis 37-48).

Those famous stories serve to show that relationships which are *good and pleasant* within families are not always the rule. When they do happen they are the result of God's blessing and generosity. The lavishness of God's love in creating harmonious families is compared to the anointing of Aaron as priest. (Leviticus 8.10). The oil poured on his head is so plentiful that it flows down his face, onto his beard and thence onto his robes. Oil itself, with all its uses, is a sign of God's blessing. Here it spills over, *running down,* like God's love which, poured into people, overflows so that they can love others. All human love is the result of the overflowing of God's love. The psalmist then compares family love to an early morning on a beautiful day on a mountainside. The dew still lies on the grass, and all is fresh and lovely before the fierce sun dries the dew and burns the grass. The oil runs down and the dew falls, just as God's love overflows to humans, enabling brothers to love one another.

As this is a Pilgrim Psalm we hear that Zion/Jerusalem is the source of God's blessing. From Zion it overflows on to the pilgrims and through them to all Israel.

What a wonderful psalm this is for family celebrations. It is not surprising that it is loved by monastic communities, male and female, for it can be heard to speak of a brotherhood and sisterhood that is wider and sometimes deeper than a blood relationship.

It can also be a source of inspiration for small groups of Christians who meet together for a particular purpose – in house groups, study groups, prayer groups, any small gathering united by a common purpose. It reminds us of the strength found in unity and the fact that the love we share is God's generous gift.

Psalm 134

This is the last of the *Pilgrim Psalms*, Psalms 120-134. It is in the form of an extended versicle and response, and was almost certainly used at night, possibly on every night of the pilgrim festival. It has been used in a similar way by the Church at Compline and other evening or night services.

Verses 1 and 2 would seem to be said or sung by the pilgrim congregation, calling the priests, Levites and other temple officials to bless Yahweh, and to perform the ritual action of raising their hands towards the ark. It was, of course, their official duty to praise, thank and bless God. But the pilgrims would consider that those officials were fortunate in their profession which took them daily into the temple, where they could be confident of being in the presence of Yahweh. The pilgrims themselves had journeyed long and far to share that privilege, and for most of them it would be one of few visits to Jerusalem, possibly the only one. Those two opening verses we can consider as being the versicle.

Verse 3 is the response from the priests. They solemnly pronounce Yahweh's blessing. It is the blessing of the Creator God, who chose Zion/Jerusalem as his earthly *habitation* (Psalm 132.13). The pilgrims have obeyed the Law, made the pilgrimage, done their duty and can now return home full of Yahweh's blessing. Perhaps the blessing the priests used at the conclusion of this psalm was the Aaronic blessing, often used by Christian priests: "The Lord bless you and keep you: The Lord make his face to shine upon you, and be gracious to you: The Lord lift up his countenance upon you, and give you peace." (Numbers 6.24-26).

The psalm is a fitting conclusion to the Pilgrim Psalms. Many pilgrims, and not only pilgrims to Jerusalem, feel the same sense of blessedness as, the pilgrimage ended, they leave for home, full of memories, having seen new places, made new friends and deepened their faith. Many people go on pilgrimage to draw closer to God, to worship him and to devote to him time that cannot be found in everyday life – to give God his due; in the words of the psalm 'to bless him'. Like the pilgrims in the psalm they usually find that what happens is that though they want to 'bless' God, God takes the initiative and they find themselves enriched by God's blessing.

The greatest of the many privileges of Christian priesthood is speaking God's words of absolution and blessing. Up to a generation ago it was the normal practice at the Eucharist for the priest to stand before the altar in what was known as the 'eastward position'. He thus faced the same way as the congregation and was clearly seen to be one with them, speaking with or on behalf of them. It was strikingly obvious, therefore, that when he spoke for God in giving absolution, in the reading of Scriptures, the preaching of the Word of God and the giving of God's blessing, he turned westward, facing the people. We have lost some of the dramatic power of those changes of position now that it is customary for the priest to face the people over the altar throughout the service, though there are undoubted advantages brought by the new position.

Psalm 135

We can best understand this wonderful hymn of praise by thinking of different sections of the psalm being sung by different voices. The psalm is something of a patchwork or mosaic as we discover that many phrases and verses are identical with words in other psalms.

In verses 1 and 2 we hear the congregation, using words very similar to those in Psalm 134, calling the temple officials to join in the praise of Yahweh. He is worthy of praise because he is *good* (v.3) and because he chose Israel, *Jacob,* as his covenant people (v.4).

They are called to *praise the name of the Lord.* That name, so sacred that it was rarely, perhaps never, spoken, reveals God's innermost nature. It is possible that the name was uttered liturgically during a festival service, perhaps as the ark was placed 'beneath the cherubim'. Such a ritual act, if it took place, must have been of the most profound and awesome significance. It would be a similar, but much rarer occasion than the showing of the reserved sacrament in the monstrance at a Christian service of Benediction or in a solemn procession. All such occasions remind us that religious faith is more than a matter of reason. The awe that is felt, the sense of unworthiness and the realisation that God is both holy and 'wholly other' take us beyond our ability to reason, and we find we need other faculties which are just as real as our rationality. Experiences of the divine are notoriously difficult to describe, and here we have the words of a pilgrim psalmist as he strives to make known to others what he, with certainty, has felt and known of the presence of God.

Perhaps a solo voice takes over in verses 5-7, recounting Yahweh's supreme power over all other so-called gods, his great creative acts and his continuing control of nature.

Verses 8-12, perhaps sung by another solo voice, recount a brief salvation history. God's special love for Israel was demonstrated by his mighty acts in Egypt which eventually persuaded Pharaoh to let them go. Then, during the conquest of Canaan and the settlement there, he enabled them to defeat the kings of neighbouring peoples, and *gave them their land as a heritage.* The success of the entry into their Promised Land was never attributed to the strength, wisdom or courage of Israel's leaders, but always to Yahweh; he *gave* the land.

Having been reminded of their wonderful history, verses 13 and 14 are the congregation's enthusiastic response to the two solo voices. Again the name of God and his choice of Israel are the cause of celebration.

Verses 15-18 again sounds like a solo voice, possibly the same one heard in verses 5-7, for again other 'gods', *the idols of the nations,* are scornfully compared to Yahweh. Unlike the unseen Yahweh, those gods are mere dolls, *the work of men's hands.* Like dolls they have hands, mouths, eyes and ears, but there is no life in them. The implication is clear. Yahweh is the source of life, which he gives to his people. The worshipper inevitably becomes like the object of his worship. Those who worship dolls become lifeless and useless.

The psalm ends with a great congregational burst of praise. All are called to worship – the nation, *Israel,* the priests, *house of Aaron,* other temple officials, *house of Levi,* and even Gentiles, *you that fear the Lord.* All are called to bless and praise Yahweh.

Names are important in the Bible, especially the name of God. It was believed that the name revealed the person's character or nature. There are important name changes in the Bible. Abram became Abraham and Sarai became Sarah. (Genesis 17.5 and 15). Jacob became Israel. (Genesis 31.28). In the New Testament Simon became Peter (Matthew 16.17, 18), and Saul became Paul. (Acts 13.9). Charles Dickens showed genius in creating names which revealed the character of whoever bore it. It isn't difficult to guess what Uriah Heep, Ebenezer Scrooge, Wackford Squeers or Thomas Gradgrind were like.

The name of God, given to Moses in Exodus 3.14 as "I am who I am," seems to state that which many men and women of deep spiritual experience and understanding have said, that God cannot be labelled. All we can say of God is that He is who He is. A whole tradition of Christian spirituality, sometimes called the Negative Way, teaches that we can only say of God that he is "not this" or "not that." Any attempt to speak positively of God will be wide of the mark. The author of the spiritual classic, *The Cloud of Unknowing* writes, "he may well be loved, but not thought. By love he can be caught and held, but by thinking never." Kenneth Leech recounts that Symon the New Theologian (949-1022) spoke of a man standing on the edge of the ocean at night holding a lighted candle. What can he see? He knows the ocean before him is huge and he cannot see it all at once. He sees a tiny bit, and then it changes and he sees another tiny bit. Such is our knowledge of God.

We must not think that this way of thinking is exclusively Christian. It has always been strong in Judaism too. A story tells of an emperor who visited a rabbi and demanded that he be shown God. The rabbi told him to look at the sun. The emperor said that he could not. The rabbi said that the sun is only one of Gods servants, and if it is impossible to look at the servant how much less can anyone look upon the glory of God. In his novel *Salvation* Sholem Asch has a dying rabbi say, "God is not to be inquired into, but to be loved; we should be consumed by our love for Him; and it is not by inquiring into His way that we shall be joined to Him, but only by love, by humbling our hearts before Him and leading a serene and holy life."

So sacred is God's name, that when in reading the Scriptures a devout Jew comes to the divine four letters, YHWH, spelling out God's name, they say in Hebrew either "The Name" or "My Lord."

From the experience and teaching of men and women who have striven to know and love God we learn that He certainly loves us and is our friend, but we can never presume to know all there is to be known about God, nor should we be presumptuously familiar with him.

Psalm 136

If we read this psalm immediately after reading Psalm 135 it is likely that the words our memory has retained are those about Sihon king of the Amorites and Og the king of Bashan. We will have realised too that verses 17-22 of this psalm repeat verses 10-12 of the previous one.

We have seen many psalms in which different voices say or sing different verses. This psalm presents that structure in its simplest form. We might assume that a priest or priests would sing the first half of each verse, itemising a particular act of Yahweh in the nation's history, and each time the congregation would make the same response, *for his steadfast love endures for ever.* That statement of faith is to be found also in the opening verses of Psalms 106, 107 and 118.

Because of its constant repetition of the call to give thanks to God this psalm is known in Judaism as 'The Great Hallel', the great hymn of praise.

The psalm is a comprehensive summary of the greatness of Yahweh. The foundation on which all his actions rest is the fact that he is God and his *steadfast love* is unending (v.1). Verses 2 and 3, with a parallelism of *God* and *gods* and *Lord* and *lords* declare his supremacy over all other so-called gods. Verses 4-10 celebrate his wonderful acts in creation. In verse 11 things move on with a summary of the mighty acts by which God freed his people from slavery in Egypt, saved them at the Red Sea, led them through the wilderness, and gave them victory over the kings of Canaan whose land God gave to Israel as *a heritage* (vv. 21, 22). Difficult times and the way God rescued the nation are remembered in verses 23 and 24. The fact that God unfailingly provides food for all the creatures he created is yet another sign of his *steadfast love (v.*25).

The end of the psalm returns, fittingly, to the thought of Yahweh as the ruler of heaven and all heavenly beings. The fact that the mighty, incomparable Creator God cares for all beings, and especially for his chosen covenant partner Israel, is cause for the giving of thanks.

The repetition might be considered tedious, but we should imagine the building up of the fervour of the congregation as the numerous causes for thanks are set before them. Repetition is a feature of much liturgical writing. Christians have only to consider the nine-fold Kyries, or hymns with the same chorus after each verse. Many modern hymns use the repetition of words like 'Jesus', 'Majesty', 'Lord', with the intention of building up a united feeling of devotion in all members of a congregation An older (18th century) and more traditional hymn which uses the same technique is "All hail the power of Jesus' name…"

Psalm 137

The psalmist is looking back to the dark days of the Babylonian exile. It sounds as if he speaks from personal experience. He had perhaps been one of a group of captives who had just crossed the border into Babylon. However, their own captivity was not their greatest woe. They had seen Jerusalem devastated; they had witnessed what is described in Psalms 74 and 79. Their guards, seeing their misery and knowing its cause, taunt them, suggesting that they should cheer themselves by singing one of their songs which praise Jerusalem.

But the songs of Zion were celebratory and full of thanks. They couldn't sing; they could only weep. Those who had carried their harps and other instruments with them, laid them aside. As Psalm 150 shows, musical instruments were commonly used to enhance songs which praise God.

The question they ask themselves in verse 4 may reveal a naïve belief about the imagined localisation of gods. In the story of Elisha's healing of the Syrian general who was a leper, Naaman asks if he may take a cart-load of the soil of Israel back with him to Syria, so that he can worship the God of Israel. (2 Kings 5). It seems to be true that, in spite of defeat and humiliation and against all expectations, Judaism benefited from the exile in Babylon because they learned that Yahweh could be worshipped there or indeed anywhere, because he was the only God and his rule reached every place.

The memories of Jerusalem lead the poet to say that he would prefer the hand with which he played the harp to wither than that he should forget Jerusalem. Also he would prefer dumbness to forgetfulness. Perhaps verses 5 and 6 together mean that he would prefer to suffer a stroke with its attendant disabilities than to forget the holy city.

Verses 7-9 are notorious among the 'difficult' passages in the psalms. There is an undiluted lust for revenge. Edom and Israel were traditional enemies, tracing the origin of their antagonism to the fierce rivalry between the brothers Jacob and Esau. Also Edom had looked on as the armies of Babylon destroyed Jerusalem (Ezekiel 25.12-14). The whole of the book of the prophet Obediah is a diatribe against Edom.

But Babylon was the great offender, and the atrocities carried out as Jerusalem was destroyed (Psalm 79. 1-4) lead to this famous and chilling cry for vengeance. We should not be too surprised. For some time after the end of the Second World War there was strong anti-German, and even stronger anti-Japanese, feelings in the hearts and minds of many people in Britain and in the United States. After terrible injury or desecration, as in rape at an individual level, or the deliberate killing of civilians, the torture and execution of prisoners of war, or the wanton destruction of homes and farm lands at a national or international level, it is hard to forgive and impossible to forget. And yet, if we do not forgive, the prospect is of reprisals without end. Just occasionally, an individual will startle us with their shocking readiness and ability to live out their Christian faith and forgive those who hurt them terribly. Marie Wilson, a nurse, was killed along with ten others, by an I.R.A. bomb at a parade in Enniskillen on Remembrance Day in 1987. Her father, Gordon, said, "I bear no ill-will. I bear no grudge… I shall pray for those killers tonight and every night." More recently the book *The Railway Man* by Eric Lomax tells of forgiveness and reconciliation of a man who suffered greatly as a prisoner of war in Japan in the Second World War.

The words of verses 5 and 6 are used in a very moving passage in Dostoyevsky's *The Brothers Karamazov*. A child, a young boy, is dying, and he is aware that his death is close. He tries to comfort his distraught father by saying, "Daddy, don't cry and – and when I die, get a good boy, another one…" "I don't want a good boy, I don't want another boy" he said in a wild whisper, grinding his teeth. "If I forget thee, Jerusalem, may my tongue…. When Alyosha Karamazov is asked what the father meant by those words," he said, "It's from the Bible. If I forget thee, Jerusalem, that is to say, if I forget all that is most precious to me, if I exchange it for anything, then…" His questioner said, "I understand. That's enough." The overwhelming nature of the father's loss was understood. That is how the psalmist and his fellow exiles felt about Jerusalem.

Psalm 138

The words of this psalm are those of a worshipper, perhaps a pilgrim, possibly the king, as he looks on the temple in Jerusalem. The sight fills him with gratitude to Yahweh, and he promises to witness, in the presence of those who do not worship Yahweh, to the *steadfast love and faithfulness* which are God's nature. The exalting of Yahweh's *name* may be a reference to a particular moment in the temple liturgy when the sacred name of Yahweh was possibly formally uttered.

He recalls (v.3) that when he has asked for Yahweh's help over some particular difficulty, the help given has been far more than he expected. His experience of the generosity of God has increased and deepened his faith.

He looks forward to the time when the rulers of all nations will worship Yahweh. This may well be the natural or inevitable hope of one who believes that Yahweh is the only God, and that eventually the reality of his rule over all nations will be acknowledged. It is also possible that it is a Messianic hope – the hope that God will make himself known to all people by a dramatic intervention in human affairs (vv. 4, 5).

In verse 7 we might imagine the king speaking the words; indeed he may have been the speaker throughout. It certainly seems to be a person of some importance. Problems have beset him and he has opponents, whether personal, military or political. In spite of this he is able to live his life in the confidence that Yahweh *preserves* and *delivers* him.

The psalm ends mentioning again Yahweh's steadfast love and asking that he should not *forsake the work of thy hands.* This may mean, as in Psalm 136.25 and 145.15,16, the remarkable way God sustains his creation. It might also refer to God's choice of the nation as his Covenant partner – Israel, the pre-eminent work of God's hands.

It is characteristic of the faith of the Old Testament that God's concern for the lowly and his displeasure with the arrogant are stressed (v.6). These words, written to be uttered in public worship, remind us of the 'social gospel' of the Old Testament, which is proclaimed again and again in the prophets and the psalms. It was clearly adopted and furthered by Jesus in his teaching and in his living. The Parable of the Sheep and the Goats in Matthew 25. 31-46 is the clearest example of this teaching. For his actions we might simply look at his touching of a leper (Mark 1.41) and his eating with people considered outcasts. (Mark 2.15). Christians pray, "Thy kingdom come, thy will be done, on earth as it is in heaven." Our prayer requires that we not only pray but also work for a just and compassionate society, seeking to transform our flawed and unjust society into the Kingdom of God.

Psalm 139

Few psalms contain such intense personal feelings as this one. It is a personal conversation with God; I and Thou.

In the opening verses the psalmist ponders God's omniscience and omnipresence. His conscience tells him that his life – his thoughts, his words, his actions – are all open and clear to God, even before he has thought, spoken or acted. He feels totally exposed; there is no hiding from God, no escaping him. In his poem *The Hound of Heaven*, Francis Thompson speaks of feeling pursued by God who is relentless in his following:

> "I fled Him, down the nights and down the days;
> I fled Him, down the arches of the years;
> I fled Him, down the labyrinthine ways
> Of my own mind; and in the midst of tears
> I hid from Him…"

Like Francis Thompson, the psalmist has tried to escape the searching judgement of God, but he has found it impossible. Neither time nor distance can separate him from God. He feels like a naughty child, hiding from his parent's expected anger, only to be found, and to discover that the parent is not chastising but gently holding his hand and guiding him in the way he should go. We might note that this experience of the psalmist, of being unable to hide from God, is just the opposite to that of Job who wants to find God and confront him. Job says, "Oh, that I knew where I might find him, that I might come even to his seat…" He continues, "Behold, I go forward, but he is not there; and backward, but I cannot perceive him; on the left hand I seek him, but I cannot behold him; I turn to the right hand, but I cannot see him." (Job 23.3, 8, 9).

In contrast to Job, the psalmist is totally overwhelmed by his awareness of the presence of God and God's total knowledge of his inmost being (v.6). Why is God so concerned about the minutiae of his life? The answer is that God is his creator and sustainer. He has been intimately concerned with him since before his birth and everything in his life is important to God. The awareness of God's care for him both amazes and humbles him (vv.17, 18).

As happens so often in the psalms, we come to an awkward passage. In verses 19-22 he prays for the destruction of the wicked. He knows that there are those who do not worship Yahweh and sometimes they display an active hatred of God. The psalmist counts it a virtue that he hates such people (vv.21, 22). In contrast however, Jesus said very clearly, "Love your enemies and pray for those who persecute you." (Matthew 5.44). More important, he practised what he preached. On the cross he said, "Father, forgive them; for they know not what they do," praying either for the soldiers who were crucifying him, or for all whose involvement in accusations, injustice, condemnation and torture had led to that moment.

Anyone who has been hurt, slighted, belittled, bullied, or cheated knows what it is to have thoughts of revenge. And it may well be that thoughts, which would not and should not be uttered out loud, have been spoken to God in prayer. We can bring all our hurts and fears to God, knowing that he understands our feelings. In exactly that way the psalmist puts his innermost thoughts to God with total honesty.

The existence of evil in a world created by a loving God, and which he declared to be 'very good' (Genesis 1.31) is a problem. The creation story in Genesis 2 and 3 attributes the presence of evil in the world to human abuse of God's gift of free will. If we believe in God's inexhaustible love, revealed in Christ, do we believe that ultimately all people will enter God's kingdom? In a sense, if they don't, then God's love is not the most powerful thing in creation. But if all do enter the kingdom, what has become of God's justice? We should be grateful that it is far more important to strive to live with love and compassion for all people, than to find a satisfactory intellectual answer to that question.

We need to be wary of the psalmist's confidence that he is on God's side, and that God hates those whom he hates. Too often in the history of the world, atrocities have been carried out by people believing that they know God's will, and are carrying it out. We see and hear reports today of suicide bombers and brutal executions carried out in the name of God, and we are rightly appalled. But we should not forget that Elijah slaughtered 450 prophets of baal, believing that it was God's will. (I Kings 18.17-40), and the heartless slaughters carried out in the conquest of Canaan are uncomfortably similar to what we see and hear of jihadists in the Middle East today (e.g. Joshua 6.21, I Samuel 15.3, 32, 33). God's will must always be beyond the comprehension of man. Our responsibility is not to indulge in fruitless attempts to guess what God's will is, but to strive to live as his Son Jesus did when he was on this earth.

Psalm 140

This is the distraught prayer of a man who is being attacked, certainly verbally and possibly physically. We are tempted to wonder who this man could be to have so many enemies, and why? Perhaps we suspect he is suffering from a persecution complex. But a few moments considering the lives of politicians in free democratic nations as well as in less stable societies around the world, including the present-day Middle East, will make us at least consider that he isn't deluded and he isn't inventing it.

In verses 1 and 4 he describes his opponents as *violent men.* Verse 3 brilliantly describes the sharpness of the attacks and the pain he feels, and in verse 5 he writes that he feels like a hunted animal, at risk from trap, net and snare.

The psalm begins by stating its main purpose, *Deliver me, O Lord,* and in verses 6-8 he asks for God's help, recalling that in the past such prayers have been answered.

In his misery and anger he calls for punishment for his persecutors. He wants the mischief they spread by their lies and slander to fall upon themselves (v.9). He then resorts to examples of God's punishment on the wicked recounted in the nation's history. Verse 10 recalls the fate of Sodom and Gomorrah (Genesis 19. 24-28), and perhaps the fate of Korah, Dathan and Abiram who rebelled against the authority of Moses and Aaron. (Numbers 16.31-33).

Both those scriptural examples suggest that the author believed himself to be exercising authority within the nation as the rightful bearer of God's rule. Those who oppose him are therefore seen as enemies of the state and of God. We can ask therefore, is this psalm the prayer of a king facing unrest and rebellion? As we read the Books of Samuel and Kings we find constant coups and changes of dynasty, making such an assumption by no means far-fetched.

If the psalmist is the king or a person in high authority in the nation, it is significant that Yahweh's care for the *afflicted* and the *needy* is mentioned. It is the vital work of compassion and justice that characterizes the exercise of authority under God, and distinguishes it from authority used for self-aggrandisement, and the lust for power or wealth.

The psalm ends on a calm note of confidence that in the end, because Yahweh is supreme, justice will be done; the needy will be cared for, and the righteous will know the joy and blessedness of the presence of God.

This psalm, very similar in many ways to Psalm 64, makes us think seriously about the qualities we wish to see in those who wield authority and influence in our society. The personal example of several exceedingly rich people is admirable as they set up charities or contribute large sums to causes which care for the needy. Sadly, but not surprisingly, such people seem to be a minority, and many of the very rich we hear about seem to care only for themselves and the image they present to the world. We have a responsibility to demand moral leadership from those in authority in the nation. We need them to consider the ethical dimensions of all their political, military, economic and other judgements. We must require them to pursue justice and compassion and to transform us from being a society of people who want to get, into one of people who want to give. Of course, to have the right to make such demands we must live by those standards ourselves.

Psalm 141

Because of verse 2, speaking of the *evening sacrifice,* this psalm has been used by the Church in some of its evening services. What the verse says, that this prayer might count as the equivalent of the evening sacrifice in the temple in Jerusalem, gives us some clue as to the time of its origin. Either the psalmist is not able to attend the evening sacrifice in the temple or there is no evening sacrifice. So it might be the prayer of an exile in Babylon, or perhaps of a person left behind in the devastated Jerusalem with its ruined temple.

The apparent disaster of the fall of Jerusalem in 586 B.C. actually contributed to the development of Judaism. They came to realise that Yahweh could be worshipped in Babylon, and indeed anywhere, just as effectively as he could be worshipped in Israel and Judah. The only God was not limited to any particular location, as was believed of the false gods worshipped by other peoples. Similarly, they discovered that Yahweh could be worshipped without the rituals of the temple. As the prophets – and many of the psalms – had often insisted, it was not the sacrifice of animals, oil or incense that God wanted. He wanted obedience to his laws demanding justice and mercy – and penitence when those laws have been ignored. (For example, see Isaiah 1.12-17 and Amos 5.21-24). Psalm 51, verse17 sums up this spiritualizing of the faith: *The sacrifice acceptable to God is a broken spirit, a broken and contrite heart, O God, thou wilt not despise.*

In verse 3 the psalmist is careful in what he says. We often find psalmists complaining to God about those who slander them or spread lies about them. This man seems to be aware that he might slip into that sort of behaviour himself. So he asks that he might not keep bad company which would lead him into bad ways. The text of verses 5-7 is very corrupt and translators struggle to make clear sense of it. It seems to be saying that he would prefer to be rebuked by the righteous than be praised by the wicked. Those sentiments are echoed many times in the Book of Proverbs, such as 12.15, 19.20, 22.17, 18 and Ecclesiastes 7.5, "It is better for a man to hear the rebuke of the wise than to hear the song of fools." Or again in

Proverbs 13.1 and 3 we read, "A wise son hears his father's instruction, but a scoffer does not listen to rebuke… He who guards his mouth preserves his life; he who opens wide his lips comes to ruin."

In verse 8 the psalmist prays for God's protection. Without God's help he would be *defenceless,* and likely to be trapped by the wiles of the wicked into joining them. He prays that they might themselves fall into the traps they have set for others, allowing him to escape to live a godly life. Despite considerable difficulty over translation and interpretation, what comes across clearly in this psalm is the poet's humility and honesty. He knows he is inclined to speak thoughtlessly and foolishly. He knows he is weak and easily tempted, and that only with God's help can he stand against temptation. If we follow the good example of the psalmist and review our day or week in an evening prayer, we should strive to be as honest about our failings and our need for God's help as is the psalmist.

Psalm 142

As we read this psalm, we can feel the weariness, anxiety and loneliness of the man who is praying. He turns to God because he has not be able to find help anywhere else. He believes that God alone understands his suffering and his needs. He knows that even when he has lost all confidence that he might understand himself, God always understands him (vv. 2, 3).

His enemies set traps for him. This seems to mean that they have spread damaging and untrue stories, destroying his reputation. In this situation he feels deserted; he has not been able to find any friend who would stand by him (v.4). God is his only *refuge* (v.5), the only one who can rescue him from the depths of despair and ruined reputation. He knows that without God's help he will be destroyed, because alone he is no match for his enemies (v.6).

The prison he speaks of in verse 7 seems more likely to be the despair from which he cannot escape, rather than a physical dungeon. He hopes that when he regains his freedom he will be able, publicly, to acknowledge that he owes it all to God. Thus restored, he will be able to take his proper place among the worshippers of Yahweh, and he looks forward to the generous welcome he will receive (v.7). So this mainly melancholy psalm ends on a note of optimism and gratitude. He knows that, forgiven and helped by God, he will be welcomed by the worshipping community.

The Church is a community of forgiven sinners, who constantly need to mend and renew their relationships with God and with each other. One reason we worship together and receive the sacrament, is so that we may receive strength from God and from each other. A parish priest, in a sermon shortly after arriving in his new parish, told the congregation he had, that week, met someone in the parish who said he was a Christian but didn't go to church because he wasn't good enough. The vicar's wise and true reply was, "Not good enough! You should see the lot we've got there." Forgiven and forgiving should be the nature of every Christian community.

Psalm 143

This is counted as the last of the Penitential Psalms and the sentiments of the psalm are, in many ways, similar to those of Psalm 142. The psalmist may be suffering unjust imprisonment, in the darkness of a dungeon (v.3). It seems more likely, however, that it is again the prison of his own sins that encloses him. The burden of guilt which he carries seems heavier in the depths of the night – as it does to all who suffer such pangs of guilt. The psalmist knows this and so he prays for the coming of morning, for a new day in which God can demonstrate again his *steadfast love (v.8)*.

In the opening two verses he prays that God will not judge him harshly. He knows that he has sinned and that in a court of law God would have a strong case against him. He also knows that his human frailty is the direct opposite of God's faithfulness and righteousness. He has enemies who, like those in Psalm 142.6, are stronger than he. He seems to speak of a particular individual who has crushed and imprisoned him (v.3). Perhaps he is speaking of a political opponent. He fears for his future and is sinking into despair (v.4).

Then he remembers the way God has saved the nation in the past (v.5). If the prison is a figurative one and the psalm is being spoken in the temple, he may have been listening to the recital of Israel's salvation history as a part of the temple liturgy. He hopes that God's remarkable acts of salvation for the nation may be repeated in his own situation. This hope is painful for him; he feels as though he is in a drought-stricken land, dying for want of the water of life – for the assurance of God's love for him. His situation is urgent. He is near to despair and near to death. He fears that if God does not answer him, he will die and will therefore be utterly cut off from the presence of God. (See comments on Psalm 88).

It is possible that his desperate prayer was made in a night vigil in the temple. He longs for the light of a new day and the hope it will bring. He looks forward to hearing and seeing the morning liturgy, which will reassure him of God's unfailing and steadfast love, renewed day by day. He will find, in the liturgy, the habitual teaching which will enable him to try once again to live as God requires. The second half of verse 8, asking that God would teach him *the way* would sit very happily in Psalm 119.

His prayer so far seems to have enabled him to cast off the gloom and pessimism with which he started. He prays that God will guide him so that he may pass through life as if walking on a smooth path with no obstacles or irregularities which may cause him to stumble (v.10).

He believes that God's acting on his behalf will vindicate God as well as himself. Acts of love and faithfulness are of the nature of God, and through them God's 'name' will be honoured. He expects that the judgement he feared would condemn him (v.2), will fall on his opponents. He sees himself as God's *servant* and necessarily thinks of his opponents as enemies of God. As is often the case, the psalm ends on an all too human note of vindictiveness.

Few conscientious people have not lain awake at night regretting things they have thought or said or done. Only the most charitable have never mulled over differences of opinion, trivial or important, and smarted with pain, and sometimes with guilt, at the outcome. How important it is to have a 'salvation history' from which to draw strength. It is a great benefit to recall events in our own life to which we can look back with gratitude to God; occasions when we have been sure of his care and blessing. It might be helpful to write them down. If we do that, we might also copy down also some of the words of John Keble's hymn, "New every morning is the love our waking and uprising prove..."

As well as a personal salvation history there is the salvation history of our faith. We may recall incidents in the gospels – Jesus healing, comforting, forgiving and suffering without bitterness or condemnation of those who hurt him. It also might help to know something of the saint to whom our local church is dedicated, or one whose day coincides with or is close to our own birthday. We might find unexpected help and strength there. When we feel burdened with guilt, anger or frustration, looking back, as the psalmist did, can give us comfort and strength.

Psalm 144

This would seem to be a prayer uttered by a king at his coronation or at a festival celebrating the anniversary of his accession.

Many words and images used, for example those describing Yahweh as a rock, a fortress, a stronghold and a deliverer, are found in many psalms. Verses 3 and 4 are almost identical with verse 4 of Psalm 8. It is likely that such words, phrases and sentences were commonly used in a number of temple liturgies, just as familiar words and phrases recur in Christian acts of worship.

The psalm begins with the king's thanksgiving to God for making him militarily successful and secure as reigning monarch. The psalm has the title, *A Psalm of David*, and certainly, the qualities mentioned are those regarded as Davidic – a king, strong and just because of God's help and the king's ready dependence on that help.

In verse 3 the frailty of all humans is noted, thus acknowledging that the king's success is due, not to his own strength, wisdom or virtue, but solely to God's help. There is the beautiful simile, found in several psalms, of all humans as a *breath,* a mere puff of wind which hardly ruffles the surface of history.

The king's role as God's chosen ruler over his people is renewed and confirmed and he prays for a clear proof of the presence and the power of God. He asks for a spectacular demonstration of that power, flashes of lightning (God's arrows), inducing fear and flight in his enemies. We might wonder if the words of verses 5 and 6 were the cue for special effects in the Temple created by drums and flashing light, driving home the message of this part of the liturgy. The psalmist's enemies are called *aliens,* probably foreign nations, and he sees deliverance from them as being deliverance from *many waters.* He is perhaps looking back to that seminal act of deliverance of the nation from the power of the king of Egypt at the Red Sea. Verse 8 makes us wonder whether he was also under attack from some within his own nation, those *whose mouth speak lies, and whose right hand is a right hand of falsehood.*

He promises that when his prayer has been answered, and God's promised protection of the house of David has been accomplished in the defeat of the nation's enemies (v.10), he will sing a new song of praise, one specially composed for the occasion and lavish in its musical setting (v.9).

Verse 11 is something of a jumble, really another version of verses 7 and 8. It has probably been miscopied at some time and

236

should be omitted, as it is in some translations. It is also possible that it was a refrain, punctuating the psalm, voicing a plea that the nation's enemies should be defeated.

Verses 12 to 15 are a lovely, lyrical vision of the peaceful and prosperous nation over which the king hopes to rule. Young men will be tall and strong. Young women will be beautiful and shapely, as if sculpted. Harvests will be plentiful and sheep and cattle will be fertile. The people will be free from *distress,* from the normal pains and problems of life. This constitutes a vision of an ideal Israel, and such blessedness can only be the lot of those who have Yahweh for their God.

Of course, no king of Judah or Israel ever ruled over such a godly nation. So the hope became a Messianic hope, a looking forward to the day when God would send his Messiah, making all things new and endowing his people with the blessings dreamed of in this psalm. Such Messianic longing is still strong within Judaism. For Christians a start has been made; the Messianic day has dawned. Jesus' first words in the earliest gospel are, "The time is fulfilled, and the kingdom of God is at hand; repent and believe in the gospel." (Mark 1.15). It is the task of each generation of Christians to work to bring the kingdom closer to its fulfilment.

Psalm 145

This wonderful hymn starts from praise of God by an individual (vv.1, 2, 5). It then widens to the nation's praise for God's *wondrous works* on its behalf, which will be remembered and passed on from generation to generation (vv.5-7). It moves to the care God has for all his creatures (vv.10-19), especially, for those who are fallen and struggling with life (v.14).

There is no sign of artificiality in the thoughts and words of the psalm, but for ease of memorising, it is in the form of an acrostic. The verses start with the successive letters of the Hebrew alphabet, though the verse that should begin with the letter N is missing.

It seems likely that the words of the psalm were spoken by the king in a festival liturgy in the temple. It may have been the annual festival, renewing the nation's acknowledgement that its real king was Yahweh. Verse 1 identifies God as king and verses 11 and 13 speak of his kingdom. His power, majesty and rule over all are declared throughout the hymn. Verses 15 and 16 suggest that the occasion might also have been a harvest celebration.

After the initial praise of God as king, the important practice, indeed the duty of passing on the nation's salvation history is declared. It is through this history that God's greatness and the nation's uniqueness are revealed. But God is known, not only for his power, but also for his *goodness* and *righteousness.* Verses 6 and 7 imply that the congregation will join the king in praising God, and that the song of praise has been composed for this very occasion.

Verses 8 and 9 are a wonderful credal statement naming the qualities which distinguish Yahweh from any other 'gods'. The only thing a Christian might like to add to that statement is that those divine qualities were demonstrated in the life of Jesus. Christ's incarnation clothed in human form the Old Testament belief about God, and showed us what exercising those qualities always costs God.

Creation praises God by its very existence, and those who recognise God's generosity (rather than just accept it) are his real worshippers, *the saints (v.*10). They will uphold and pass on the faith, and thus God's kingdom will be remembered and sustained generation after generation (v.13).

God cares for people in need, the fallen and those who are bowed down by life. Indeed God's care extends to all creation, and the needs of every creature are supplied by God (vv.15, 16). It is not surprising that those two verses have often been used as a grace before a meal.

People are encouraged to pray by being told that God is close to all who turn to him. He not only pays heed to their words, but is close enough to know their very thoughts, their *desires (v.*19). Verse 20 reflects on the justice of God in a world of imperfect humans. The psalmist can see no other outcome than that of favour for the faithful and punishment for the wicked.

The psalm ends with the king promising his personal devotion to Yahweh, and looking to the time when the whole creation will similarly acknowledge God. One is tempted to regard the final half verse as a congregational response to bring this hymn to a resounding conclusion, *Let all flesh bless his holy name forever and ever.*

Psalm 146

This great hymn of praise begins with the psalmist exhorting himself to praise Yahweh. Immediately, in verse 2, he responds that he will indeed praise God *as long as I live.* Perhaps saying that reminds him that sooner or later his life will end, and with it his ability to praise God. He ponders the limitations of all human life. Leaders of nations, *princes,* have no lasting power, nor are they any less mortal than other men. All men die, and with them their thoughts and hopes; *his plans perish.*

Because of man's limitations the only sure source of hope and help is the limitless power and supreme goodness of Yahweh (v. 5). He is the Creator-God who constantly upholds those he has created; *he keeps faith forever (v.*6). The psalmist then rehearses some of the things which characterise Yahweh's loving-kindness. He is known by his care for those in need. The psalm lists *the oppressed, the hungry, prisoners, the blind, those who are bowed down, strangers, widows and orphans.* In the midst of that list of the needy, he mentions *the righteous.* Those who honour and worship Yahweh are also objects of his care. But because Yahweh is a just God, the way of the wicked will be destroyed. We should note that it is not the wicked themselves, but their *way,* not the sinner but the sin, which God will destroy (v.9).

The final verse, rejoicing that Yahweh's kingship over Israel will last for ever, suggests that the psalm may have been used at the annual renewal of the Covenant and celebration of God's reign. We might speculate that different verses of the psalm were spoken or sung by different voices. Verses 1 and 2 might have been sung by a single voice which would speak for every individual in the congregation. Verses 3 and 4 could be a choir, a small group of voices, warning against dependence on human strength, even that of the human king of Israel. A greater number of voices would bring weight to the rehearsing of the greatness of the power and compassion of Yahweh. Verse 10 would be the response of the whole congregation, a joyful shout of praise.

A number of Christian hymns follow the pattern of this psalm, with its continual praise of God and his graciousness. Such psalms and hymns of praise are designed for congregational use. They can, and often are, used by individuals as a prayer, but their real meaning and power only comes out when they are spoken or sung by a number of people.

Psalm 147

This psalm celebrates the power of Yahweh – in creation, in his compassion and in his choice of and care for Israel. There are three calls inviting people to join in worship. The first of these, in verse 1, gives Yahweh's graciousness as the reason for singing his praise.

The building up of Jerusalem, mentioned in verse 2, suggests, as does verse 13, that the psalm was composed in the time of Nehemiah's rebuilding of the temple and reconstruction of the devastated city after the return from the exile in Babylon. The gathering of outcasts and the healing of broken hearts fits well with the circumstances and feelings of returned exiles. But it could equally well apply to the unburdening of guilts and fears by all pilgrims who make their way to Jerusalem as required by the law set out in Deuteronomy 16.16.

Verses 4 to 6 celebrate God's majesty as it is seen in his creation, the wonder of the night sky being a clear and unmissable example of his power. But his wisdom and power is exercised too in the rescue of the persecuted and judgement on the wicked.

The call to worship is renewed in verse 7, the song of praise being accompanied by musical instruments. Again Yahweh's providential care for all his creatures is seen in the balance of nature, his sustaining of vegetation and animal life. Unlike humans, God is not impressed by physical strength in either animals or humans. What he cares about is devotion and hope sustained by faith in his *steadfast love (v.*11).

The call to worship sounds out again in verse 12. God is to be thanked for having made possible the rebuilding of Jerusalem and the strengthening of its defences against possible future attack. The future is secure because God's blessing is on the next generation and on the fields surrounding Jerusalem which supply food for the people of the city (vv.13, 14).

Again the wonders of God's creation are pondered. Most impressive are snow, frost and ice, rare in the Middle East and quite beyond the wisdom and ingenuity of man to copy. The cold comes and water becomes solid until God sends a warm wind and again the waters flow. The psalmist knows that humans cannot imitate that (vv.16-18).

The final two verses celebrate the other great wonder – God's choice of Israel as his covenant partner, the recipient of his Law. The nation can only wonder in gratitude that it has been chosen in this way. The consequence of Israel's status as God's special people is its responsibility. It was chosen for service not for privilege. That was not always remembered and acted upon, and the prophets constantly point out that the dereliction of this duty will inevitably lead to punishment. Amos (3.2) says, "You only have I known from all the families of the earth; therefore I will punish you for your iniquities."

Christians believe that Jesus fulfilled all the hopes and promises of the Old Testament and set up a new Israel on the foundation of The Twelve, the new sons of Israel. At the Last Supper he spoke of "a new covenant" (I Corinthians 11.25), which he would inaugurate by his blood shed on the cross, just as the original covenant had been sealed by blood. (Exodus 24.8). To hold such a belief is an awesome responsibility, and we have to remember that if Christians, as members of the New Israel, have inherited the promises, they have also inherited the responsibilities.

Psalm 148

There is a very clear shape to this psalm as all things and all people are called to give praise to Yahweh. Such praise should be a natural response because he is the source and reason for all things. The psalm is in effect a vision of the kingdom of God.

First, those closest to God in the thought of the day, heaven itself and all heavenly beings, are called to worship (vv.1, 2). Then the heavenly objects visible to humans – the sun, the moon and the stars are called to join in the praise (v.3). The waters above the heavens, ordered and controlled by Yahweh's power in the act of creation (Genesis 1. 6, 7) are summoned to worship their Lord and creator (vv.4-6). The land and sea, sea-monsters and other frightening and destructive aspects of nature – fire, hail, snow, frost and tempest are called. They are beyond the power of man to tame or regulate. Only Yahweh is their master.

The earth is more familiar and less frightening. The slopes of mountains and hills have been cultivated, providing food and materials for human living. Unlike the monsters of the sea, many creatures of earth have been tamed and domesticated. They are called to worship along with the more baffling and untameable reptiles and birds.

In verses 11-13 the rulers of all nations and their people are called to acknowledge that Yahweh is their God too, because he is the only God. The vision is of all people, young and old, male and female from all nations joining in joyful praise of their creator and sustainer.

The psalm reaches its climax recalling Yahweh's choice of Israel as his covenant partner. The *horn* or 'power' he has raised up probably means the Davidic dynasty. This glorying in the nation's special status in relation to God might at first appear to be a narrowing of the thought of earlier verses. This is not so. The choice was made so that God's promise to Abraham could be fulfilled. God's blessing on all people would be achieved through the dedication and example of Abraham and his descendants. This vision of the universal rule of God, the kingdom of God, is still the hope of Judaism. It is now also the hope of all Christians.

A fuller and perhaps more polished version of this psalm is found as the *Song of the Three Holy Children* which, in the Greek version of the Hebrew Bible, is added to chapter 3 of the *Book of Daniel*. The Three Holy Children are Shadrach, Meshach and Abednego, who were thrown into "the burning fiery furnace" by king Nebuchadnezzar, but who, because of their faith in God, did not perish. Daniel 1.7 tells how they had been given the names by which they are generally known to take the place of their original Hebrew names, Hananiah, Mishael and Azariah. The song was included as an optional canticle in the service of Morning Prayer in the Book of Common Prayer. It is commonly known by its opening word in Latin, Benedicite. The original names of the singing men in the furnace appear in the closing verse of the Prayer Book version of the hymn or psalm, but have been omitted from more recent orders of Morning Prayer – which is a pity. The omission was probably made because people would ask "Who on earth are Hananiah, Azariah and Mishael?" Although, as we have seen, the answer is slightly complex, it is worth knowing.

Psalm 149

From Psalm 145 there has been a steady build-up in fervour in the singing of the praises of Yahweh. Psalm 149 is a fitting preliminary to the final outburst of praise which is Psalm 150.

Verse 2 suggests that the psalm was for use in the temple at the festival celebrating the kingship of Yahweh, and the role of the earthly king of Judah, Yahweh's viceroy. The gathered worshippers are called to praise Yahweh with song, music and dance. What they will take part in is to be no staid act of piety, but a joyous, triumphant, confident celebration (v.3).

Verse 4 rejoices in God's choice of Israel as his special people, his covenant partner. It is Yahweh's favour that has given them victory in battle. This is probably a recalling of the conquest of Canaan, when often their enemies seemed stronger than they. The acknowledgement of Yahweh's vital role in their victories is very clearly stated in Psalm 44, verses 1-3.

The whole nation is called to praise God. Those who are not in the temple, that is the vast majority of the population who are at work or at rest in their own homes, they too must join in the praise. Verse 6 reminds us of the rebuilding of the temple under Nehemiah, after the return from exile in Babylon. Neighbouring kingdoms did not welcome the prospect of a renewed and strong Judah and they harassed the builders as much as they could. As a result, "each of the builders had his sword girded at his side while he built." (Nehemiah 4.18).

The final verses are another reminder from the psalmist of the seriousness of God's judgement. Part of the role of those who worship and obey God is to challenge the way of life of the unfaithful, offering a different and better way. Blurring the distinction between right and wrong and behaving as if "it doesn't matter what I do, God will forgive me," is what Dietrich Bonhoeffer called 'cheap grace'. Bonhoeffer was martyred in a concentration camp in 1945, shortly before the end of the Second World War. In 1937, when Hitler had been in power in Germany for four years Bonhoeffer wrote, "Cheap grace is the grace we bestow on ourselves. Cheap grace is the preaching of forgiveness without requiring repentance, baptism without Church discipline, Communion without Confession, absolution without personal confession. Cheap grace is grace without discipleship, grace without the cross, grace without Jesus Christ, living and incarnate."

The psalm calls us to praise God. Bonhoeffer reminds us that we can only truly praise God by the way we live – keeping God's commandments and striving to be Christ-like – and that is a costly business as Bonhoeffer well knew. Christians are called to follow the One whose whole life praised God. Never was that praise more real than when he gave up his life on the cross.

Psalm 150

The Psalter reaches its intended climax in this great outburst of praise. It is sparing in its words and there are none of the beautiful and striking similes or word pictures found in many of the psalms. Its allusion to God's *mighty deeds* is all we hear of the nation's salvation history.

The praise of Yahweh, of which this psalm is a part and perhaps an introduction, is a part of a joyous festival liturgy in the temple in Jerusalem, *his sanctuary,* his earthly home. The fervent praise in the temple may be wonderful and impressive to those present, but in reality it is very limited. It is a small part of the endless praises of Yahweh which resound through the heavens, God's greater home, where, as many psalms have told us, he is worshipped by all heavenly beings as well as by sun, moon and stars.

From verse 3 onwards the psalm celebrates the way musical talents arc to be offered as part of the congregation's praise. The words of the psalm were perhaps a single unaccompanied voice in the silence, calling for the great surge of musical praise which was to follow.

But the psalm was not speaking only to the musicians, nor even simply to the congregation in the temple. All people are called to praise Yahweh: *Let everything that breathes praise the Lord.* That means every human being, as we are pointed back to the second creation story in Genesis, where God, having moulded Adam from the dust of the earth, "breathed into his nostrils the breath of life; and man became a living being." (Genesis 2. 7, 8).

Christianity has inherited and developed the love of praising God through wonderful music. How good it is that cathedrals and many churches and chapels continue the practice, enhancing their acts of worship with great music, beautifully performed. The organ, a one-instrument orchestra, with stops to enable the sound of many instruments to be heard, became a rival to the groups of local musicians who used to accompany and lead the worship in many parish churches. Eventually the convenience of relying on only one person to produce the required music meant that organs were installed in most churches. Thomas Hardy, in *Under the Greenwood Tree,* amusingly and sensitively records some of the problems which such changes caused in small communities. Today, some less traditional congregations have formed music groups, which use a variety of instruments, not very different from those mentioned in this psalm, to lead their worship.

It is significant that much of the greatest music of western civilisation has been inspired by the Christian faith and its festivals. Hearing the wonderful music, in Masses, Oratorios, Passions, seasonal hymns and anthems inspires worshippers and confirms and deepens their faith. God's mighty acts, the wonders of his creation, his justice, his steadfast love and mercy, his revelation of himself in Jesus, and the continuing work of the Holy Spirit are all celebrated in magnificent and inspiring music and continue to draw people to wonder and to worship.

***

Closing Reflections

What have we found or noticed as we have read, prayed and searched the psalms? The thing that strikes me very strongly is how little human life, and indeed human nature, has changed. Like the psalmist we are sometimes filled with a lively awareness of God's presence and his love for us and for all his creation. At other times, we find belief difficult and wonder if God is punishing us or has forgotten us. Like the psalmist we often feel hard done by, as though everything is against us and life is not fair. We see the wicked flourishing, and too often we see the good suffer. Wars continue, injustices abound, poverty and hunger are the lot of many. The leaders of nations are filled with good intentions and fine words, but all too often their practice falls short of their promises. All these things we find in the psalms, in our daily newspapers and in our own experience.

In a largely godless world, awe of the divine is still felt by those who are touched by the presence of God, who have experienced his grace and felt his forgiveness. For such people, the reality of God is inescapable, and praise of God seems to be a natural and necessary part of human life. Also, like the psalmist, the present-day believer finds that such praise is best done in the company of fellow believers.

One cannot read the psalms without there lingering in the mind the choice of Israel as God's special people, his covenant partner. "How odd of God to choose the Jews" light-heartedly wrote W.N. Ewer. But it is not the oddness that worries us, it is the fairness. It is therefore important that we realise that this belief needs to be understood as a responsibility rather than as a privilege. The task, placed upon Abraham and his descendants, was no easy task. It has not been changed or removed, and since the coming of Jesus those who are part of the New Israel, the Christian Church, share the responsibility of bringing God's blessing to all people. As we constantly pray 'Thy kingdom come', we are joining with the psalmists and the prophets in dedicating ourselves to the bringing in of the kingdom of God, in which his just and gentle rule will bring peace, harmony and justice to all.

Perhaps the most powerful message emerging, time after time in the psalms, is the conviction that God's steadfast love for all his creatures is focused particularly on the poor, the weak and the oppressed. That is the divine preoccupation, and it must never be overlooked or displaced in our enthusiasm for personal religious experience. Many people would like Christians to concentrate wholly on personal experience of God – the saving of souls. Too often we hear people, often people of influence, say that the Church should stay out of politics. Such thinking betrays a sad ignorance or misunderstanding of what Judaism and Christianity are about. It is, of course, possible that those who make such statements actually know the truth, and fear that a strong Christian voice and involvement in the life of the nation and in the making of its laws, might reveal the weakness or selfishness of their policies and perhaps of their lives. Living a truly Christian life is never an easy matter. All Christians find it hard to imitate the unconditional love and generosity of God, and some find it hard to accept it.

The psalms teach us that we are never beyond the justice, love and mercy of God. In the happiness of human love, in the warmth of fellowship in the Church, in our delight at the wonder and beauty of creation as well as when we feel in the depths, alone, misunderstood and misused, in all the circumstances of life we can join with the psalmist and say, "O give thanks to the Lord, for he is good, for his steadfast love endures for ever."

How important it is that the Book of Psalms ends as it does, with a wonderful crescendo of praise and thanksgiving. The Christian's knowledge of the nature of God as revealed in Christ makes joy, perhaps with music and dancing accompanying the songs of celebration, the most appropriate treasure to take away from our reading, praying and searching of the psalms.

***

Psalms which may be helpful on Particular Occasions (The lists are not exhaustive).

The Importance of Caring for those in Need. Psalms 12, 14, 41, 55, 58, 68, 72, 108, 111, 112, 132, 146.

The Duties of Rulers and Leaders. Psalms 2, 12, 20, 21, 46, 64, 94, 101, 140.

The Building of God's Kingdom. Psalms 82, 85, 89, 138, 144.

Difficulties in Prayer. Psalms 9, 10, 25.

Feelings of Guilt, Unworthiness or Depression. Psalms 4, 6, 13, 17, 22, 31, 36, 38, 51, 130, 142, 143.

Penitence and Forgiveness. Psalms 5, 6, 25, 30, 32, 38, 41, 106, 116.

Praise and Thanksgiving. Psalms 30, 32, 126, 148, 149, 150.

Family Life. Psalms 127, 128, 133.

Riches. Psalms 37, 49, 51, 73.

The Brevity of Human Life. Psalm 39, 62, 78, 90, 102, 146.

Purity of Heart. Psalms 1, 66, 112.

God Revealed in Creation. 8, 19, 29, 33, 65, 67, 93, 104, 147.

God's Care and Protection. Psalms 7, 17, 23, 28, 40, 63, 100, 103

God's Dependability: God as Rock. Psalms 18, 27, 28, 31, 42, 61, 62.

The Importance of Passing on the Faith. Psalms 71, 78, 81, 145.

The Two Ways. Psalms 1, 32.

References

Some of the books which I have read and pondered over the years and which have been immensely useful and inspiring:

A. Weiser: "The Psalms." (London, SCM Press, 1962).

A.R. Johnson: "Sacral Kingship in Ancient Israel." (Cardiff: University of Wales Press, 1955) and the essay in "The Old Testament and Modern Study" edited by H.H. Rowley (Oxford University Press, 1952).

D. Bonhoeffer: "The Psalms." (Fairacres Publications, 1994).

W. Brueggeman: "Israel's Praise." (Fortress Press, 1988).

T. Merton: "Bread in the Wilderness." (Burns & Oates, 1986).

J. Day: "Psalms" (Continuum, 1990).

P.S. Johnson and D.G. Firth "Interpreting the Psalms." (Leicester, Apollos, 2006).

References in the Text
The Introduction

Page 3. Luther and Calvin quoted in Patrick Miller "Interpreting the Psalms." (Minneapolis, Fortress, Press 1986).

Page 4. Philip Toynbee: "Part of a Journey 1977-1979" (Collins, London, 1981).

Page 6. J.H Newman "Apologia Pro Vita Sua" (Longmans, Green and Co., 1890).

Page 7. Poems of William Wordsworth. Elson (Thomas Nelson and Sons Ltd.)

Page 10. A. Weiser (see above).

Page 11. W. Brueggeman (see above).

Page 12. C.S. Lewis: "Reflections on the Psalms."

Page 14. Thomas Merton: "Bread in the Wilderness" (Burns & Oates, 1986).

The Individual Psalms

Psalm 7: John V. Taylor: "The Go-Between God." (SCM Press Ltd. 1972).

Psalm 17: Francis Thompson: "The Hound of Heaven." (Burns Oates and Washbourne Ltd. 1913).

Psalm 21: Dennis Potter: "Son of Man." (BBC play, April, 1969)

Psalm 23: Sholem Asch: "Salvation." (Macdonald. London. 1953).

Psalm 25: George R. Potter, Evelyn M. Simpson: "Sermons of John Donne" (University of California. Press, 1953-1984).

Psalm 27: Simon Sebag Montefiore: "Jerusalem: The Biography." (Weidenfeld & Nicolson, 2011).

Psalm 29: Evelyn Underhill: "Concerning the Inner Life with the House of the Soul." Page 87. . . (Methuen, 1947).

Psalm 31: Evelyn Underhill (ibid) page 103.

Dietrich Bonhoeffer: "The Cost of Discipleship." p.31 (S.C.M. 1959)

Psalm 32: John V. Taylor: "The Go-Between God" page 172, 3 and 180. (SCM Press Ltd. 1972).

Psalm 33: W. H. Vanstone: "Love's Endeavour: Love's Expense." (DLT, 1977).

Graham Kendrick: "The Servant King." (Thank you Music/Adm. Kingsway Music. 1983).

Psalm 37: Kathleen Ferrier: "Elijah" Mendelssohn. Boyd Neel Orchestra. September 1946.

Psalm 39: Richard Morris: "Leonard Cheshire" page 401. (Penguin Books, 2001).

Psalm 41: Rupert Shortt: "Christianaphobia" pages 117,118. (Ryder 2012).

Psalm 55: Karl Jenkins: "The Armed Man" (2001 Karl Jenkins Music Ltd; 2001 Virgin Records Ltd.

Psalm 58: Kenneth Leech: "True God" page 66 (Sheldon Press, S.P.C.K. 1985).

Hilary Mantel "Wolf Hall." (Fourth Estate, 2009).

Ken Follett "The Pillars of the Earth" (Macmillan 1989).

Psalm 63: Geoffrey Moorhouse: "Sun Dancing" (Weidenfeld & Nicolson (Phoenix Paperback), 2001).

Psalm 84: Gerald Hughes: "Walking to Jerusalem." page 140. (Darton, Longman and Todd, 1991) Thomas a Kempis: "The Imitation of Christ" Book 4, chapter 10.7. Burns and Oates, 1963).

Psalm 93: W.H. Vanstone (op. cit. Psalm 33).

Psalm 99: W.H. Vanstone (op. cit. Psalm 33).

Rudold Otto: "The Idea of the Holy." (Pelican Books, 1959).

Psalm 106: Talmud story found in Elie Wiesel: "Messengers of God" page 140. (Touchstone (Simon and Schuster Inc.) 1976).

Psalm 109: Bonhoeffer: "The Cost of Discipleship" page 132. (S.C.M. 1959).

Psalm 119: Thomas Traherne "Centuries of Meditation III," 92. (P.J. & A.E. Dobell, 1950).

Psalm 130: Kenneth Leech: "True God" page 66. (Sheldon Press, S.P.C.K., 1985)

John V. Taylor: "The Go-Between God" page 180. (S.C.M. Press., 1972).

Psalm 135: Kenneth Leech: "True God." page 213 (Sheldon Press, S.P.C.K. 1985) page 180.

"The Cloud of Unknowing," chapter 6. (Penguin Books, 1954) page 180.

Scholem Asch: "Salvation" (Macdonald, London, 1953).

Psalm 137: Gordon Wilson with Alf McCreary: "Marie." (Collins, 1990) Fyodor Dosteyevsky: "The Brothers Karamazov" pages 158, 9. (Penguin Classics, 1958) page 183.

Eric Lomax: "The Railway Man" (Vintage Books, 2014).

Psalm 139: Francis Thompson: "The Hound of Heaven." (Burns, Oates and Washbourne, 1913).

Psalm 149: Dietrich Bonhoeffer: "The Cost of Discipleship" page 36. (S.C.M., 1959)

Psalm 150: Thomas Hardy: "Under the Greenwood Tree" (Penguin English Library, 1979).

***